MRS. GOODFELLOW'S

COOKERY AS IT SHOULD BE.

A NEW MANUAL OF

THE DINING-ROOM AND KITCHEN.

CONTAINING

ORIGINAL RECEIPTS ON EVERY BRANCH OF COOKERY; DOMESTIC BEVERAGES; FOOD FOR INVALIDS; BRANDYING FRUITS; PICKLING; PRESERVING; SALTING AND CURING MEATS; ETC., ETC.;

TOGETHER WITH

RULES ON CARVING, WITH FULL ILLUSTRATIONS OF THE SAME; SUGGESTIVE HINTS TO YOUNG HOUSEKEEPERS; TABLE CUTLERY; WINES; YEASTS AND FERMENTED BEVERAGES; ALSO BILLS OF FARE FOR EVERY DAY IN THE YEAR;

FORMING

ONE OF THE MOST COMPLETE COOK AND HOUSEHOLD RECEIPT BOOKS EVER PUBLISHED.

Who would suppose, from Adam's simple courses,
That Cookery could have called forth such resources,
As form a science and a nomenclature,
From out of the commonest demands of nature.—BYRON.

Philadelphia:
T. B. PETERSON & BROTHERS,
306 CHESTNUT STREET.

PUBLISHER'S PREFACE.

THE publishers, in presenting this Cook Book to the public, feel an assurance of its being well received, from a knowledge of the source from whence they come. They are by the justly celebrated MRS. GOODFELLOW, who was for many years in Philadelphia, pre-eminent in the art of cooking. Besides this advantage of being a practical cook, she obtained some of the best receipts from experienced housekeepers of the south, who understood well the art of compounding good things. Many of the receipts are from Europe, presented to her by travelling friends, and experimented on by the authoress, and adapted to American palates. All these considerations are calculated to make it not only an acceptable, but a valuable household assistant, in arranging that most important branch—the culinary department. As such, the publishers have great pleasure in offering it to the American public, with the belief that, if they will only follow the rules herein set forth, they will be enabled to become as good housekeepers as the authoress of this celebrated work.

A RECEIPT

FOR IMPROVING AN INDIFFERENT DINNER.

"A clean table cloth and a smiling countenance."

The former may be commanded; but there *are dinners* over which the mistress of the house cannot smile; they are too bad for dissimulation: the dinner is eaten in confusion of face by all parties.

INTRODUCTION.

FROM a peculiarity of position the writer has had occasion to regret the very defective domestic education of American women. It is the only country where women in the middle ranks of social life consider domestic avocations as unlady-like—in England and on the Continent it is a part of the home training. Education must be given not as an end but as a means to an end, and that end, to woman, a clearly defined one. Her destiny has by a holy law been fixed, and she when rightly educated is fitted for her sphere, and when she keeps in it, is happy in the fulfilment of her duties. In times past she was only given a domestic education. Her mental training was not considered necessary—her sympathies were limited solely to household cares—and her conversation to domestic detail. Now she is taught every accomplishment possible to be taught, and all her time is devoted to the acquisition of showy accomplishments or to the society of those whose pursuits are of the same character. Both extremes are reprehensible, but of the two the olden time practical system was more calculated to render her happy and beloved; her destination being her home. There, and there only must she look for compensating enjoyment in duties fulfilled.

An intellectual and domestic woman is most attractive—knowledge does not unfit her for the attention to be given to the comfort of those about her. Mental culture strengthens the judgment and the understanding—when this effect is not produced better limit her information as the women of bye-gone times, to the compounding of receipts and the use of the distaff, for then she will at least be useful—not the mere drawing-room ornament which we now see. I fear much that is in the present age termed education is like that spoken of by the Poet in relation to our first Parents:

"Knowledge of good, bought dear by knowing ill."

In no country as in this does its future destinies so entirely depend on woman. Her influence will be felt by future generations, for from that home circle over which it is her privilege to preside, will come—the lawgivers and the legislators of this our favoured land. If the discipline there received has not been of a healthy, moral character, and obedience and truth, the first principles inculcated, then must we expect from those thus so neglected—misrule and political dishonesty when placed in power. In this Country where every avenue to distinction is open, a mother cannot know to what high place of trust her son may be elevated should he be endowed with abilities. Therefore so train the daughters that they may fulfil this holy mission in the domestic sphere, and send forth their children from their Christian nests, provided with those principles which will prove their safeguard in passing through the Scylla and Charybdis of this world. So guarded, a mother may trust her children in the world's great sea; without it many a soul freighted bark is lost in the Maelstrom of temptation and sin. And what agony for a parent to bear the reproaches and remorse of conscience, and to be obliged to say, "I have not fulfilled my trust." Not to the gay butterfly of fashion is this addressed; she has her season and is content.

And how is this best to be effected? By educating mothers and making home what it should be, a spot dearer than all others, a haven of rest. Poets have sung—travellers written about the comforts of a well regulated "English home," why cannot we have our model "American homes?" And to do this is woman's privilege. A precious boon of Christianity, she can by the sunshine of love and the exercise of the domestic affections, dispel all the vapour and malaria threatening moral destruction to home influence.

Let her not listen to that mental ignus fatuus, "women's rights," but keep her head and heart clear from all that may cause her to lose sight of her true destiny, and be content to be the keystone in that beautiful temple of liberty, designed and executed by those noble spirits who risked all in its erection. To woman is entrusted the training of the heart and head of those who are to guard this model fabric.

She must render that home happy where all these virtues are to be fostered, and it is by attention to the domestic duties, that this is to be accomplished, and this is compatible with the highest intellectual attainments.

But few of the young ladies now floating on the summer sea of thoughtless enjoyment, can realize the Poet's description of an accomplished woman:

——— "She had read
Her Father's well-filled library with profit,
And could talk charmingly. Then she could sing
And play with taste and feeling—and dance with grace.
She sketched from nature well—and studied flowers—
Which was enough to love her for—
Yet she was knowing in all needle-work,
And shone in Dairy—and in Kitchen too
As in the Parlour."

Time was when ladies looked to the ways of their household. Now such matters are left to inexperienced foreigners who swarm our shores. On them has fallen the domestic mantle. The consequence is, the young and uninitiated wife must be taken to a hotel or boarding-house to spend that most important period of her married life, instead of enjoying the quiet of their own fireside, there to become familiarized with each other's characters, and binding their young hearts more closely by domestic intercourse, for a man feels his responsibility more in his own home. Their individuality is lost in a crowd, and they soon cease to be necessary to each other's happiness. How many estrangements if nothing worse will boarding-house annals give, all arising from maternal neglect. Club houses are increasing; what a commentary on the times! American mothers must cease to be like Circassian parents—giving their daughters Mahommedan educations—training them for the ball-room and gala nights as for a market arena.

But render them true hearted women, fitting them for each department in the domestic cabinet, and thus enabling them to fulfil the positive duties of life with credit to themselves, and comfort to those whose happiness they have assumed.

The first object of a woman's care must be the family laboratory—the kitchen. On that being well looked to, the health and happiness of the household depend.

She need not degenerate into a drudge, but let her initiate her uninstructed domestic—and then she be only supervisor, not operative. Surely she has a compensation sufficient for a daughter, wife, or sister, in witnessing the pleasure with which those so nearly allied to her, assemble around a neatly arranged table, spread with wholesome food, if not prepared by her hand, at least under her direction; which will produce in her mind the most pleasant emotions? A morning spent often in idle loungings and heartless visits, or one given to these much neglected household duties?

I would not be understood as countenancing the "Gourmand," but only giving attention to that which nourishes, thereby producing health and comfort. One of the most fruitful causes of dyspepsia in our country is the manner in which the food is prepared. We have every thing that can be desired either in the animal or vegetable kingdom, and yet nature's best gifts are rendered poisonous by the preparation. We leave the family laboratory too often in the hands ot the ignorant and inexperienced. What chemist would commit such a folly as to entrust to an uninitiated workman the preparation of a chemical test? How much more that which is to be taken into that delicate organ, the stomach—which is in the present arrangement sadly taxed by the compounds introduced by ignorance and consequent want of skill.

One who does not attend to the domestic details and has not a well regulated home, cannot enjoy or fulfil the rites of hospitality, one of the pleasures and duties of life inculcated by Scripture. Being always ready, is the result of well administered household laws, and makes the guests feel welcome, not by words alone but by evident facts. How often is the pleasure of a long anticipated visit to a friend, entirely destroyed by finding on your arrival that it is inopportune, in consequence of some rebellion in the "Kitchen Cabinet," or absence of one of the operatives; and scarcely are the first greetings over, before the budget of domestic troubles is opened, and you are without it being intended, made to feel an intruder by apologies for things being out of sorts, and by a detail of the catalogue of trials occasioned by servants. Quickly vanishes all those long anticipated quiet chats of "Auld lang syne," and pleasant readings of books once enjoyed together, until in very weariness you are ready to exclaim "I wish I was away."

How easily all this might be obviated, if left without assistants, by a knowledge of domestic avocations, and by going to work with a willing spirit and a skilful hand. 'Tis true it is annoying, but if skilled, it is not perplexing. Besides you are independent, and believe me, in domestic duties, as in the affairs of life, "knowledge is power." There are cases where ill health prevents such attention to family concerns, as is necessary for home comforts; then, some experienced person should be procured, and not the whole family be made uncomfortable by the incapacity of one member, even if that is the head. Much of the ill health of our American women arises from defective and often neglected physical training. The habits of life pursued by girls is calculated to produce delicacy of constitution, and unfit them for the duties of wives and mothers. Parents are responsible for this also; often are girls enfeebled by luxury, and softened by sloth, when strength forsakes their limbs, and health their constitution. Instruct them in the laws of nature, and of the effects which will necessarily follow when these physical laws are neglected or violated; this is a *mother's* duty.

"The practical duties of life enrich the heart and fancy; for action, like a strong current, clears and deepens the affections; the discontent induced by a consciousness of wrong-doing will render turbid the whole temper of the mind. Whereas, having done to the best of our abilities, produces a peaceful and happy influence, before which irritability vanishes like a cloud—the for a time withered sympathies of this world and home, again revive and bloom. Do the right and your ideal is perfected; the exercise of the affections has a most purifying effect on the character." Turn not the daily routine of life's duties into slave labour imposed by a hard task master, although self-sacrifice is needful for the growth and health of conscience; but feel that all the trials of domestic life are ordered by one who formed woman for the niche she fills, man's counsellor and friend, therefore, let all her duties be performed in a cheerful and affectionate spirit. The acts of housewifery are professional—and consequently must be early commenced. They demand energy of mind and body, every thing must be done by maternal care to produce this. When troubles darken the domestic horizon, woman must be at her post to meet the storm and if possible avert it. And in the performance of all these duties, she must "be happy without witnesses, and content without panegyrists"—the exercise of which will not bring celebrity, but improve her usefulness.

Let the American woman only desire from those she loves the praise that "she presideth in her house, and there is peace, she commandeth with judgment and is obeyed, the care of her family is her whole delight: to that alone she applieth her study, and elegance and frugality are seen in her mansion."

CONTENTS.

ADVICE FOR KITCHEN AND DINING-ROOM.

Of all the apartments in a house, this for the health and happiness of the family is the most important, and strange to say, in modern days the most neglected. It is the family laboratory. All the utensils should be kept in order, and of them a plentiful supply for the proper preparation of the food. Let cleanliness and order be the presiding spirits, for without either there can be nothing satisfactorily accomplished, and although economy should regulate the household, yet it is a mistaken economy which pinches the kitchen for the embellishment of the drawing-room, or the wardrobe. Economy is essential in a woman for her properly performing the duties of a wife and mother. Care and economy should therefore be exercised, but let it characterize *every* expenditure, as economy and a well spread board are perfectly compatible.

Much depends on the articles to be prepared, and then the vessels in which they are cooked. Copper utensils are altogether objectionable. The use of saleratus is another injurious habit. A little best quality soda, in judicious hands is not hurtful. Doubtful meats should never be used—the least taint may produce in the stomach most serious consequences, while good meat is necessary for nourishment and consequent health: sometimes tainted meat is prepared and so disguised by spice that the palate does not discover it, but the poor digestive organs become deranged if not materially injured.

A vessel should be set apart for each particular purpose,

and held sacred to it, thus, a milk sauce-pan should be used for no other purpose. A "soup pot" the same; vegetable pots the same, and so on through the whole list of culinary vessels. Not as is too often, one made to pay not a "double debt" only—but many. Care should be exercised in their use, and with the requisite supervision of the mistress they will last a long period. In modern days the progress of invention has supplied us with articles which are labor-saving, and most important aids in perfecting the culinary art. The "Jelly strainer" is a great improvement on the jelly bag; the "Digestor" on the ordinary "Soup Pot;" the variety of ladles, strainers, and spoons are all important to the skilful housewife.

The table arrangements require the careful eye of the mistress. An elegantly prepared dinner may have all the effect destroyed by untidiness in the laying of the table. A clean cloth and napkins, sharp knives, the castor in order, the plates, in winter especially, well heated. All these details are important as involving the comfort of the family. For guests or set company they are always looked to, but I am now pleading for every day life—the family board, which influences the character by the observance of the little courtesies in household intercourse. The first impressions are received under the domestic roof, how necessary that order and regularity should be amongst the first lessons taught. There are many little details which cost a trifle, yet give a table an inviting appearance: and as to that which is denominated the administration of the "honours of the table," how often those who serve seem not to understand the art of dispensing judiciously the "loaves and fishes!" A good carver will help in an equitable manner the dainty before him. It is an accomplishment which should be learned by men and women. Chesterfield says, "A man who tells you gravely he cannot carve, may as well tell you he cannot feed himself. It is both as necessary and easy."

Prime joints are often mutilated by inexperienced carvers, and rendered unfit for a second appearance. With a good carving knife, which should be sharp and light, a lady may soon learn to be a carver. It requires more skill than strength. If the butcher has properly divided the bones, nothing but practice will make a carver, although there are illustrations given of the style in which it is done.

The suggestions and receipts here given are the experience of a practical housekeeper who has kept a manual, and recommends all housekeepers to do the same, by which means she has been enabled to collect much that is valuable in domestic concerns.

> "Experience is by industry achieved
> And perfected by the swift course of time."

ILLUSTRATIONS OF CARVING.

On Carving.

One of the most important acquisitions in the routine of daily life is the ability to carve well, and not only well but elegantly. It is true that the modes now adopted of sending meats, &c., to table are fast banishing the necessity for promiscuous carving from the elegantly served boards of the wealthy; but in the circles of middle life, where the refinements of cookery are not adopted, the utility of a skill in the use of a carving knife is sufficiently obvious.

It must not be supposed that the necessity for this acquirement is confined to the heads of families alone, it is as important for the bachelor visitor to be familiar with the art, as it is for the host himself; indeed he is singled out usually for the task of carving a side dish, which happening to be poultry of some kind, becomes a task most embarrassing to him, if he should happen to be ignorant of the *modus operandi* of skilfully dissecting a fowl. He may happen to be on the right hand of the lady of the house, and at her request, very politely conveyed, he cannot refuse: he rises, therefore, to his task as though one of the labors of Hercules had been suddenly imposed on him; he first casts around him a nervous glance to ascertain whether any one else is carving a fowl, in order to see where they insert their fork, at what part they commence, and how they go on; but it generally happens that he is not so fortunate as he desires, and therefore he is left to get through the operation as well as he can. He takes up his knife and fork desperately, he knows that a wing is good, a slice of the breast is a dainty, and that a leg is a gentleman's portion, so he sticks his fork in at random, and slashes at the wing, misses the joint, and endeavours to cut through the bone; it is not an easy task, he mutters something about his knife not being sharp, essays a grin and a faint *jeu de mot* at the expense of the fowl's age, and finding the bone will not sunder by fair means, he puts out his strength, gets off the wing with a sudden dash which propels the mangled member off the dish upon the cloth, sends the body of the fowl quite to the edge of the dish, and with the jerk splashes a quantity of gravy over the rich dinner dress of the lady seated next to him, much to her chagrin at the injury to her robe, and her contempt for the barbarous ignorance he has displayed. He has to make a thousand apologies for his stupidity, which only serve to make his deficiency more apparent, he becomes heated, suffused with blushes and perspiration, continues hacking and mangling the fowl until he has disjointed the wings and legs, and then, alas! the body presents itself to him as a *terra incognita*, what to do with it he is at a complete loss to imagine, but it must be carved, he has strength of wrist, and he crashes through it at the hazard of repeating the mishaps he commenced with. His task over, he sits down confused and uncomfortable to find his efforts have caused the rejection of any portion of the fowl he has wrenched asunder by those who have witnessed his bungling attempt; he is digusted with the fowl, himself, carving, and everything else; loses all enjoyment for his dinner, and during the remainder of the evening cannot recover his equilibrium.

He will possibly too have the very questionable satisfaction of witnessing an accomplished carver dissect a fowl; he perceives with a species of wonder that he retains his seat, plants his fork in the bird, removes the wings and legs as if by magic, then follows merry-thought and neck bones, then the breast, away come the two sides men, and the bird is dissected; all this too is accomplished without effort and with an elegance of manner as surprising as captivating; the pieces carved look quite tempting, while there is no perceptible difference in the temperature of the carver, he is as cool and collected as ever, and assists the portions he has carved with as much grace as he displayed in carving the fowl. The truth is, he is acquainted with the anatomy of the bird, he has felt the necessity of acquiring the art, and has taken advantage of every opportunity which has enabled him to perfect himself in the requisite knowledge to attain the position at which he has arrived.

Ladies ought especially to make carving a study; at their own houses they grace the table, and should be enabled to perform the task allotted to them with sufficient skill to prevent remark or the calling forth of eager proffers of assistance from good natured visitors near, who probably would not present any better claim to a neat performance.

Carving presents no difficulties; it requires simply knowledge. All displays of exertion or violence are in very bad

taste; for, if not proved an evidence of the want of ability on the part of the carver, they present a very strong testimony of the toughness of a joint or the more than full age of a bird: in both cases they should be avoided. A good knife of moderate size, sufficient length of handle, and very sharp, is requisite; for a lady it should be light, and smaller than that used by gentlemen. Fowls are very easily carved, and in joints, such as loins, breasts, fore-quarters, &c., the butcher should have strict injunctions to separate the joints well.

The dish upon which the article to be carved is placed should be conveniently near to the carver, so that he has full control over it; for if far off, nothing can prevent an ungracefulness of appearance, nor a difficulty in performing that which in its proper place could be achieved with ease.

In serving fish, some nicety and care must be exercised

here lightness of hand and dexterity of management is necessary, and can only be acquired by practice. The flakes which, in such fish as salmon and cod are large, should not be broken in serving, for the beauty of the fish is then destroyed, and the appetite for it injured. In addition to the skill in the use of the knife, there is also required another description of knowledge, and that is an acquaintance with the best parts of the joint, fowl, or fish being carved. Thus in a haunch of venison the fat, which is a favourite, must be served with each slice; in the shoulder of mutton there are some delicate cuts in the under part. The breast and wings are the best parts of a fowl, the trail of a woodcock on a toast is the choicest part of the bird. In fish a part of the roe, smelt, or liver should accompany the piece of fish served; the list, however is too numerous to mention here; and indeed, the knowledge can only be acquired by experience. In large establishments the gross dishes are carved at the buffet by the butler, but in middle society they are placed upon the table. In the following directions accompanied by diagrams, we have endeavoured to be as explicit as possible; but while they will prove as landmarks to the uninitiated, he will find that practice alone will enable him to carve with skill and facility.

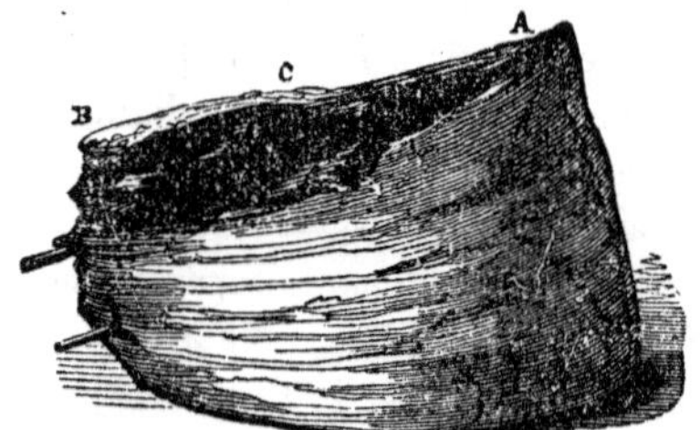

Aitch-Bone.

An Aitch-bone of Beef. This is a simple joint to carve, but the slices from it must be cut quite even, and of a very moderate thickness. When the joint is boiled, before cutting to serve, remove a slice from the whole of the upper part of sufficient thickness, say a quarter of an inch, in order to arrive at the juicy part of the meat at once. Carve from A to B, let the slices be moderately thin—not too thin; help fat with the lean in one piece, and give a little additional fat which you will find below C; the solid fat is at A, and must be cut in slices horizontally. The *round of beef* is carved in the same manner.

RIBS OF BEEF. There are two modes of carving this joint; the first, which is now becoming common, and is easy to an amateur carver, is to cut across the bone commencing in the centre, and serving fat from A, as marked in the engraving of the sirloin, or it should be carved in slices from A to C, commencing either in the centre of the joint or at the sides, Occasionally the bones are removed, and the meat formed into a fillet; it should then be carved as a round of beef.

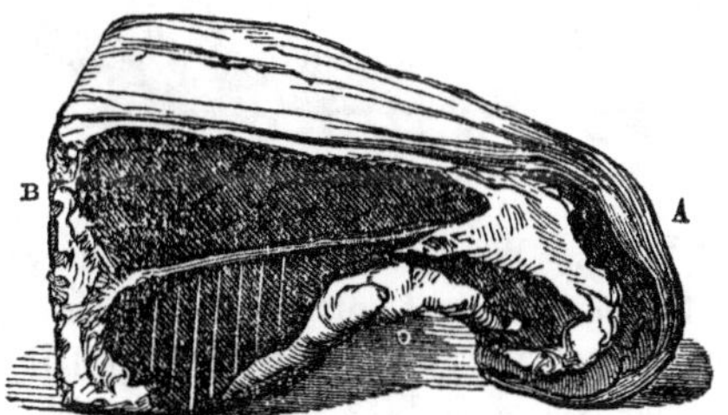

Sirloin of Beef

THE SIRLOIN OF BEEF. The under part should be first served, and carved as indicated in the engraving, across the bone. In carving the upper part the same directions should be followed as for the ribs, carving either side, or in the centre, from A to B, and helping the fat from D.

Fillet of Veal.

FILLET OF VEAL. Cut a slice off the whole of the upper part in the same way as from a round of beef; this being, if well roasted, of a nice brown, should be helped in small pieces with the slices you cut for each person. The stuffing is skewered in the flap, and where the bone comes out there is some placed; help this with the meat with a piece of the fat.

Neck of Veal.

NECK OF VEAL. Were you to attempt to carve each chop, and serve it, you would not only place a gigantic piece upon the plate of the person you intended to help, but you would waste much time, and should the vertebræ have not been jointed by the butcher, you would find yourself in the position of the ungraceful carver being compelled to exercise a degree of strength which should never be suffered to appear, very possibly, too, assisting gravy in a manner not contemplated by the person unfortunate enough to receive it. Cut diagonally from B to A, and help in slices of moderate thickness; you can cut from C to D in order to separate the small bones, divide and serve them, having first inquired if they are desired.

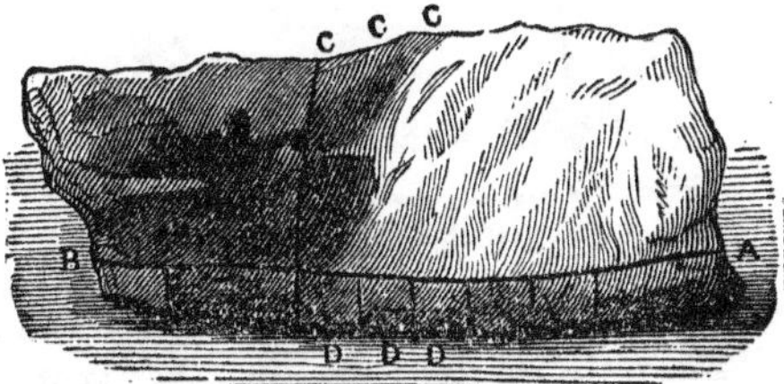

Breast of Veal.

THE BREAST OF VEAL. Separate the ribs from the brisket, cuting from A to B; these small bones, which are the sweetest and mostly chosen, you will cut as at D D D, and serve; the long ribs are divided as at C C C, and having ascertained the preference of the person, help accordingly; at good tables the scrag is not served, but is found, when properly cooked, a very good stew.

LOIN OF VEAL. This joint is sent to table served as a sirloin of beef. Having turned it over, cut out the kidney and the fat, return it to its proper position, and carve it as in the neck of veal, from B to A; help with it a slice of kidney and fat. The kidney is usually placed upon a dry toast when removed from the joint.

SHOULDER OF VEAL is sent to table with the under part placed uppermost. Help it as a shoulder of mutton, beginning at the knuckle end.

A TONGUE. Cut nearly through the middle, at the line 1, and take thin slices from each side. The fat is situated underneath, at the root of the tongue.

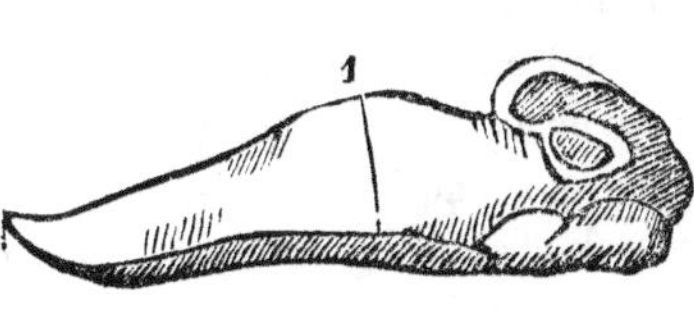

A Tongue.

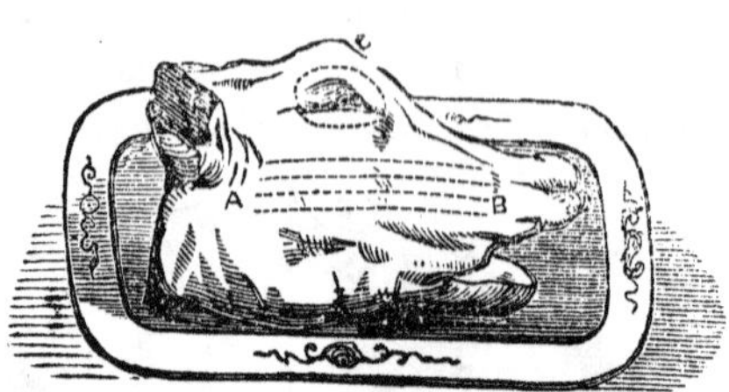

Half of Calf's Head.

CALF'S HEAD. There is much more meat to be obtained from a calf's head by carving it one way than another. Carve from A to B, cutting quite down to the bone. At the fleshy part of the neck end you will find the throat sweetbread which you can help a slice of with the other part; you will remove the eye with the point of the knife and divide it in half, helping those to it who professs a preference for it, there are some tasty, gelatinous pieces around it which are palatable. Remove the jaw bone, and then you will meet with some fine flavoured lean; the palate, which is under the head, is by some thought a dainty and should be proffered when carving.

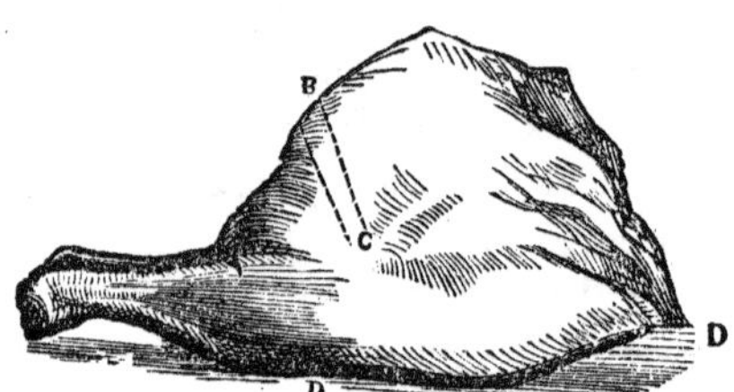

Leg of Mutton.

LEG OF MUTTON. The under or thickest part of the leg should be placed uppermost and carved in slices moderately thin from B to C. Many persons have a taste for the knuckle, and this question should be asked, and if preferred should be assisted. When cold, the back of the leg should be placed uppermost, and thus carved : if the cramp bone is requested, and some persons regard it as a dainty, hold the shank with your left hand, and insert your knife at D, passing it round to E, and you will remove it.

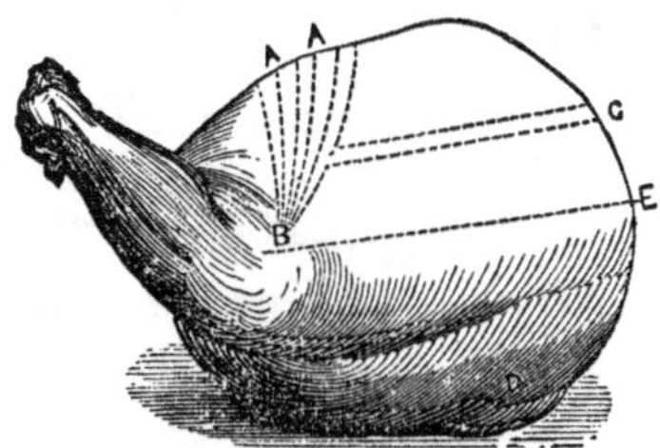

A Shoulder of Mutton Boiled.

A Shoulder of mutton. This is a joint upon which a great diversity of opinion exists, many professing a species of horror at its insipidity; others finding much delicacy of flavour in certain parts. In good mutton there is no doubt but that if properly managed it is an excellent joint, and if judiciously carved will give satisfaction to all who partake of it. It should be served and eaten very hot. It is sent to table lying on the dish as shown in the annexed engraving. Commence carving from A to B, taking out moderately thin slices in the shape of a wedge ; some nice pieces may then be helped from the blade bone, from C to B, cutting on both sides of the bone. Cut the fat from D, carving it in thin slices. Some of the most delicate parts however lie on the under part of the shoulder ; take off thin pieces horizontally from B to C, and from A ; some tender slices are to be met with at D, but they must be cut through as indicated.

The shoulder of mutton is essentially a joint of tit-bits, and therefore when carving it, the tastes of those at table should be consulted. It is a very insipid joint when cold, and should therefore be hashed if sent to table a second time.

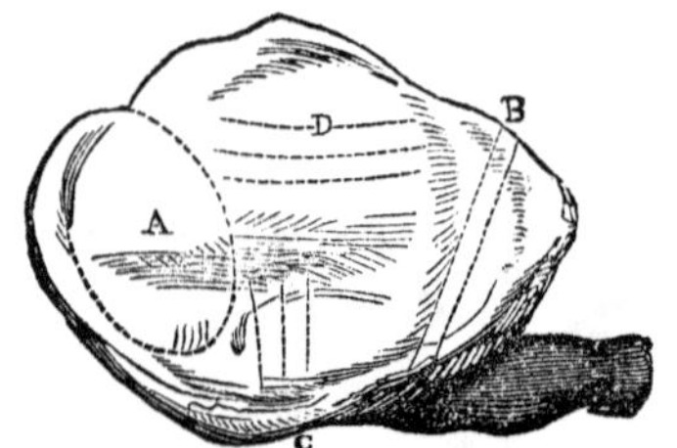

A Shoulder of Mutton, Boiled or Stewed, with celery sauce.

THE LOIN OF MUTTON, if small, should be carved in chops beginning with the outer chop; if large, carve slices the whole length. A neat way is to run the knife along the chine bone and under the meat along the ribs, it may then be cut in slices as shown in the engraving of the saddle of mutton below; by this process fat and lean are served together; your knife should be very sharp and it should be done cleverly.

NECK OF MUTTON, if the scrag and chine bone are removed, is carved in the direction of the bones.

THE SCRAG OF MUTTON should be separated from the ribs of the neck, and when roasted, the bones assisted with the meat.

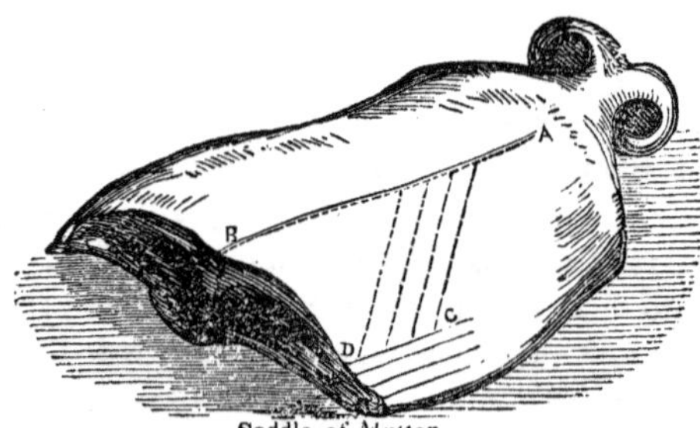

Saddle of Mutton.

SADDLE OF MUTTON. The tail end is divided in the engraving and the kidneys skewered under each division; this is a matter of taste, and is not always done. Carve from A to B in thin slices, help fat from C to D. You may help from the vertebræ on both sides of the loin, and then carve cross-wise as marked in the engraving, which gives you both fat and lean; help a slice of kidney to those who desire it.

HAUNCH OF MUTTON is carved as *haunch of venison.*

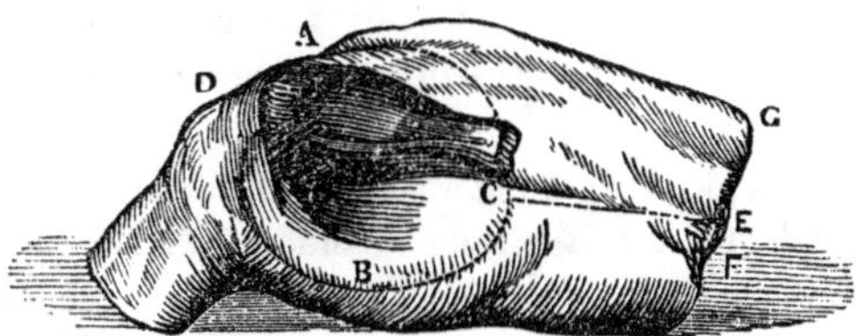

Fore Quarter of Lamb broiled.

FORE QUARTER OF LAMB. Place your fork near the knuckle and cut from A, to C, to B, and on to D; pass your knife under, lifting with the fork at the same time. The juice of half a lemon or Seville orange which has been sprinkled with salt and pepper, is then squeezed under the shoulder, and a slice of fresh butter placed there also, the parts are re-united until the butter is melted, and the shoulder is then placed upon a separate dish; separate the neck from the ribs, from E to D, and then assist the breast G, or the neck F, according to the palate of your guest.

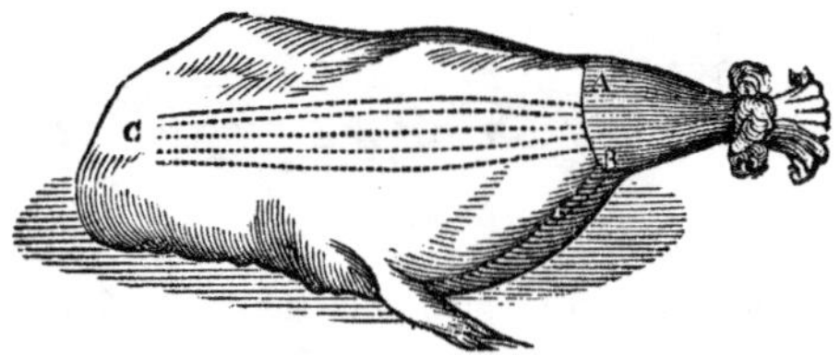

Haunch of Venison.

HAUNCH OF VENISON. Have the dish placed before you so that the loin is nearest to you, and the knuckle farthest.

then cut from A to B, sufficiently near the knuckle to prevent the escape of any gravy, then make your first cut from A to C, with a slanting cut, and then let each succeeding slice be sloping so that all the gravy may be retained in the hollow thus formed ; the fat will be found at the left side, and must be served with the meat.

NECK OF VENISON should be carved across the ribs, as in the neck of veal, or length-wise, from one end of the neck to the other.

KID, if kept until the age at which lambs are killed, is served and carved in the same manner ; if killed at a month or five weeks, they are roasted whole and carved in the kitchen.

PORK. The leg when sent to the table should be placed with the back uppermost and the crackling be removed ; if sufficiently baked, this may be done with ease ; the meat should be served in thin slices cut across the leg, the crackling being served with it, or not, according to taste ; the loins are cut into the pieces as scored by the butcher

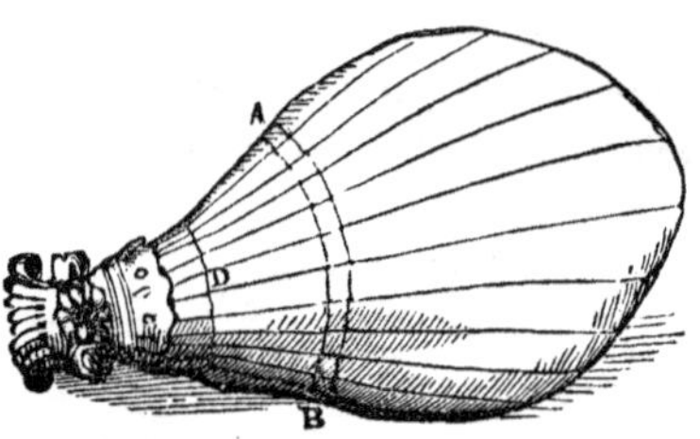

Ham

HAM. It is served as placed in the engraving, and should come to table ornamented. Carve from A to B, cutting thin slices cut slantingly, to give a wedge like appearance. Those who prefer the *hock* carve at D, in the same direction as from A to B, then carve from D to C, in thin slices, as indicated in the diagram:

BOILED TONGUE. Carve across the tongue, but do not cut

through; keep the slices rather thin, and help the fat from underneath.

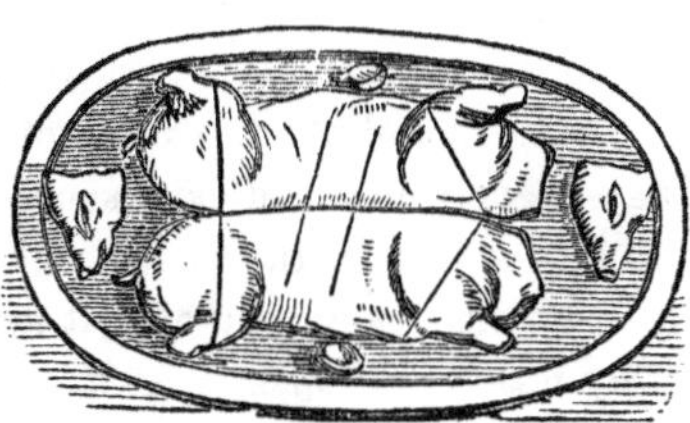

Roast Pig.

SUCKING PIG. The cook should send a roast pig to table as displayed here, garnished with head and ears, carve the joints in the direction shown by the lines in the diagram, then divide the ribs, serve with plenty of sauce ; should one of the joints be too much it may be separated ; bread sauce and stuffing should accompany it. An ear and the jaw are favourite parts with many people.

Roast Turkey.

POULTRY. Poultry requires skilful carving ; the requisites are, grace of manner, ease in the performance, a perfect knowledge of the position of the joints, and the most complete mode of dissecting, so as to obtain the largest quantity of meat: In no case is this ability more demanded than in carving a Roast Turkey. Unless this is done well, there is not only much waste, but the appearance of the turkey is spoiled. You will commence by carving slices from each side of the breast, in the same directions as the lines marked in the engraving, cutting from A to B. Now remove the legs, dividing the thighs from the drumsticks, and here an instrument termed a *disjointer* will be found serviceable. for unless the turkey be very young, and the union of the joints very accurately taken, dislocation becomes difficult: the disjointer effects the separation at once, and it possesses also the advan tages of enabling the carver to divide a thigh into two, thus permitting a less bulky portion of a part much esteemed to be served. The pinions and that portion of body removed with it, are always a delicacy, and care should be taken to carve them nicely; the joint of the pinion will be found at B. The stuffing, whether truffles or whatever it may be made of, you will obtain by making an opening at C.

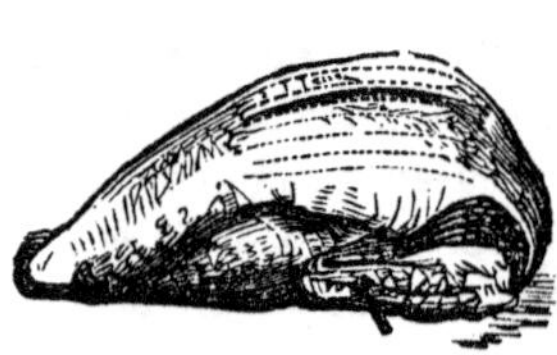

Boiled Turkey.

BOILED TURKEY is trussed in a different fashion to the roast, but the same directions given for the first applies to the second. The legs in the boiled turkey being drawn into the body may cause some little difficulty at first in their separation, but a little practice will soon surmount it:

TURKEY POULTS. Refer to directions for carving pheasants.

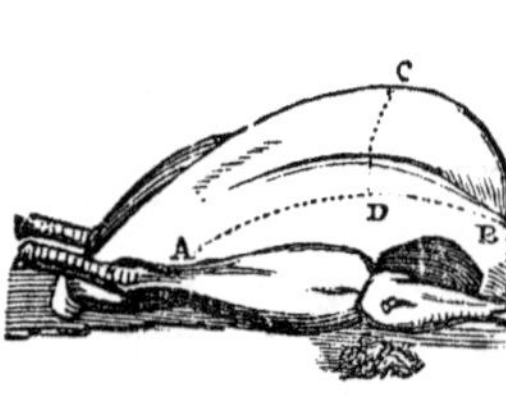

Roast Fowl.

ROAST FOWL: This operation is a nice and skilful one to perform, it requires both observation and practice. Insert the knife between the legs and the side, press back the leg with the blade of the knife, and the joint will disclose itself: if young it will part, but at best, if judiciously managed, will require but a nick where the joints unite. Remove your wing from D to B, cut through and lay it back as with the leg, separating the joint with the edge of your knife, remove the merrythought and neck bones next, this you will accomplish by inserting the knife and forcing it under the bones, raise it and it will readily separate from the breast. You will divide the breast from the body by cutting through the small ribs down to the vent, turn the back uppermost, now put your knife into about the centre between the neck and rump, raise the lower part firmly yet gently, it will easily separate, turn the neck or rump from you, take off the side bones and the fowl is carved.

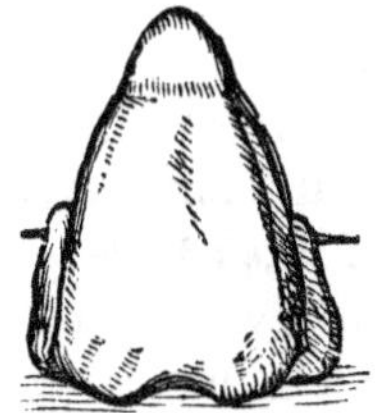

Boiled Fowl (breast).

Boiled Fowl (back).

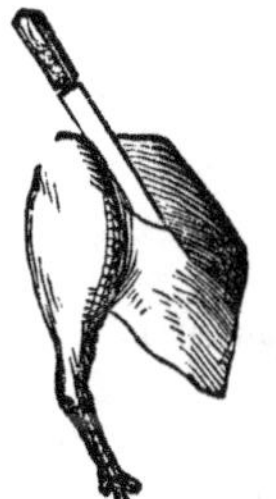

In separating the thigh from the drumstick, you must insert the knife exactly at the joint as we have indicated in the engraving, this however will be found to require practice, for the joint must be accurately hit, or else much difficulty will be experienced in getting the parts asunder. There is no difference in carving roast and boiled fowls if full grown; but in a very young fowl when roasted, the breast is served whole. The wings and breast are in the highest favour, but the leg of a young fowl is an excellent part. Capons when very fine and roasted, should have slices carved from the breast.

Roast Goose.

GEESE. Follow with your knife the lines marked in the engraving, A to B, and cut slices, then remove the wing, and if the party be large the legs must also be removed, and here the *disjointer* will again prove serviceable. The stuffing, as in the turkey, will be obtained by making an insertion at the apron C.

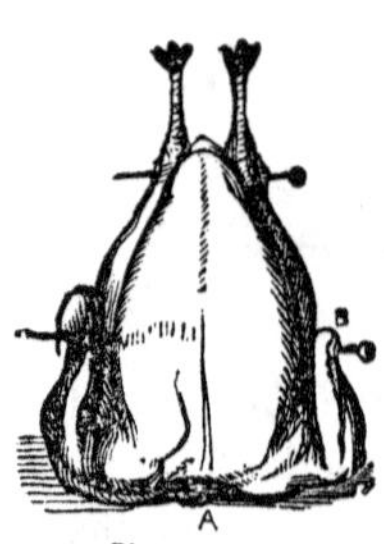

Pheasant.

PHEASANT. Clear the leg by inserting the edge of the knife between it and the body, then take off the wings, B to A, but do not remove much of the breast with them, you are thus enabled to obtain some nice slices; the pheasant is then carved as a fowl. The breast is first in estimation, then the wings, and after these the merry-thought: lovers of game prefer a leg.

GUINEA FOWL are carved in the same manner.

Partridge.

PARTRIDGE. Separate the legs, and then divide the bird into three parts. leaving each leg and wing together. The breast is then divided from the back, and helped whole, the latter being assisted with any of the other parts. When the party consists entirely of gentlemen only, the bird is divided into two by cutting right through from the vent to the neck.

Quails, Landrail, Wheat-ears, Larks, and all small birds are served whole.

Grouse and Plover are carved as partridges.

Snipe and Woodcock, are divided into two parts; the trail being served on a toast.

Wild-duck and Widgeon. The breast of these fowls being the best portion is carved in slices, which, being removed, a glass of old port made hot is poured in, the half of a lemon seasoned with cayenne and salt should then be squeezed in, the slices relaid in their places, and then served, the joints being removed the same as in other fowl.

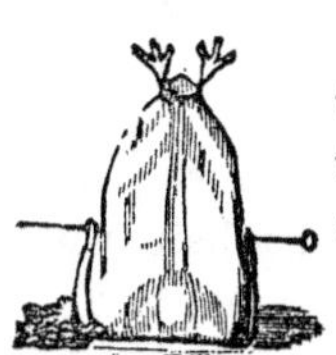

Pidgeon (breast).

Pidgeon. Like woodcock, these birds are cut in half, through the breast and back, and helped.

Pidgeon (back).

FISH.

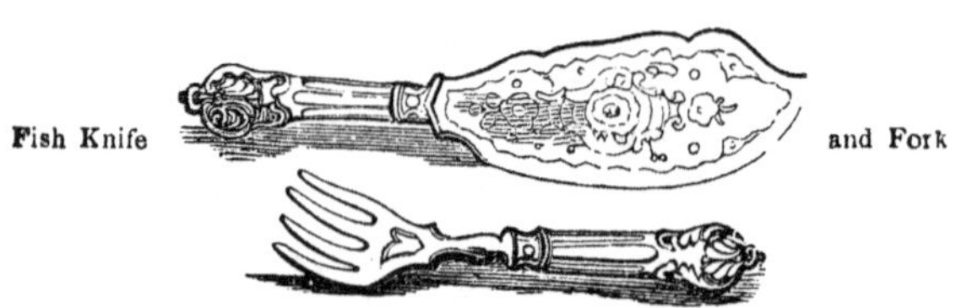
Fish Knife and Fork

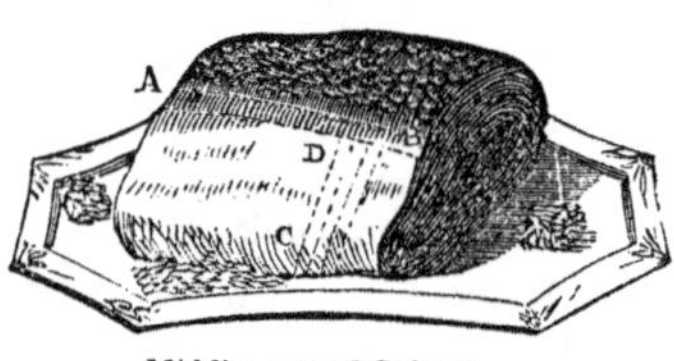

Middle cut of Salmon.

Fish should never be carved with steel; assisting requires more care than knowledge; the principal caution is to avoid breaking the flakes. In carving a piece of salmon as here engraved, cut thin slices, as from A to B, and help with it pieces of the belly in the direction marked from C to D; the best flavoured is the upper or thick part.

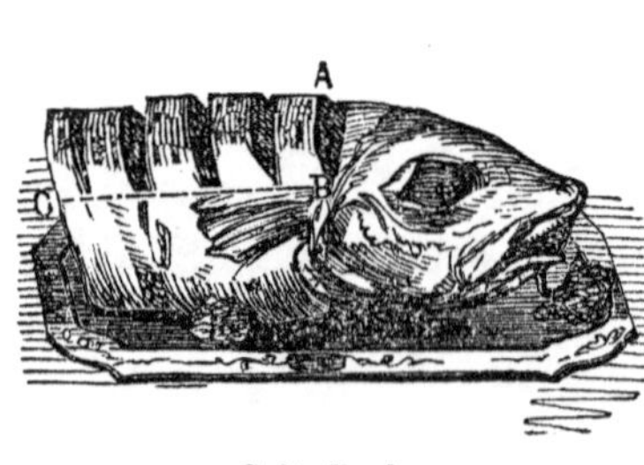

Cod's Head

Cod's Head and Shoulders. Carry the knife from A to B, and then along the line to C, help slices accompanied by some of the sound, which is to be found lining the back, and which you may obtain by passing the knife under the back-bone at C, serve also a piece of liver. Many choice parts lie in this dish, and by inquiry you will soon ascertain the parts preferred. The jaw-bone from its gelatinous nature is considered by some a dainty, and the head generally, including eyes and palate, is a favourite with many.

HADDOCK. It is dressed whole, unless unusually large. When sent to table it is split its whole length, and served one-half the head to the tail of the other part; it is carved across

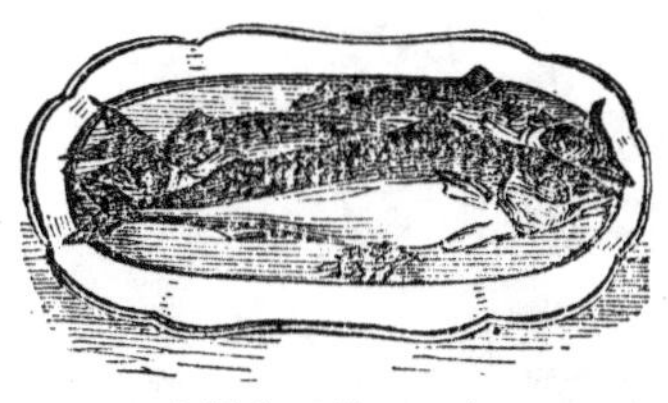

A Dish of Mackerel.

MACKEREL should always be sent to table head to tail, divide the meat from the bone by cutting down the back length-wise, the upper part is the best.

All small fish, such as perch—herrings—smelts—mullets, &c., are served whole.

MUTTON.

The Sheep is thus apportioned by butchers.

- A The Leg.
- B Loin (the best end).
- C Loin (chump end).
- D Neck (best end).
- E Neck (scrag end).
- F Shoulder
- G Breast.

The Saddle of Mutton is the union of the two loins—the Chine is the union of the two necks.

BEEF.

A Bullock marked as cut into joints by the Butcher.

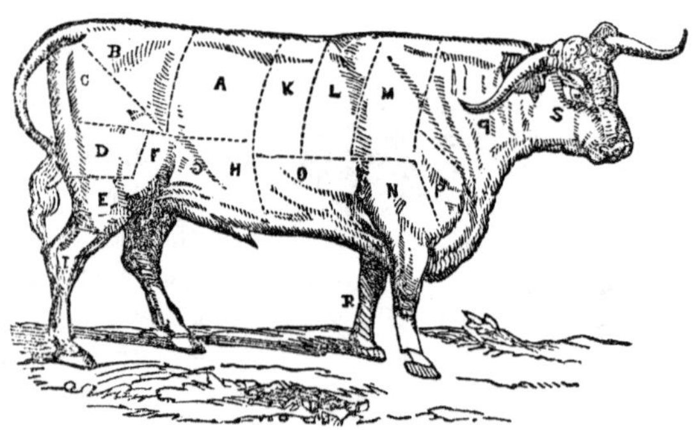

A Sirloin.
B Rump.
C Aitchbone.
D Buttock.
E Mouse Buttock.
F Veiny Piece.
G Thick Flank.
H Thin Flank.
I Leg.

K Fore Ribs, containing five ribs.
L Middle Rib, containing four ribs.
M Chuck Rib, containing three ribs
N Shoulder or leg of Mutton piece
O Brisket.
P Clod.
Q Neck, or Sticking Piece.
R Shin.
S Cheek.

The baron of beef is formed of the pieces marked A. B. united on both sides

VEAL.

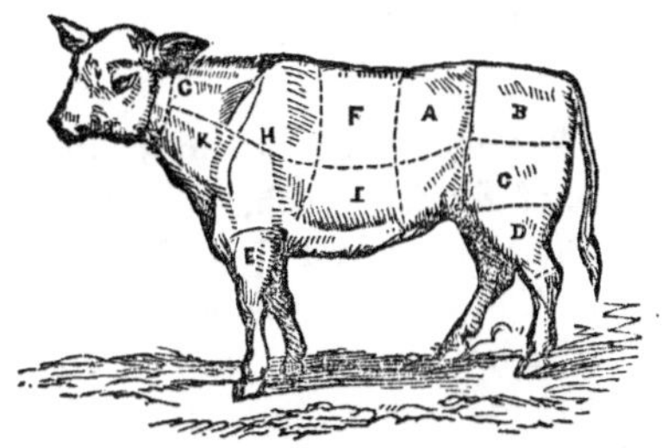

The Calf is divided into joints by the butcher, upon a system which unites the methods employed for cutting up both beef and mutton.

A The Loin (best end).
B The Loin (chump end).
C The Fillet.
D The Hind Knuckle.
E The Fore Knuckle.

F Neck (best end).
G Neck (scrag).
H Blade Bone.
I Breast (best end).
K Breast (Brisket).

PORK.

The Pig is thus divided :—

A The Fore Loin.
B The Hind Loin.

C The Belly, or Spring.
D The Hand.

E The Leg.

The spare rib is under the shoulder, which, when removed in a porker, leaves part of the neck without a skin upon it, forming the spare rib. The head is much liked by many, and appears at table dressed in various ways.

TO CHOOSE MEATS.

Venison.—The choice of venison should be regulated by the appearance of the fat, which, when the venison is young, looks bright, thick, clear, and close. It first changes towards the haunches. To ascertain whether it is sweet, run a knife into that part; if tainted it will have a rank smell. It should not be cooked if too high.

Beef.—True, well-fed beef may be known by the texture and colour; the lean will exhibit an open grain of deep coral-red, and the fat will appear of a healthy, oily smoothness, rather inclining to white than yellow. The suet firm and white. Yellow fat is a test of meat of an inferior quality. Heifer beef is but little inferior to ox beef; the lean is of a closer grain, the red paler, and the fat whiter. Cow beef may be detected by the same signs, save that the older the beast the texture of the meat will appear closer, and the flesh coarser to the sight, as well as harder to the touch.

Veal.—When you observe the kidney well surrounded with fat, you may be sure the meat is of a good quality. The whitest is not the best veal; but the flesh of the bull-calf is a brighter colour than that of the cow-calf. The fillet of the latter is generally preferred, on account of the udder. There is a vein in the shoulder very perceptible; and its colour indicates the freshness of the meat; if a bright red or blue, it is recently killed; if any green or yellow spots are visible, it is stale. The suet will be flabby, and the kidney will smell.

Mutton.—The best is of a fine grain, a bright colour, the fat firm and white. It is better for being full-grown. The meat of the ewe is not so bright, while the grain is closer The ram mutton may be known by the redness of the flesh, and the sponginess of the fat.

LAMB should be eaten very fresh. In the fore quarter, the vein in the neck being any other colour than blue betrays it to be stale. In the hind quarter, try the kidney with your nose; the faintness of its smell will prove it to be stale.

PORK.—In young pork the lean when pinched will break; the thickness and toughness of the rind shows it to be old. In fresh pork the flesh is firm, smooth, a clear colour, and the fat set. When stale it looks clammy and flabby. Measly pork may be detected by the kernels in the fat; it should not be eaten. Dairy-fed pork bears the palm over all others.

BACON.—Excellent young bacon may be thus known:—the lean will be tender and of a bright colour; the fat firm and white, yet bearing a pale rose tinge; the rind thin, and the lean tender to the touch. Rusty bacon has yellow streaks in it.

HAMS.—The test of a sweet ham is to pass a sharp knife to the bone, and when drawn out smell it; if the knife is daubed greasy, and the scent disagreeable, it is bad. A good ham will present an agreeable smell when the knife is withdrawn.

POULTRY AND GAME, TO CHOOSE.

TURKEY.—The cock bird when young has a smooth black leg with a short spur. The eyes bright and full, and moist supple feet when fresh; the absence of these signs denotes age and staleness; the *hen* may be judged by the same rules and is the best.

FOWLS like a turkey; the young cock has a smooth leg and a short spur; when fresh the vent is close and dark. Hens when young have smooth legs and combs; when old these will be rough; a good capon has a thick belly and large rump, a poll comb and a swelling breast.

GEESE.—In young geese the feet and bills will be yellow

and free from hair. When fresh the feet are pliable; they are stiff when stale.

DUCKS may be selected by the same rules.

PIGEONS, when fresh, have supple feet, and the vent will be firm; if discoloured and supple they are stale.

PLOVERS, when fat, have hard vents; but, like almost all other birds, may be chosen by the above rules.

HARES.—When a hare is young and fresh, the cleft in the lip is narrow, the body stiff, the ears tear easily, and the claws are smooth and sharp; and old and stale hares will be the opposite of this. Rabbits the same.

PARTRIDGES.—Yellow legs and a dark bill are signs by which a young bird may be known, and a rigid vent when fresh. When this part is green the bird is stale.

PHEASANTS may be chosen as above; the young birds are known by the short or round spur, which in the old is long and pointed.

TABLE CUTLERY.

THE same rule applies to Table Cutlery as to all other cutting instruments, viz., that they must be frequently sharpened. A servant who understands knife-cleaning, will, before taking them off the board, draw them briskly a few times from back to edge (raising the back a little) first on one side, then on the other, and thus produce an excellent edge; whereas a clumsy inexperienced hand will (by not holding them flat on the board) contrive to give the best steel a dull edge. Hence the necessity of an efficient steel, in using which, care should be taken to raise the back of the knife a quarter of an inch from the steel. Servants are apt, in cleaning knives, to allow the arm to take its natural ball and socket, or half-circular movement, this of course, must completely *round and thicken the edge and wear the back.* Strict injunctions should be given to keep the knife *always flat on the board.* The best knives when new, will not cut, unless the above directions are strictly enforced.

ROASTING MEATS.

THE operation of roasting is intended to loosen the fibres, and prepare it for digestion in the stomach.

In roasting, meat will bear a greater and longer heat than in either boiling or stewing. Roasting is considered by very many, if rightly done, more digestive than boiling or stewing; for although roasting is one of the commonest and most simple processes, yet it requires more attention than to make most made dishes—" to have it done to a turn."

The cook must have her roaster clean and bright; a clear, brisk fire. It is impossible to give a specific rule as for time, but slow roasting is important. The season of the year—the length of time which the meat has been kept—all has an influence. As a general rule, a quarter of an hour to the pound is the best. The young and tender should be roasted; the strong and full grown animal boiled or stewed. Basting is a most important operation in roasting, as the more meat is basted, the sooner and better it is roasted. Never pour gravy over either roasted or boiled joints, as many prefer the juices of the meat to gravy which is made.

A well selected roasting piece of beef—the noble sirloin of about fifteen pounds—will require about three hours and a half. The beef should be kept for several days after it is killed, if the weather will allow; in winter a week.

Have ready the spit and roaster before putting it down. Rub the beef all over with white ground ginger—nothing else ; never salt roasted meat, it draws out the juice ; do not place it too near at first, but allow it to gradually warm ; baste it well at first with a little cold water. When it begins to cook, pin a thick piece of paper on it, to preserve the fat. Keep the fire clear and brisk. Continue every quarter of an hour to baste it. The last half hour remove the paper ; then sprinkle over it a little salt, baste it with a little melted butter, and dredge it with flour ; then let it remain until the froth rises ; then serve on a hot dish. Take the drippings, skim off all the fat, (which must be saved for the dressing of made dishes ;) thicken the gravy with a very little browned flour, which is done by sifting flour on to a tin plate and browning it in an oven. This is nice for all kinds of brown gravies.

SIRLOIN OF BEEF.

This is one of the best dishes that can be put upon a table, and most properly knighted by Charles II., the merry monarch of England. In the cooking, observe strictly the above directions for roasting.

RIBS OF BEEF.

This should be kept some days before eating ; prepare it exactly as the sirloin ; keep the bones next to the fire when first put down—basted and dredged as the other piece. Do not pour gravy over roast beef.

RIBS OF BEEF BONED.

Keep two or three ribs of beef until quite tender ; take off the bones carefully, and skewer it as round as possible, (like a fillet of veal ;) stuff it with a veal stuffing as follows : Quarter of a pound of finely chopped beef suet, three spoonsful of crumbs of bread, a very little sweet marjoram, the grated rind of two lemons, one onion chopped as fine as possible, a little salt and pepper, a half teaspoonful of ground cloves, all mixed together with the yolk of two eggs; stir all well. Secure it in the beef with skewers, and twine crossed over the top, the beef having been previously rubbed with white ground ginger. Then press the spit through it, and cook slowly, basting it as the other. Being a more solid mass, it will require more time, and must be kept down four hours and a half. Just before it is done, dredge it as the other. Make a rich gravy by taking the drippings, remove all the fat and thicken with a little flour, and just before dishing pour over the beef some of this gravy; send the rest in sauce-boat. Serve hot.

ROAST MUTTON.

Mutton should be hung some time before using. All animal food should be hung up in the open air until its fibres have lost some of their toughness, but be careful not to let it hang until it loses its natural sweetness; in that state, it is detrimental to health. The time it should hang to be tender depends on the heat and humidity of the air; if not long enough, it is hard and tough; if too long, it loses its flavour. Care must be taken to hang it in the open air, and dried night and morning, to keep it from damp and mustiness. When the weather is very cold, bring the meat required for dinner into the kitchen early in the morning. Cooked frozen meat is tough. Clean the outside by paring off a thin slice. In summer, if you fear its keeping, either par-roast or parboil, which will keep it surely. Beef requires a large sound fire—mutton a brisk, sharp one. On mutton put neither salt, pepper, or any kind of seasoning when first put to the fire; baste it well, and dredge just before it is done, as the beef. Serve hot.

A LEG OF MUTTON

Weighing eight pounds requires an hour and a half, and is much improved by pouring over it a wine glass full of mushroom catsup or wine when dished. Never put any gravy in the dish, but send it separately, in a sauce-boat. Serve currant jelly with roast mutton.

A SADDLE OR CHINE OF MUTTON

Of ten or twelve pounds, two hours and a half. Have the skin taken off, and skewer it on to preserve the succulence. If this is not done, tie on a piece of paper in roasting; and before it is done, remove the paper and dredge it to froth it, having previously well basted it. Eat with currant jelly or cranberry jelly.

A SHOULDER OF MUTTON.

This is always better boiled than roasted. One of seven pounds, an hour and a half. Introduce the spit at the shank bone, and pass it along the blade bone. Roast as above. A rich gravy from the meat; stir in a little flour to thicken.

A LOIN OF MUTTON

Requires from one and a half to two hours. Never run the spit through the prime part, but skewer and tie on the spit. Baste and dress it as the leg. Serve with currant jelly. But we think this joint is better boiled.

MUTTON VENISON FASHION.

Take a fat loin, remove the kidney, as that will sometimes spoil; let it hang at least a week, if the weather permits. Two days before dressing it for cooking, take ground allspice, ground cloves and black pepper, mix them and rub well into the meat about a tablespoonful of each twice a day for two days. Before dressing it, wash it off and roast as a leg. To preserve the fat of the loin, and keep it in, make a paste of flour and water, and spread very thickly over the meat. Over this tie a double sheet of coarse paper, well buttered. About a quarter of an hour before it is done, remove the paper and paste carefully; then baste and dredge with flour. This is equal to venison. Serve with currant jelly. Pour over the mutton when dished a glass of good cooking wine, but no gravy—serve that in a sauce-boat.

VEAL.

Veal requires particular care to roast a nice brown. Let the fire be the same as for beef. Put it at some distance from the fire at first, to let it roast thoroughly, as it must be well done, but not dried; then draw it near to finish it brown—basting well. For sauce, remove the juices of the meat from the bottom of the roaster, and skim all the fat off, mix in a little flour, salt and pepper, then simmer and serve hot.

FILLET OF VEAL.

A fillet of twelve or fourteen pounds will require nearly four hours' roasting before a good fire. Make some stuffing of a quarter of a pound of finely chopped beef suet, and as much bread crumbs, a large spoonful of finely chopped parsley, a little sweet marjoram, the rinds of two lemons grated, a tablespoonful of grated horse-radish, a little black pepper and salt; these all mixed together well with two hard-boiled, smoothly-rubbed yolks of eggs. Introduce this through the fillet, secure the stuffing with skewers and twine, baste it well, and make a gravy of the dripping, skim off the fat and thicken with flour. Serve hot.

VEAL SWEETBREAD.

Take two fresh sweetbreads, par-boil them for five minutes, then lay them in cold water. This process is called blanching. Beat up the yolks of two eggs, grate some bread crumbs. When the sweetbreads are quite cold, wipe them very dry, run a skewer through them, dip them in the egg and then into the bread crumbs; tie them on a spit, or lay them in a stew-pan with a little butter and a very little veal gravy, and cook them a nice brown. For sauce, take the gravy in which they were cooked, and pour into a saucepan; add the juice of two lemons, a little salt and pepper; toast thin slices of bread, dip them into the gravy and lay the sweetbread on. Serve hot.

LAMB.

This requires much attention in the roasting. All young meats should be well cooked. For a sauce, wash clean a handful of fresh green mint, remove the leaves from the stems, mince it very fine and put it into a sauce boat, and stir in one teaspoonful of brown sugar and four tablespoonfuls of good wine vinegar. Green peas is the vegetable eaten with lamb.

HIND QUARTER.

If eight pounds, it will require nearly two hours roasting. Baste it and froth it by dredging, flour over it as the other roasts.

PORK.

The prime season for pork is from November to March. Great care must be taken that it is sufficiently done. Other meats may be underdone, but pork is uneatable and indigestible, if not well cooked.

QUARTER OF PORK.

A quarter of good young pork is nice cooked in this way. If very young, the leg and loin should be roasted together. For sauce, nicely stewed apples.

A LEG OF PORK.

One of eight pounds requires three hours. The skin must be scored across in narrow stripes, about a quarter of an inch apart Rub it with sage, pepper and salt, well. Do not put it near the fire, when first put down. When it begins to roast, brush it over with a feather dipped in sweet oil. This will render it a better colour than any other method, and is the best way of preventing a blistering of the skin. For a sauce, put three onions finely chopped, and a spoonful of rubbed sage leaves, into a saucepan with four spoonsful of water, cover tightly and simmer gently for ten minutes, then stir in half a teaspoonful of salt and the same of black pepper; add this to the dripping, skim the fat off, and strain the whole through a sieve; then mix in a tablespoonful of browned flour, simmer a few minutes, and send up in a sauce boat with the pork. Stewed apples are always necessary with roast pork.

A NICE ONION SAUCE.

Peel and thinly slice four or five onions, put them into a saucepan with a piece of butter; stir the onion until browned; then stir in slowly a spoonful of flour, four tablespoonfuls of any kind of nice broth, a little pepper and salt; boil this for a few minutes; watch, to prevent its scorching; then add a wine glass full of claret, and the same of mushroom catsup. Strain it through a hair sieve. Serve hot. This is a very nice gravy for steaks.

SAGE AND ONION STUFFING.

Chop very fine three onions, a tablespoonful of sage leaves rubbed very fine; put them into a saucepan with four large spoonsful of water; simmer for ten minutes, covered tightly; half a teaspoonful of salt and the same of black pepper, three tablespoonfuls of bread crumbs, mixed well in; then pour over it three tablespoonfuls of broth or gravy. Stir the whole well together, and use for pork stuffing.

A Sucking Pig Roasted.

A three weeks old pig is the required age; it should be freshly killed. If not fresh, it has lost its crispness. This requires skill and care both in the preparing for the spit and the roasting. The ends require more heat than the middle, and it will take an hour and a half to cook. A small piece of iron, called a "pig iron," should be hung in front of the roaster. This is only a sheet of iron about a foot wide, and a foot and a half long, suspended by wires from the middle of the roaster, and is a most useful appendage to the roaster for moderating the heat in roasting. For a stuffing, use the "Onion Stuffing," with the addition of four good sized boiled and mashed white potatoes. While the potatoes are hot, stir in a lump of butter the size of a walnut.

The pig must be wiped very dry after it is ready for the spit, and rubbed with nice lard. This prevents the blistering of the skin. Baste well while roasting; and just before it it is done, rub it over with a feather dipped in olive oil. Whilst at the fire, and when quite done, cut off the head, take out the brains, and drain all the gravy from the roaster; put the gravy into a saucepan, skim off all the fat, mix a large spoonful of browned flour with the brains and liver, chopped very finely; add a little pepper and salt; then stir it into the gravy and let it simmer fifteen minutes, and serve up in a tureen with the pig. Apple sauce is always eaten with roast pork.

Roast Pork and Beans.

A bacon spare rib, weighing eight or nine pounds, will take three or four hours to cook—not so much from weight as thickness. Lay the thick end near the fire, and cook slowly.

It must be well jointed: crack the ribs as ribs of lamb. When put down to roast, dust on some flour, and baste with melted butter; dry some sage leaves in the oven, rub them very fine, and put into the pepper box and dust it over the pork. While cooking, never pour gravy over anything that is roasted, by so doing the dredging is washed off, and it eats insipid. Have boiled some nice white homony beans, and when the pork is nearly done, lay the beans very dry in a dripping pan, and remove the pork from the spit, and lay it on the beans. Set the pan with the beans and pork in an oven and brown the beans. Make the gravy of drippings in the roaster, skim off the fat, stir in a large spoonful of browned flour, let it simmer ten minutes, add salt and pepper, and serve hot with the pork and beans.

ROAST CORNED PORK.

Take a leg of lightly corned young pork, weighing about eight or nine pounds, make a nice sage and onion stuffing, and stuff the thick end well. Tie over it a piece of well greased, thick paper. Dredge it and prepare it exactly as the fresh pork. Roast slowly about three hours. The sauce the same as for roast pork, and serve stewed apples with it. This is very nice if the meat is carefully roasted, and is good cold.

ROAST TURKEY

Must be well selected. A small hen turkey, weighing eight or ten pounds is the best. This should be kept in a cool, dry place several days before cooking. Poultry should not be allowed to freeze, it affects the flavor.

A turkey of the above size will require about two hours. First singe it with lighted clean paper, then with a penknife pick out the pin feathers; break the breast bone to give it a plump appearance, and pull the sinews out of the legs, then draw it very carefully, and do not break the gall-bag, as no after washing will take off the bitter taste after once broken. In trussing, do not cut off the legs, only the toes ; press them tightly to the sides ; pass a skewer through each foot; they present a better appearance. For a stuffing,—four tablespoonsful of bread crumbs, one lemon grated carefully, a very little pepper and salt, half a nutmeg grated; mix this all well together with a large spoonful of finely minced butter, and stuff well the craw and belly of the turkey. Put the gizzard and liver, when cleaned, into a saucepan with half a pint of cold water and a little salt. Let it cook while the turkey is roasting. When the turkey is first put down, dredge it with flour. When it begins to cook, put a large spoonful of butter into a ladle, and as it melts baste the bird. Keep it at a distance from the fire for the first half hour, to let it warm gradually; then nearer, and when it is plumped, it is near enough. Then dredge it lightly with flour, and baste it with butter. This will raise a fine froth, and is much better than the drippings out of the roaster.

The gravy must be made of the liver. When cooked, rub the liver with a large spoonful of flour, to a smooth paste, chop very fine the gizzard and mix with it, boil an egg very hard and mix in the yolk only; stir all these together; then drain off the drippings, skim every particle of fat from off the top, and stir the above ingredients into the gravy. Put it into a saucepan, and let it simmer ten minutes; serve this in a sauce tureen, very hot, with the turkey. Cranberry sauce is a necessary accompaniment to roast turkey. Turkey legs are very nice when cold, "devilled." Warm them on a gridiron, then have heated some of the turkey gravy, and add a spoonful of mushroom catsup, a teaspoonful of mixed mustard. Stir this well together, simmer for ten minutes, or less, only while the legs are broiling; then lay the legs on a hot dish, and pour over some of the gravy. Send the remainder to table in a sauce boat. Serve hot.

ROAST CAPONS AND FOWLS.

They must be killed, in warm weather, two days before cooking; in cold weather, several days. A good criterion of the ripeness of poultry for the spit is the ease with which the feathers can be plucked; always leave a few on to pluck to ascertain this. A full grown fowl requires about an hour and a quarter for cooking; it is prepared and dressed exactly as a turkey, only not much, if any, stuffing in the belly of the fowl. The craw requires some for plumpness, but the stuffing absorbs the flavour of the fowl. The gravy is made like the turkey, of the liver and gizzard. Cranberry sauce is a necessary companion of roast poultry.

A GOOSE.

This requires keeping the same as fowls, some days before cooking. The goose is best in the autumn and early part of winter—never good in spring. What is called a green goose is four months old. It is insipid after, although tender. Pick well and singe the goose; then clean carefully. Put the liver and gizzard on to cook as the turkey's. When the goose is washed and ready for stuffing, have boiled three white potatoes, skin and mash them; chop three onions very fine, throw them into cold water; stir into the potatoes a spoonful of butter, a little salt and black pepper, a tablespoonful of finely rubbed sage leaves; drain off the onions, and mix with the potato, sage, &c. When well mixed, stuff the goose with the mixture, have ready a coarse needle and thread, and sew up the slit made for cleaning and introducing the stuffing. A full grown goose requires one hour and three quarters. Roast it as a turkey, dredging and basting. The gravy is prepared as for poultry, with the liver and gizzard. Apple sauce is indispensable for roast goose.

HAUNCH OF VENISON.

To preserve the fat, make a paste of flour and water, as much as will cover the haunch. Wipe it over with a dry cloth in every part. Rub a large sheet of paper all over with butter, and cover the venison with it; then roll out the paste about three quarters of an inch thick; lay this all over the fat side, and cover it well with three or four sheets of strong white paper, and tie it closely with packthread. Have a sharp, close fire, and baste your venison as soon as you lay it down to roast. It must be basted continually while roasting. A buck haunch weighs usually twenty pounds, and will take about four hours and a half to roast. One weighing twelve or fourteen pounds requires three or three and a half hours. It is in perfection about Christmas. About a quarter of an hour before it is done, cut the twine and remove carefully all the paste; now baste it with butter, dredge it with flour; send it to table very hot. For a sauce, drain off all the drippings in the roaster, skim with care all the fat off; then stir in a little browned flour, a wine glass full of port or claret wine, and let this only just simmer. Send hot to the table. Currant jelly is indispensable with venison.

PHEASANTS

Should be hung up by the tail feathers some time before cooking—some say till they drop, but that is a matter of individual taste. Thirty minutes will roast a young bird, but ¾ of an hour for a full grown. Pick and draw it out by a slit in the back of the neck, and take out the craw, but do not cut off the head; wipe very carefully the inside of the bird; twist the legs close to the body; leave the feet on, but cut off the toes; truss the head like fowls, back. Baste it with butter, and dredge like poultry. For sauce, take the liver, &c., and prepare it as for fowls. Serve with currant jelly and wine.

DUCK.

Clean and wipe dry your duck; prepare the stuffing thus; chop fine and throw into cold water three good sized onions; rub one large spoonful of sage leaves, add two ditto of bread crumbs, a piece of butter the size of a walnut, and a little salt and pepper, and the onions drained. Mix these well together, and stuff the duck abundantly. Always keep on the legs of a duck; scrape and clean the toes and legs, and truss them against the sides. The duck should be kept a few days before cooking to become tender. Three quarters of an hour is generally enough for an ordinary sized duck. Dredge and baste like a turkey. A nice gravy is made by straining the drippings; skim off all the fat; then stir in a spoonful of browned flour, a teaspoonful of mixed mustard, and a wine glass full of claret; simmer this for ten minutes. Serve hot. With the duck currant jelly is necessary.

GUINEA FOWLS, OR PEA HENS,

Are dressed as pheasants, and if kept until tender are better.

PARTRIDGES

Are kept for several days, then cleaned and trussed. They require care in cleaning, and are very nice if properly dressed; they are basted and dredged like poultry; thirty minutes will roast one. They are never stuffed, as the stuffing absorbs the flavour of the bird. A piece of butter the size of a walnut must be put into the body of the bird. For sauce, take a cup of rice, steep it in a pint of milk, with an onion and a dozen whole berries of black pepper, let this stand on the fire until the rice is perfectly tender; then take out the pepper, and rub the rice and onion through a sieve into a clean saucepan. If too thick, add a little cream ; let it simmer once ; add a little salt, and serve hot with the bird This is a delicate and nice sauce.

TEAL.

It requires the same cooking as a duck, and dressed in the same manner. Onion sauce only must be served with teal, prepared as follows : Take six good sized white onions, peel them, cut them in half, lay them in cold water for half an hour, drain off that water and boil in fresh water a quarter of an hour. Take them out of the water and chop them very finely ; cut up with them a stick of celery washed carefully. Put them into a clean saucepan, with a large spoonful of butter, set on a slow fire, keep turning until the onion is browned, then dredge in a little flour. Pour over this any nice broth or stock, which a careful cook is never without. Stir it well, add a little salt and very little pepper ; let this simmer for ten minutes, then rub it through a seive, and add a wine glass full of claret wine. Serve this hot with the bird.

PIGEONS.

Pigeons are better for being freshly cooked ; their flavour passes off in a day or two. When cleaned and ready for roasting, prepare some stuffing of bread crumbs and about three oysters to each bird, a spoonful of butter, a little salt and nutmeg. Mix these well together, and fill the belly of the bird. They must be well basted with melted butter, and require thirty minutes careful cooking. When full grown, and in the autumn, they are best. For a sauce, take the gravy which runs from them, thicken with a very little flour and some chopped parsley. Serve hot. This bird is in perfection when it has just done growing.

REED, AND OTHER SMALL BIRDS.

Reed birds, and all other small birds, when picked and cleaned, must have a lump of butter the size of a hickory nut put into the belly; then roll them in the yolk of an egg—then in bread crumbs; tie them and truss them on the bird spit; baste them well. While they are roasting, sprinkle bread crumbs over them. They require only fifteen minutes if they have a quick fire. Garnish them with sliced lemons.

WILD DUCKS, OR TEAL.

You must be very particular in not roasting these birds too much; teal about twenty minutes, with a good fire; baste them very frequently; your fire and motion of the spit must be attended to, and when you dish it, unless preferred to be done by the gentleman at the table, draw your knife four times down the breast; have ready a little hot butter, and juice of a lemon, cayenne pepper, a little dust of sugar, a glass of port wine, pour it all hot, the last minute, over your teal; the remainder left of these birds the next day makes excellent hash, taking care of all the gravy that may remain, to stew it in.

WILD DUCKS.

These birds require clean plucking and washing, which may be done by pouring warm water through the body after it has been drawn; half an hour before a brisk fire will suffice to roast them, and stuffing is not required. When it is sent to table, the breast should be sliced, and a lemon squeezed over it. The slices of the breast and the wings are the only parts really worth eating to a sensitive palate, the strong flavour of the bird rendering it a dish only for those with peculiar tastes. Currant jelly must be served with them.

BOILING.

THIS most simple culinary process is not often done properly. The great requisites are, to skim your pot well, and keep it boiling slowly, and to know how long it requires boiling, and to take the article from the pot at the moment it is cooked. These comprehend the whole mystery and art. This, however, demands vigilance. The cook must take care that the pot is kept boiling; on the scum being carefully removed as it rises depends the good appearance of all boiled things. When the scum is first removed, throw in some cold water, which will cause the rest of the scum to rise. The oftener skimmed, the cleaner and sweeter will be the meat. If thoroughly and often skimmed, there is not any necessity of wrapping in a cloth; and, in fact, muffling affects the flavour of meat or fowls. Put your meat into cold water in the proportion of about a quart of water to a pound of meat, and it should be kept covered during the whole process of boiling. It is desirable that boiling pieces should be of an equal thickness, if not, the thick parts are not done before the thinner are overdone. The water should be gradually heated; if the water boil before the meat becomes thoroughly heated, the meat will be rendered hard, and shrink up; by keeping the water a certain time heated before boiling, the fibres of the meat are dilated, and it yields a quantity of scum, which must be taken off as soon as it rises. All meat is better and more juicy for slow simmering; the slower it boils the tenderer, plumper and whiter it will be. Twenty minutes to the pound for fresh, and rather more for salted meat, allowing for the weather and the thickness of the joint. In cold weather, meat requires more cooking than in warm. This, also, requires practice and experience. Fresh killed meat takes longer than that which butchers call ripe; if frozen, it must be thawed before cooking. For a small family, the best article for boiling purposes is a tinned saucepan, of a large size, with a closely fitting top, to prevent evaporation by which the nutritive parts are lost. Never allow the meat boiled to remain soaking in the water after it is done, excepting ham, which should always remain until the water somewhat cools, as it re-absorbs the juices let out. Beef and mutton a little underdone is better, but pork and poultry must be thoroughly cooked—or they are uneatable—but not overdone. It is an excellent plan to place a trivet in the bottom of the pot, and then lay that which is to be boiled on it; it prevents contact with the bottom of the pot. An inverted soup plate answers as well as a trivet.

A good housekeeper never has a boil without converting the broth into soup, either the same day or the next. The broth should always be put away carefully in a clean vessel kept exclusively for that purpose. As all salted meat should be well washed before boiling, the broth is very useful for seasoning stews.

BOILED TURKEY.

A turkey weighing eight or nine pounds, boiled an hour and a half. Clean it and wash it carefully; then stuff the belly and craw; chop very fine a teaspoonful of fat salt pork. To this add four large spoonsful of bread crumbs, half a teaspoonful of grated lemon peel, and a very little pepper. This must be well mixed, and the turkey stuffed with it; then truss the turkey, and lay it on the trivet in the pot. Fill it with cold water and simmer slowly. Be attentive to the skimming, or the turkey will not be white, and the flavour also affected. An oyster sauce is best for boiled turkey. Strain fifty oysters, put the juice into a saucepan; to this add one pint of new milk, let it simmer and skim off any froth which may rise; then rub a large spoonful of flour and a quarter of a pound of butter together, stir this into the milk and juice, add a little salt, some chopped parsley and very little pepper. Give this a simmer for five minutes, and just as the turkey is dished, throw the oysters into the sauce, as, if they are too much cooked, they become hard. Garnish the turkey with fresh parsley.

FOWLS

Are prepared in the same manner. A large-sized fowl requires an hour slow boiling; a chicken three-quarters of an hour; it can be served with oyster, egg, or celery sauce. The egg sauce is made by cutting a half a quarter of a pound of butter into very small pieces; mix well together a tablespoonful of flour and a cup of new milk, stir this very smoothly and let it simmer for five minutes, then stir in the butter; boil two eggs very hard, and throw them into cold water, until required; this makes the yolk harder, and the shell is more easily removed; chop the whites and yolks, and stir into the sauce; then stir in half a pint of the chicken broth, simmer this up for a few minutes, and serve hot with the fowls. Celery sauce is prepared in the same manner, only the celery is used instead of eggs. Garnish the fowl, and dish with sprigs of parsley.

LEG OF MUTTON.

A leg of nine pounds will take two hours and a half. For sauce, make some drawn butter, as follows:—Rub together three tablespoonfuls of cut up butter, and two of sifted flour. When well mixed, pour on it a tea cup full of boiling water; put it into a saucepan, stirring constantly, and let it simmer up quickly for a minute. If allowed to remain boiling, the butter becomes oily. Chop up some parsley and throw in after it is cooked; then add a tablespoonful of capers or nasturtions. Pour some over the mutton when dished, and if too thick, stir in some of the broth of the mutton. Garnish with nasturtions and parsley.

A Loin of Mutton.

Joint well all the ribs; roll it and tie the two ends together. It requires the same proportion for boiling as the leg. Serve it with drawn butter, and garnish it with carrots sliced and parsley.

Beef Bouilli.

Select a nice juicy piece of fresh beef. A piece of nine pounds requires three hours boiling slowly. The broth of this makes the best soup. A mushroom sauce is the nicest for bouilli. Clean half a pint of mushrooms, put them into a saucepan with half a pint of the beef broth and a spoonful of butter; cut up and rub with it a spoonful of flour; set this all on the fire to simmer; add a little salt; then strain them through a seive. Serve this hot with the bouilli. Garnish with parsley.

Corned Beef.

The round and brisket pieces are the best; skewer it up tight. Eight pounds will require three hours slow boiling. Put it into cold water, and observe the rules given; take off all the skum as it rises. If allowed to boil quick at first, no art can make it tender—the slower the better in appearance and flavour. A head of young Savoy cabbage is very nice served with it. Before putting into the pot, cut the head in half, and pour boiling water over it. This prevents all that unpleasant odour so disagreeable in cabbage. It requires half an hour's cooking. The broth of corn beef is very useful in gravies and soups, and should be saved for that purpose, or can be used for boiling the cabbage in.

CALF'S HEAD.

Let the butcher split the head in half. One with the skin is better; take out the eyes and the snout bone; then lay it in cold water to soak for two hours before boiling, to whiten; take out the brains and wash them well in several waters; then lay them in cold water. Put the head together, and lay it in a good sized pot; cover it with cold water entirely; throw in a large spoonful of salt. Let it boil slowly for two hours and a quarter. Skim it carefully, or it will not be white. Beat up an egg very lightly, with two tablespoonfuls of flour; then carefully remove all the skin from the brains and stir them into the flour and egg. This must be well beaten; chop up some parsley and stir in, grate a little nutmeg, add a little salt. When this is mixed, just before sending to table, have ready some boiling lard and drop into it a spoonful of this brain batter. These brain fritters must not stand after they are cooked, but sent directly to table and served with the head.

In dishing the head, remove all the large bones, clean the tongue, and keep the head as whole as possible. If prepared as directed, it is a very wholesome and nice dish. For a sauce, take a large spoonful of butter, and one of flour, and rub together; take half a pint of the broth, put it into a saucepan to boil, then stir in slowly the flour and butter and some chopped parsley; stir it until perfectly smooth. Serve it with the head. Garnish the head with sprigs of parsley Save all the bones and broth for soup.

CALVES' FEET.

Clean and wash a set of feet (four); put them on in cold water and let them boil slowly two hours. Whilst boiling, throw in a teaspoonful of salt; skim them carefully. Dish them, but remove the large bones. Sauce, the same as for calf's head; they are very delicate and nice. The broth is good for jelly.

CORNED PORK

Must be soaked for three or four hours before dressing; it must be well washed and scraped. When delicately dressed, it is a favorite dish. It must not be boiled fast; put on in cold water and gradually warm through; skim it frequently whilst boiling. A leg weighing seven pounds requires three hours and a half slow simmering. When you dish the pork, skin it very carefully. Some prefer the skin remaining on, as it loses much of its juices by skinning;—and is very nice cold. Pork must be well cooked. Parsnips are usually eaten with corned pork, but nicely boiled homony and beans are very necessary with boiled pork.

BOILED BACON.

If much salted, it must be scraped and soaked in warm water for two hours before dressing. A piece of three pounds will require two hours very slow boiling; remove all the scum as it rises. A nice way of dressing it is (after it is boiled,) to take off the skin, and grate bread crumbs over it and set it in the oven to brown. Do not let it remain longer than browned, as it will dry too much.

HAM.

Give it plenty of room; put it in cold water, and let it heat gradually; it must remain an hour heated before it boils; keep it simmering very gently. A ham of fifteen pounds requires four or five hours, according to its thickness. A ham is better for not cutting before it is cold—it is more juicy. Remove the skin carefully; keep it as whole as possible, as the ham should be kept covered with it to keep it moist. After the ham has been boiled the required time, let it remain ten or fifteen minutes in the pot, as it re-absorbs the essence thrown out in boiling. Ham is a necessary accompaniment to roast and boiled poultry.

TONGUE.

A tongue should be soaked twelve hours in cold water, if salted and dried; if a green or fresh one from pickle, two hours soaking in cold water is sufficient. Put it on to cook in plenty of cold water, and let it gradually warm; give it four hours slow cooking. In selecting a tongue for cooking, ascertain how long it has been dried; pick the plumpest and smoothest, which is an evidence of its being young and tender. Never cut off the root of the tongue before boiling. When boiled, let it stand as the ham for ten or fifteen minutes in the water; then take it out and skin it. Garnish it with mashed white potatoes and parsley sprigs.

TRIPE.

Select fresh, fat tripe; it is usually prepared by the butcher—cleaned and laid for several days in salt and water. Then it only requires to be well washed before cooking. Then roll it and tie it with white twine; then put into cold water, and boil it slowly for three hours; skim it carefully whilst boiling or it will not be white. Make an onion sauce; take six white onions, peel and cut them in half, lay them in a pan of cold water for half an hour to remove the strong taste; then put them into fresh cold water and boil for half an hour, and throw in a little salt. Throw off that water, and cover them with new milk; let it simmer for fifteen minutes; mash them well; then rub a large spoonful of butter and a spoonful of flour together; stir this into the milk and onions; let it simmer; then rub this through a seive, and add a cup full of cream or milk. Serve very hot with the tripe, which must be cut into slices before sending to table, keeping it rolled in cutting.

A Fresh Cod.

This is very nice. Clean it, and before putting it on the strainer rub it with salt, then lay it on the strainer, and cover it plentifully with cold water, and a tumbler full of vinegar; cook it as directed for other fish. An egg sauce must be served with this, which is made by chopping up three hard-boiled eggs, and stirring in well made drawn butter. Serve very hot. Garnish the fish with sprigs of parsley.

Boiled Haddock.

This is preferable to the salted cod, which is strong and requires so much soaking before it is fit for use, and can be easily obtained; if taken out of pickle for dressing, it only requires to be well washed, but if dried, it must be put to soak over night. Lay it in the kettle and cover it plentifully with cold water, but no salt; let it simmer slowly, and skim constantly as the other. If weighing eight or nine pounds, it will require, from being salted, one hour and a half slow simmering. When done, take it out of the water, pick out with care every bone and little particle of skin; put the shredded fish into a very clean saucepan; chop up four hard boiled eggs; take two and mix with the fish. Mash seven or eight good sized, well boiled white potatoes, and when quite smooth, stir them into the fish; cut up and add a quarter of a pound of butter; mix these well, set the saucepan near the fire to keep hot, then make some nice drawn butter, and stir in the other two chopped eggs. Serve this hot with the fish. Garnish the dish with sprigs of parsley. This is very nice if the above rules are observed. Should there be any of the dish left, it is nice made into little cakes, and fried brown for breakfast.

Any boiled fish left from dinner is very nice for tea. Remove all the butter, and pour on boiling vinegar, in which a few whole pepper grains and allspice have been boiled; cover it up and serve cold, with the vinegar and spice.

To Boil Rock.

Scale and clean with care, and lay it in water and salt until required for dressing. Lay the fish on a fish strainer; then cover it entirely with cold water; set the fish kettle on the side of the fire to simmer. (Remember,—if it boils, the fish breaks to pieces.) Skim it carefully while simmering. It will require twenty minutes, if weighing eight or nine pounds —and fifteen minutes if of less weight. For sauce, stew with care twenty-five oysters, chop up some parsley and stir into the oyster sauce, and garnish the dish with parsley sprigs.

Boiled Halibut.

A nice thick slice weighing about six pounds will require thirty minutes' slow simmering; always put on the fish in cold water, with a teaspoonful of salt in the water. For a sauce, make nice drawn butter, as directed for other boils; chop up some parsley and put into the butter, boil an egg very hard, and cut it into thin slices and lay on the halibut Serve hot.

SALMON BOILED.

Select a fresh and firm fish, wash and prepare it for dressing. Lay it on the strainer, sprinkle salt over it very thickly; then cover it plentifully with cold water, let it warm slowly, and only simmer, allowing for one of eight or nine pounds, three quarters of an hour or an hour slow boiling. For sauce, make a drawn butter, and chop finely some parsley and stir it in; boil an egg, cut it in slices and lay on the fish. Garnish with sprigs of parsley. Serve hot. Walnut catsup is necessary with boiled fish at table.

BOILED FRESH MACKEREL

Are prepared in the same way as the other fish. Sauce—drawn butter.

BOILED SHAD.

When in season, the most delicate manner of dressing a shad, is with drawn butter sauce.

BOILEAU.

Ten pounds of the second cut of the rump—have the bone taken out, take a spoonful each of ground cloves, allspice, black pepper, and salt, sweet-marjoram, and sweet basil rubbed fine; rub the ingredients well into it, roll it up tightly, and tie it; put it on in a pot half full of water, with four potatoes, two carrots cut lengthwise, two onions, and let it stew six hours

SOUPS AND BROTHS, AND STOCK GRAVIES

When you make any kind of soups that have roots or herbs in them, lay the meat in the bottom of the pot with a lump of butter; then cut the herbs and lay them over the meat, cover the pot close and set it over a very slow fire, this draws the flavour from out of the herbs, produces a nice gravy and gives the soup a very different flavour from putting water on the meat at once. When the gravy is almost dried up, fill up the pot with some water—more than the soup requires, as much of it evaporates and in skimming some is lost. When it begins to boil, remove all the fat and scum, which should be put into the soap fat. Always keep a jar expressly for cold soups or scraps, which is useful for making what is termed "stock." A scrap jar is indispensable in a kitchen; it must be kept very clean, and scalded with hot soap-suds once a week, and kept in a cool, dry place. A soup pot should be of iron, with a tightly fitting cover—what is called a "digester" is the best and most proper thing to cook soups in. They require so long cooking, that the vessel in which they are prepared should be very thick, being less liable to scorch, and for retaining the heat longer.

Shin of Beef Soup.

Break a shin of beef into three or four pieces. Put it into a pot, pour on it four gallons of cold water and simmer it for four or five hours, When any water is wanted to fill up the pot, add only enough, calculating to make a gallon and a half of soup; throw in a teaspoonful of salt. When this has simmered about two hours, grate five or six raw turnips, the same of raw potatoes, and three carrots; cut up the half of a cabbage very finely; put this into the pot; stir and skim it well while simmering, and be careful to remove all the fat, as no grease should float on the surface. The little red garden pepper is the best seasoning, but, being strong, must be carefully used, as a very little piece will season a large pot of soup. Before dishing, take all the meat and bones from out of the soup, and the meat will, if nicely seasoned, make a good force meat for stuffing.

VEAL BROTH.

Break a knuckle of veal into two or three parts, lay it, as directed, in the soup pot, with a lump of butter and one pint of cold water; lay in with the knuckle, a bunch of thyme and two or three celery heads; let this heat well and simmer for half an hour; then pour on two gallons of water, cover it tightly and let it simmer slowly for four hours; then strain it through the cullender, pour the broth again into the pot, and skim it thoroughly free from fat; then wash a tea cup full of rice well, put it into the broth, slice two carrots rather thinly, and add to the broth, with a teaspoonful of salt and a very little cayenne; let this simmer slowly for half an hour; chop up parsley and put into the tureen, and pour the broth on it in dishing. The knuckle is very nice sent to table with slices of lemon for a garnish, and nice drawn butter, with chopped parsley.

MUTTON BROTH.

Take about three pounds of a neck or scrag of mutton, wash it well, lay it in a stew-pan and cover it well with cold water. When the water becomes milk warm, pour it off;

then lay the meat in the "digester," or soup pot; pour on this five quarts of water, one teaspoonful of salt and two onions peeled and cut up, set this on a moderate fire to simmer slowly for three hours; then strain it through a cullender; cut up three or four potatoes, and the same of turnips, and put into the broth; let this simmer for half an hour, removing all the fat; chop up some parsley and put into the tureen—on this pour the broth. The neck is very nice sent to table with parsley and finely minced celery put into the drawn butter and poured over the mutton.

GRAVY SOUP.

Cut half a pound of nice fat ham into thin slices, and lay them at the bottom of a stew-pan or soup pot; on these place three pounds of beef and two pounds of veal; break the bones and lay them on the meat. Peel and slice two onions, two turnips and two carrots, and cut up two heads of celery, a blade of mace, four cloves and a teaspoonful of salt. Set the pot on a hot place, and cover it tightly. As soon as the ham begins to brown, pour into the pot about one gallon of hot water. As soon as it begins to boil, remove all the scum and pour in a pint of cold water, which causes the scum to rise—and continue to skim well until done, which will be in about four hours and a half, slow cooking. Strain this through a hair sieve. This is the basis of all soups and gravies. Bottle and keep it for use. This makes a fine vegetable soup. Boil peas, potatoes, and whatever vegetables used, then mash them and add a quart of the above "stock," and one quart of hot water; let it simmer about fifteen minutes, and then serve hot.

ORIENTAL MULLIGATAWNY.

This is the true Oriental recipe for making this delicious soup. Boil a pair of fowls with care, skimming continually whilst boiling, and keeping them covered with water. When tender, take out the chicken and remove every bone from the meat; put a large lump of butter in a frying pan, and dredge the chicken meat well with flour; lay it in the hot pan and fry it a nice brown, and keep it hot and dry. Take a pint of the chicken water, and stir in two large spoonsful of curry powder, two spoonsful of butter and one of flour, one tea-spoonful of salt and a very little cayenne. Stir this until smooth; then mix it with the broth in the pot; when well mixed, simmer five minutes; then put in the browned chicken. Boil a pint of rice very dry to serve with it.

POTÁGE A L'ANGLAISE.

Put a good sized marrow bone into a soup pot, and pour on it one gallon of water; wash one pint of split pease and put in; let this simmer slowly three hours; add a half tea-spoonful of salt and a little black pepper. Toast nicely two or three slices of bread, butter them and cut into square pieces. Put them into the tureen, and pour the potáge through a cullender, and mash the pease through into the tureen. Serve hot.

NEW ORLEANS GUMBO.

Take a good sized pair of chickens, and cut them as for a fricassee; flour them well and put them into a pan with a good sized piece of butter, and fry them a nice brown; then lay them in a soup pot and pour on three quarts of hot water, let them simmer slowly two hours; then rub some flour and butter together for a thickening, and stir in a little cayenne and salt. Strain fifty oysters, and pour the juice into the soup. Just before serving, stir into the soup two large spoonsful of finely powdered sassafras leaves; let this sim-mer five minutes, and then add the oysters. Have ready some rice boiled dry, and garnish the chicken, which can be taken out of the gumbo, and makes a nice dish. Serve all hot.

CLAM SOUP.

Wash fifty of the small sand clams very clean. Put them into an iron pot, set it in a hot place and cover it up. When they become heated, the clams open; then take them from the shells. Put the clams aside in a pan, and pour the juice into a stew-pan; let it simmer for five minutes, strain it and rub two tablespoonfuls of butter and one of flour smoothly together; put the juice on to cook, and slowly add the flour and butter, stir it well together, add half a teaspoonful of salt, half of a nutmeg grated, and a pint of good cream; stir this well, let it simmer for ten minutes, chop up some parsley and throw in; then pour in the clams. One boil-up finishes, as the clams, like oysters, require very little cooking. If you use the large clams, they must be chopped.

PILLAFF—AN ORIENTAL DISH.

Take a leg of mutton, cut off the meat into small slices, put them into a pan with a good sized lump of butter and fry them a light brown. With the remainder of the meat and bone make a rich soup, by pouring on three quarts of cold water and letting it simmer three hours, tightly covered. The meat must not be fried until the soup is nearly done. Put into the soup ten skinned, sliced tomatoes, three thinly sliced onions, fried a light brown, and a small piece of garden pepper—it is strong and requires but little—salt to the taste. About half an hour before the soup is done, add a large tea cup full of well washed rice, stirring it all constantly until cooked—then put in the slices of fried meat; let it simmer for five minutes. When properly prepared, the grains of rice are all whole but cooked. Cold roast beef is equally as good as mutton for a pillaff. Serve hot.

OYSTER SOUP.

Take two hundred oysters from their liquor, strain it and put it into a saucepan to simmer; rub a spoonful of flour and two large spoonsful of butter together, a very little cayenne, half a teaspoonful of salt, some grated nutmeg or mace, but not both, and a teaspoonful of allspice, whole; set this on the fire for ten minutes, and then pour in a pint of good cream; let this simmer five minutes, and then add the oysters. A few pieces of celery gives a very nice flavour. Serve hot. Do not more than scald the oysters, as they shrink and become hard by cooking.

CALF'S HEAD SOUP, OR MOCK TURTLE.

Have cleaned a good fat head, with the skin on; let it be well washed and the eyes removed, the skull cracked and the brains taken out. Prepare a set of calf's feet, and put the head and feet into the soup pot; pour on a gallon and a half of cold water and a teaspoonful of salt. Let this simmer for three hours the afternoon before it is required. The next morning, early, after having skimmed it well, again put the whole on to boil, adding four peeled onions, which have had boiling water poured on them to take the strong odour off—a bunch of parsley and two or three heads of celery; let this simmer and add eight cloves, twelve allspice, the same of pepper corns; if not enough salt, add more to the taste. Let this only simmer for three hours; then strain it through a cullender; pour back the soup into the pot; rub very smoothly and stir in the yolks of three hard boiled eggs, and half a pint of nicely browned flour, mixed with a wine glass full of mushroom catsup and two large wine glasses of good wine. Mix this all smoothly with the brains, and pour into it half an hour before dishing, and keep it covered tightly; take all the bones from the meat, and chop it and season with a little cayenne and half a teaspoonful of finely powdered basil; rub this well together, and make of it forcemeat balls the size of a hickory nut, dredge them with flour and fry them in boiling lard to a nice brown, drain all the fat off by laying them in a hot cullender or drainer. When ready for dishing, put the forcemeat balls into the tureen, and slice two fresh lemons very thinly and lay on them; then on these pour the boiling hot soup. This, if prepared as directed, is delicious.

PEA SOUP.

Save the water in which corned beef or pork has been boiled. If too salt, only use one half, and the other half plain water. Into this put either some beef bones or mutton bones, to give it a relish. Take some of this broth—only a little—and after having washed them, put in a quart of split peas; simmer them for three hours slowly, and then pass them through a cullender to remove the skin; mash them finely, and on them pour two quarts of the broth in which the bones have been boiling; grate two carrots and two turnips, and stir in; cut finely two heads of well cleaned celery and add an onion finely chopped; stew this very slowly for an hour. When ready, fry two slices of stale bread a nice brown; cut them into small squares, lay them in the tureen and dust on a little cayenne over them; then pour on your hot soup. Serve very hot.

PEPPER POT.

To four quarts of water put one pound of corned pork, two pounds of the neck or scrag of mutton and a small knuckle of veal. Let this simmer slowly three hours, skimming all the while, and then take out the mutton (as that will serve for a dish for table, with drawn butter and celery.) Into this broth put four sliced white turnips—if in season, six or eight tomatoes—if not, a tablespoonful of the tomato catsup, an onion sliced thinly, a small piece of the garden pepper and half a teaspoonful of salt. Have ready boiled a quarter of a pound of nice white tripe; cut this into strips of an inch in length; add six potatoes thinly sliced, about a dozen whole cloves and a pint bowl full of nice little light dumplings the size of a walnut; let this simmer slowly for an hour. Serve hot,—but take out the pork and veal bone before serving.

A NICE CLAM SOUP.

Take one hundred small clams, wash them and put them into a pot in a warm place and covered; let them stand until they open their shells; take out the clams and juice, and put on a knuckle of veal to boil with two quarts of cold water, let it simmer until reduced to one quart; then add this broth to the clam juice, put it into a saucepan and let it simmer for an hour; then skim carefully,—chop the clams and put into this broth; then add half a teaspoonful of salt, a cup full of cream, a large spoonful of flour and a quarter of a pound of butter rubbed together, some finely chopped parsley, and a very little pepper and grated nutmeg. Cover tightly and just scald up. Immediately before serving beat the yolks of two eggs, and stir into the soup. Serve hot.

SOUTHERN OCHRA SOUP.

Wash a shin of beef, break it into two or three parts, put it into the soup pot and pour on it a gallon of cold water; cut lengthwise into small pieces a quarter of a peck of green ochra, and put into the soup pot, with a teaspoonful of salt, let this simmer very slowly three hours, skimming constantly. Then scald and skin a quarter of a peck of tomatoes, and press them through a seive to prevent any seeds or pulp from getting in. Stir this into the soup about twelve o'clock, and let it continue to simmer until two o'clock—the time for dinner. Be careful not to use an iron ladle or spoon with the ochra soup, as it discolours the ochra. The soup must be made in a tinned or porcelained stewing pan. A very little cayenne should be shaken in whilst simmering. The shin of beef must be taken out before dishing, which is best done by pouring the soup through a cullender into the tureen, and forms a nice dish with drawn butter for sauce—garnished with parsley.

NORTHERN OCHRA SOUP.

Take a pint of young tender ochras, wash and slice them, chop two onions finely, and put these into a gallon of water; skin and slice half a pint of tomatoes; add a small piece of garden pepper—a very little piece will answer,—and half a teaspoonful of salt; put all on to cook at seven o'clock in the morning, and let it simmer until noon; then add a large handful of Lima beans. At half past one, add two young squashes, cleaned carefully and cut into small pieces. A knuckle of veal washed and broken and put in, (or a pair of chickens is better,) and a piece of cold, cooked pork or bacon. Let this all boil gently for an hour and a half, and then take out all the meat, and rub together one large spoonful of flour and one of butter, and stir into the soup. The fowls are served with egg sauce. Be careful to remove all scum from the soup while cooking. Boil some rice very dry and serve with the soup. The knuckle of veal is very nice dished with drawn butter and parsley. This preparation of soup has been timed for a three o'clock dinner. Avoid the use of an iron spoon or ladle in skimming or stirring the ochras.

SOUP WITH BOUILLI.

Take the thick part of a brisket of beef—about eight pounds,—lay a piece of butter in the bottom of the soup pot, and on it lay your beef; then tie in a little bundle some thyme and parsley, and two heads of celery, and let this stew for twenty minutes slowly, covered very tightly; then sprinkle in a teaspoonful of salt and a little cayenne, and pour in a gallon of hot water. Let this cook slowly for four hours, skimming with care. Then take out the beef, have ready boiled four or five white potatoes, three turnips and three carrots, and mash into the soup; cover this up and let it simmer, and now prepare the bouilli; remove all the skin from the beef, beat up the yolk of an egg, spread it well on the top of the beef with a feather, and then sprinkle over it stale bread crumbs; put this in the oven to brown. Prepare a gravy from the soup; take a bowl full of the liquor freed from the vegetables, add to it a wine glass full of good cooking Malaga wine and a table spoonful of mushroom catsup, rub together a spoonful of flour and butter; stir this all well together, and let it simmer for ten minutes. Lay the beef on a hot dish, and garnish with slices of green pickles; pour on the gravy and send some to table in a sauce boat. This makes two courses—the soup and bouilli. Toast a slice of stale bread, cut it into squares and put into the tureen; on them pour the soup.

GREEN PEA SOUP.

Put a knuckle of veal and about three pounds of fat corn pork into the soup pot. On these pour one gallon of cold water; let it slowly simmer for three hours, skimming carefully. Shell a peck of pease, wash and put them on to boil, which will require about thirty minutes; pour them through a cullender; take out the meat and mash the pease through the cullender into the broth, and let it simmer for fifteen minutes; chop up a handful of green mint and put into the soup, and stir in a little salt and a tablespoonful of nice brown sugar. Toast a slice of bread, cut it into squares and lay on the soup when dished. The veal is a nice dish, served for the second course.

SPLIT PEA SOUP.

Take beef bones, or any cold meats, and two pounds of corned pork; pour on them a gallon of hot water, and let them simmer three hours, removing all the scum. Boil one quart of split pease two hours, having been previously soaked, as they require much cooking; strain off the meat and mash the pease into the soup; season with black pepper, and let it simmer one hour; fry two or three slices of bread a nice brown, cut into slices and put into the bottom of the tureen, and on them pour the soup.

EEL SOUP.

Take two good sized onions, peel, wash and slice them, and put them into the soup pot; put a lump of butter in and brown them. Have ready cleaned and washed five or six good sized eels, cut them into pieces and pour on them three quarts of boiling water; remove all the scum; when the pot begins to boil, tie in a bundle some thyme, summer savoury and parsley, and also add half a teaspoonful of allspice and the same of pepper corns and salt. Cover this tightly and let it boil slowly for two hours; then strain it carefully. Have ready, in a stew-pan, some thickening—two spoonsful of butter melted in the pan and flour dredged in to a paste—on this pour the soup, and let it simmer ten minutes. While it is simmering, fry some pieces of eels a nice brown and lay in a tureen; on these pour the soup. Serve very hot.

OX-TAIL SOUP.

Three tails divided at the joints, washed and laid in hot water half an hour to soak. Put into the pot about three onions peeled, nine cloves, twenty or thirty allspice, ten or twelve pepper corns, a teaspoonful of salt, and the tails. On this pour one gallon of cold water, remove all scum while boiling, and keep it gently simmering two hours. When quite tender, take the bones from the meat, and cut it up in nice pieces ; strain and skim the soup ; strain it through a sieve ; rub a large spoonful of flour and the same of butter together, and stir it into the soup ; let this simmer for five minutes ; skim it well, and then add the meat and a wine glass full of mushroom catsup. Simmer this a few minutes. Serve hot.

GOOSE GIBLET SOUP.

Scald and pick clean two sets of fresh goose giblets, wash them well in two or three waters, cut off the noses and split the heads, cut the gizzards and necks into mouthfuls, and crack the bones of the legs ; put them all into a soup pot, cover them with cold water ; remove all the scum as it rises ; then put into the pot a bundle of herbs—thyme, a little marjoram and parsley, an onion peeled and cut up, twenty berries of allspice, twenty of pepper corns and a little salt ; tie the herbs and spice in a little bag, so as to remove it before dishing ; let this simmer slowly two hours, and then remove the bag ; take out all the giblets with a skimmer and put them into a pan, and keep it in a hot place ; then thicken the soup —put two tablespoonsful of butter into a hot pan and stir in as much flour as will make it into a paste ; then pour in by degrees a ladle full of the soup, stir it very smoothly and pour into the soup ; let this boil half an hour, stir it and skim it well, add a wine glass full of good cooking wine, and a tablespoon ful of mushroom catsup, and let it it boil up once or twice ; then stir in the giblets. Serve hot.

GAME SOUP.

In the season for game, it is easy to have good game soup at very little expense, and very nice. Take the meat from off the bones of any cold game left, pound it in a mortar and break up the bones, and pour on them a quart of any good broth and boil for an hour and a half; boil and mash six turnips, and mix with the pounded meat; then pass them through a sieve; strain the broth and stir in the mixture of meat and turnips, which has been strained through the sieve. Keep the soup pot near the fire, but do not let it boil. When ready to dish the soup for table, beat the yolks of five eggs very lightly and mix with them half a pint of good cream; set the soup on to boil, and as it boils, stir in the beaten eggs and cream, but be careful that it does not boil after they are stirred in, as the egg will curdle. Serve hot.

MELTED BUTTER.

This is very easy to prepare, but rarely well done, and yet one in such general use for meats, fish, fowls and vegetables. It requires being rightly proportioned. Generally, do not pour sauce over meats or put it in the dish, as many have an antipathy to it, preferring the juices which flow from the meats.

Keep a saucepan exclusively for sauces. Cut two large spoonsful of good butter into very small pieces—it mixes more readily for being cut small; put it into the saucepan with a large spoonful of flour and two large spoonsful of new milk. When thoroughly mixed, add six large spoonsful of water; shake it, and hold it over the fire until it begins to simmer, shaking it always the same way; then let it stand quietly and boil up. It should be of the consistency of rich cream, and not thicker. Two tablespoonsful of mushroom catsup, instead of the milk, will make a delicious accompaniment to either fish, flesh or fowl. Should the butter oil, put a spoonful of cold water to it, and stir well with a spoon, but if properly done it will not oil.

THICKENING.

Put some fresh butter over a fire in a clean stew-pan; when melted, dredge in sufficient flour to make a thick paste; stir this well together with a wooden spoon for fifteen or twenty minutes until it is quite smooth, and the colour of gold; this must be done slowly and with care—if over too much heat, it will become bitter and oily; pour it into a pan and keep it for use; it will keep good for a fortnight. One spoonful of this will thicken a quart of gravy. This, by the French cook, is called "Roux." Be very careful in making it—if it becomes the least scorched, it will spoil everything it is put into. When cold, it should be thick enough to cut out with a knife like a solid paste.

This is a most essential article in the kitchen, and is the basis of all gravies, and of most made dishes, soups, sauces and ragouts. If gravies are too thin, this added makes it the consistency desired. In making this thickening, the less butter and the more flour used the better. In using it, always be careful to mix a little of the gravy or broth with it at first, and then mix it with the whole and stir it well in; if not, the sauces will have a floury taste and a greasy appearance. When you have thickened your sauces, add to it some broth or warm water, in the proportion of two table-spoonsful to a pint; set it by the side of the fire, when mixed, to raise any fat that is not thoroughly incorporated with the gravy, which must be carefully removed as it appears. This is called cleansing the sauce.

CLARIFIED BUTTER.

Put the butter into a very clean saucepan over a clear, slow fire. Watch it,—and when melted, skim off the butter-milk, &c. carefully, and let it stand a minute or two, for all impurities to sink to the bottom; then pour the clear butter through a sieve into a clean basin, leaving the sediment at the bottom of the stew-pan. Butter thus purified will be as sweet as marrow—a useful covering for potted meats, and for frying fish is equal to the finest olive oil, for which purpose it is commonly used by those whose religion will not allow them to eat viands fried in animal oil.

CELERY SAUCE.

Pick and wash two heads of celery, cut them into pieces an inch long, and stew them in a pint of water and a tea-spoonful of salt, until the celery is tender. Rub a large tablespoonful of butter with a spoonful of flour well together; stir this into a pint of cream, and put in the celery and let it boil up once. Serve hot, with boiled poultry.

TOMATO SAUCE.

Scald and skin fifteen ripe tomatoes, squeeze them through a sieve to get out the seeds, put them into a saucepan with half a pint of good beef gravy, a little salt and white pepper, and set them in a hot place for an hour to simmer. This is nice with beef-steak, or any made dishes.

BROWNING FOR SOUPS AND SAUCES.

This is a most convenient article to colour soups or sauces, whose richness is judged of by the colour.

Put half a pound of crushed sugar and a tablespoonful of water into a clean saucepan; set it over a slow fire and keep stirring with a wooden spoon until it becomes a bright brown colour and begins to smoke; then add to it a spoonful of salt, and dilute it by degrees with water until it is the thickness of cream; let it boil and remove all the scum; strain off the liquor into very clean bottles, which must be well corked. A little of this will colour gravies or soups a nice brown.

GRAVY FOR ROAST MEATS.

Save all the nice bits of roast in a jar for the purpose—then you are never at a loss for gravies; take some of these pieces and cut them very small and put them into a saucepan; pour over them one pint of boiling water; let it simmer very slowly (tightly covered) for an hour; strain through a seive and add this to melted or drawn butter. Send to table in a sauce boat. A careful cook will always save all the meat gravies left, and have a vessel for keeping them.

GRAVY FOR CHOPS.

Take out your chops when cooked; keep a large spoonful of fat in which they were cooked, in the pan; dredge in as much flour as will make it a paste; rub this well together over the fire, until a light brown; then pour in as much boiling water as will reduce it to the thickness of cream, and add a tablespoonful of mushroom catsup and a little salt; let this simmer five minutes, and pour it through a seive over the steak.

SAUCE FOR HASHED MUTTON OR BEEF.

Break the bones and the fragments left of the joint from which the hash has been made; pour on one pint of boiling water, six pepper corns, six or seven allspice, a head of celery cut up, a few sprigs of parsley and basil, and some salt; let this simmer (tightly covered) for three quarters of an hour; slice one onion and fry it a nice brown; then stir into it as much flour as will make it a stiff paste; pour into it slowly the gravy made from the bones and scraps; let it simmer fifteen minutes and add one tablespoonful of walnut or mushroom catsup; strain this through a seive, and into this gravy put your minced meat; let it stand in a warm place only until thoroughly heated; toast a couple of slices of bread, lay them in the dish and pour on the hash.

A MIXTURE FOR SALAD.

Boil two fresh eggs very hard, and when done, lay them for a quarter of an hour in cold water; rub the yolks through a sieve with a wooden spoon, and mix with the yolk a large spoonful of good cream; then add one large spoonful of olive oil, and stir them well together; then add by degrees a teaspoonful of dry mustard, the same of powdered loaf sugar and the same of salt. These must be well mixed, then very slowly add three large spoonsful of the best wine vinegar; rub it with the other ingredients until thoroughly incorporated with them; cut up the white of the egg into small square pieces, and garnish the salad with it. Put the sauce into a sauce boat, and serve with the salad.

CELERY VINEGAR.

Dry and pound half a pound of celery seed, pour upon it one quart of the best wine vinegar, and let it steep ten days, shaking every day. This is very nice, and has a fine flavour for salads and cold meats.

Vinegar can be flavoured with anything. The red garden pepper cut up in strong wine vinegar, as the celery, is very nice for seasoning. Sweet basil is very fine to impregnate vinegar with, and used for sauce.

ESCHALOT WINE.

Peel, mince and pound in a mortar three ounces of eschalots, and infuse them in a pint of sherry fourteen days; then pour off the liquor, and chop up three ounces more and pour in the wine, and let it stand ten days longer. This is very fine with an ounce of scraped or grated horse-radish and the rind of a lemon thinly cut--added with the first infusion. This has an advantage over the onion, as it never leaves an unpleasant taste in the mouth, or affects the breath, and imparts to chops, steaks, hashes or sauces a fine flavour.

CHILI VINEGAR, OR ESSENCE.

Those who are fond of cayenne will find this far superior to the article sold as cayenne.

Cut in half or pound fifty red English chilies, which can be purchased at the wholesale druggists;—it is a peculiar fine flavour. On the chilies pour a pint of the best wine vinegar or good brandy; put it into a bottle, cork tightly and let it stand fourteen days. A very little of this seasons delightfully, and is preferable to the deleterious substance sold as cayenne.

ESSENCE OF LEMON PEEL.

Wipe six fresh lemons and cut the rind very thinly; put it into a quart of good brandy. This, in three weeks, will have a very fine flavour. For sauces or cake.

ESSENCE OF GINGER.

Take three ounces of fresh grated green ginger, and the rinds of two lemons, thinly cut; put them into a quart of the best brandy or proof spirit. Cork.

ESSENCE OF ALLSPICE.

Take three ounces of allspice and put into a pint of good brandy. In two weeks it has all the flavour of the spice. For sauces, hashes or soups.

ESSENCE OF CINNAMON.

Take three ounces of cinnamon (cassia will not do,) break it up and put it into a bottle ; on this pour a pint and a half of the best brandy, and let it stand two weeks. This is very fine for flavouring puddings, cakes or sauces. Cloves are good prepared the same way, for sauces.

A DELICIOUS SAUCE.

Claret wine, or good Port, one pint; half a pint of walnut pickle ; three fresh lemon peels, thinly sliced ; peel and slice six eschalots ; scrape or grate three large spoonsful of fresh horse-radish, half an ounce of allspice and the same of pepper corns powdered, two Chili peppers chopped and a teaspoonful of celery seed. Put all these into a wide-mouthed bottle, and pour on them a pint of mushroom catsup ; shake well and cork tightly. In fourteen days, it is fit for use. This is a delightful and really economical seasoning for broths, stews, and sauces, as a little answers in drawn butter or gravies. No housekeeper should be without it.

STEWS, MADE DISHES AND FRIES.

These are very economical, and, if rightly prepared, exceedingly palatable. Cold meats are rarely acceptable, with the exception of roast beef, ham, pork and poultry, but if reheated, without being overdone, lose none of their flavour or nutrition.

Mutton Stew.

Cut the cold mutton into not very thin slices; trim off all the sinew, gristle and skin; put into the stew nothing but that which is to be eaten; lay the prepared pieces into a saucepan, and put the scraps into a jar, which should always be kept as a reservoir for scraps, to be converted into soups, broths or gravies. If you have no mutton or beef gravy, make some from these scraps, by putting them into a saucepan and pouring over them a pint of boiling water; then add a bundle of sweet basil and celery heads tied together, a little salt, and a few whole pepper corns. Cover it up and stew it for half an hour, and then pour it over the prepared slices of mutton; let the meat slowly warm in this gravy. Just before dishing, take out the meat, cover it and keep it warm; then dredge some flour into the gravy to thicken it; simmer it five minutes, and serve very hot. This is a nice dish.

A VEAL HASH.

Take the bones of cold meats—roast or boiled—dredge them with flour and put them into a saucepan with a pint and a half of hot water or cold broth ; cut up a peeled onion, slice a lemon thinly, a little salt, a few small blades of mace and a few whole pepper corns ; stew it for half an hour ; then strain this through a sieve and rub a large spoonful of butter and one of flour well together ; hash up the veal rather finely, and stir into this hot gravy. Let it stew for a quarter of an hour very slowly. Serve hot, and garnish with sprigs of parsley.

A BEEF HASH.

If you have any pieces of cold ham, lay them in the stew-pan with any scraps of bones or meats from the jar for such things ; tie up a few sprigs of sweet basil and parsley, a few pepper corns and a little salt. Pour on all these a pint and a half of boiling water ; let this simmer for half an hour and strain through a sieve. Rub together a large spoonful of butter and one of flour ; stir this into the gravy, and a large tablespoonful of mushroom catsup. Then have ready the beef nicely hashed, but not so small as the veal, and put into the gravy. Let this simmer for ten minutes, just to warm the meat. Serve very hot, and garnish it with hot, well-boiled slices of carrots.

STEWED BEEF.

Make a rich gravy, as above, and take any nice piece of cold beef which may be left—corned beef is very nice. Stuff it with a cooked onion finely chopped, and a large spoonful of bread crumbs, rubbed together with some powdered basil and a little horse-radish. Make incisions in the beef, and stuff it well; then lay it in a stew-pan, and pour the hot gravy over; cover tightly and let it warm slowly for half an hour in a hot place. Garnish with carrots sliced. Serve hot.

AN IRISH STEW.

Take a loin of mutton, cut it into chops, season it with a very little pepper and salt, put it into a saucepan, just cover it with water and let it cook half an hour. Boil two dozen of potatoes, peel and mash them, and stir in a cup of cream while they are hot; then line a deep dish with the potatoes, and lay in the cooked mutton chops, and cover them over with the rest of the potatoes; then set it in the oven to bake. Make some gravy of the broth in which the chops were cooked. This is a very nice dish.

HARICOT OF MUTTON.

Cut a neck or loin of mutton, that has been kept until tender, into chops; trim off some of the fat, and lay them in a stew-pan with a large spoonful of butter. Have a quick fire, or they will not brown nicely. While the chops are browning, peel and boil one dozen of little white button onions in three pints of cold water for twenty minutes; set them aside and pour the water in which they were boiled into the stew-pan with the chops, as soon as they are brown. If that does not cover them, add more boiling water; then set them on the fire to stew slowly for half an hour, skimming carefully. When tender, pour off all the gravy through a sieve, and skim off every particle of fat. Have ready boiled four or five turnips and two or three carrots; pour all the water from them and cut them into slices; thicken the gravy with a spoonful of butter; stir it in and let it simmer five minutes, then add the carrots, turnips and onions.

Lay the chops around the dish, the vegetables in the centre, and pour the gravy over, and send some to table in a sauce boat.

SHIN OF BEEF STEWED.

Have the bone sawed into three parts, put it into a stew-pan and just cover it with water. When it simmers, skim it well, and clean and tie a small bundle of basil and parsley together, two heads of celery, two good sized onions, about a dozen of pepper corns and the same of allspice, and salt to the taste. Cover this tightly, and let it stew three hours very slowly. Take three scraped carrots, two peeled turnips, five or six peeled onions, and boil them together until quite tender; the carrots will require a much longer time than the others. When the beef is quite tender, take it out and keep it hot. Mix three tablespoonsful of flour with a tea cup full of the liquor; stir this quite smooth; then put it into a pint of the liquor of the beef, and add a wine glass full of mushroom catsup. Be careful to leave no fat on the gravy; skim it well. Then let it simmer five minutes; cut the carrots and turnips into slices, and cut up the onion; stir all in the gravy, and then lay the beef in and keep them warm until dishing time. Lay the beef in the centre, and the vegetables around, and pour over the gravy.

The broth from this beef will make an excellent soup, with the bone and meat left, for the next day. A knuckle of veal is very nice prepared the same way.

A LEG OF MUTTON STEWED.

A leg of mutton which has been kept for some few days is better than a fresh one. Prepare a stuffing of three spoonsful of finely chopped beef suet, three spoonsful of bread crumbs, an onion chopped very finely, a little pepper and salt and half a teaspoonful of pounded cloves. Make incisions in the leg and stuff it well; tie a little bundle of parsley and basil together, and lay this in the bottom of the stew-pan and on it place the mutton; just cover it with water and stew slowly. This will require two hours slow cooking and kept tightly covered. When quite tender, take out and mix with the liquor a large spoonful of flour, then stir it into the stew-pan, simmer it for five minutes and strain off the gravy, then pour it back into the stew-pan and skim off every particle of fat, and add a wine glass full of walnut catsup, then lay the leg of mutton in until dished. Pour over some of the gravy when dished, and the rest in a sauce boat. This is a delightful dish, and is called "*le gigot de sept heures*," so famous in the French kitchen. Some of the loin is left on for a "*gigot en verité*." Currant jelly to be served with it.

STEWED RUMP STEAKS.

The steaks must be thicker than for broiling, but all the same thickness. Put two tablespoonsful of butter with two sliced onions into a stew-pan, and when the butter is melted lay in the steaks and let them stand over a slow fire for five minutes, tightly covered; then turn the steaks and fry the other side; have ready boiled a dozen small sized onions, pour the water in which they were boiled over the steaks, and if it does not cover them pour more over them, and put in a dozen pepper corns and a little salt. Let this simmer for two hours very slowly, then pour off about half a pint of the gravy, then skim off all the fat and mix in a spoonful of flour with a cup of the gravy, then add it to the whole with a wine glass of tomato or mushroom catsup, a little pepper and salt, and let it simmer for five minutes; (a wine glass of Claret is a great improvement,) and lay the steaks in until they are dished. Serve hot.

HAM AND CHICKEN PIE.

Cut some thin slices of cold cooked ham, lay them in the bottom of a dish, and cut a cold boiled fowl up as for a fricasse; lay one half of the fowl on the ham, and season with a very little pepper and salt, and a little grated nutmeg. Rub the hard boiled yolks of two eggs, a spoonful of flour, and a large spoonful of butter, and stir this into half a pint of any nice broth, then pour this over the chicken, then another layer of thin slices of ham, and then the remainder of the chicken; then pour on a little more broth, and cover the whole with a nice paste, and bake it slowly half an hour. Serve hot.

ALAMODE BEEF OR VEAL.

Take about ten pounds of the round, let it be fat and juicy. Make a stuffing of four tablespoonsful of fat corned pork chopped finely, and the same of bread crumbs; cut an onion in slices into cold water, and drain off the water and chop it up, then mix these together, adding a little ginger and salt; make deep incisions in each side of the beef and introduce freely this stuffing, tie a string two or three times around the beef to keep it in shape, then dredge it well with flour and lay the meat into a stew-pan and pour over it two quarts of cold water, one teaspoonful of whole allspice, a little bundle of basil and parsley tied together; let this only simmer for three hours,—skim it carefully whilst cooking. When quite tender take out the beef and make a nice gravy of about one pint and a half of the broth; skim all the fat off of that intended for the gravy, then dredge in some flour, a wine glass of tomato catsup, and if made in summer put some thinly sliced tomatoes in the broth while the beef is stewing. Pour some of the gravy over the beef and some in a sauce-boat. The beef is better if laid for twelve hours in good wine vinegar, before preparing it for cooking.

MALINA PIE.

Take cold mutton or veal, chop it very finely; then to one pint of minced meat, stir in the yolks of four well beaten eggs, the juice of one lemon, and the rind thinly grated, two small onions very finely chopped, half of a grated nutmeg, two large spoonsful of mushroom catsup, a very little cayenne, and salt to the taste. Mix this well together, and cut up into very small pieces a half quarter of a pound of butter and stir through it, then line a dish with good paste, and put this in to bake until it is a nice brown. Serve with a nice gravy made of the bones of the cold meats

CALF'S LIVER FRIED.

Lay the liver in vinegar for twelve hours, it will render it firm; dip it in cold spring water and wipe it dry, cut it in even slices, sprinkle herbs, rubbed finely, over it, add pepper and salt, and dredge with flour; fry in rather thin slices of corn pork or bacon laid in the bottom of the frying-pan; this is preferable to lard, or butter; remove the liver when fried a nice brown, pour away a portion of of the fat, and pour in a cup full of water with a small lump of butter well rolled in flour, in which a spoonful of white wine vinegar or lemon juice has been stirred; boil it up, keeping it stirred all the while, and serve the liver up in it. The thin slices of hot fried bacon should be sent to the table with it. All served hot.

ANOTHER.

Cut the liver and heart across the grain, wash it well, pour boiling water on, and let it stand a few minutes, then drain and season it with salt and pepper, flour it and drop it in hot lard; when it is brown on both sides, dish it; dust a little flour in the pan, and pour in some water, let it boil a minute, stirring in a seasoning of parsley, thyme, or sweet marjoram; pour the gravy over the liver. This is a good breakfast dish.

BEEF KIDNEY, ROGNON DE BŒUF SUPERBE.—FRIED.

Remove all the fat and the skin from the kidney, and cut it in slices moderately thin. Mix with a teaspoonful of salt, grated nutmeg and cayenne pepper. Sprinkle over them this seasoning, and also parsley and eschalot, chopped very fine. Fry them over a quick fire until brown on both sides, pour into a cup of good gravy a glass of Madeira, and when the slices of the kidney are browned, pour it into the pan gradually; just as it boils throw in a spoonful of lemon juice, with a piece of butter the size of a nut. Have ready a dish, garnished with fried bread cut in dice; pour the whole into it.

BEEF KIDNEYS STEWED.

Procure a couple of very fine beef kidneys, cut them in slices, and lay them in a stew-pan; put in two ounces of butter, and cut into very thin slices four large onions; add them, and a sufficiency of pepper and salt, to season well. Stew them about an hour; add a cup full of rich gravy to that extracted from the kidney. Stew five minutes, strain it, and thicken the gravy with flour and butter and give it a boil up. Serve with the gravy in the dish.

CALVES' FEET FRICASSEED (PIEDS DE VEAU EN FRICASSEE.)

Soak them three hours, simmer them in equal proportions of milk and water, until they are sufficiently tender to remove the meat from the bones, in good sized pieces. Dip them in yolk of egg, cover with fine bread crumbs; pepper and salt them, fry a beautiful brown, and serve in white sauce.

TO BONE BIRDS, OR POULTRY.

Begin to bone any birds by first taking out the breast bone, when you will have sufficient space to remove the back with a sharp knife, and then the leg bones; the skin must not be broken, but the meat of the legs must be pushed inwards.

TO BROWN CHICKENS.

Bone the chickens, stuff them with a veal force-meat; place in the stew-pan the bones and trimmings, lay the chickens upon them with a bunch of sweet herbs, onions, mace whole, some thin slices of bacon, about three parts of a pint of water and two glasses of sherry: the bacon should be added last. Cover close, and stew for two hours. Then take out the chickens, strain the gravy, remove the fat, and boil the gravy rapidly, paint it over the chickens with a brush while the gravy is being boiled; brown the chickens before the fire—it adds to their appearance. Serve the rest of the gravy in a sauce-boat.

FRIED CHICKEN A LA MALABAR.

The Indian receipts for cooking chicken are very numerous; we select the following. Cut up the fowl as for a stew, removing the joints carefully and carving the body into handsome shapes, remove all moisture with a clean dry cloth, and powder every part with curry; fry it in fresh butter a pale brown, cut into small pieces two or three onions, and fry in clear butter, sufficient to keep the pan from burning, be very particular respecting that, but not more butter than should be absorbed by the onion after some time frying. It is as well here to say, that as onions are frequently used in the curried poultry by the Indian cooks, they employ the following method. When to be cut small they slice the onions and then separate them into rings, cutting these rings into the sizes they may require, which, if a little more labour, yet presents a better appearance; when they are fried sufficiently to have absorbed the grease in the pan without in any degree having been burned, spread them over the chicken and serve.

a whole lemon should be sent to the table with them. Serve dry boiled rice.

BLACK PUDDINGS.

Stir three quarts of sheep's blood with one spoonful of salt till cold, boil a quart of very fine homony in sufficient water to swell them until cooked, drain, and add them to the blood with a pound of suet, a little pounded nutmeg, some mace, cloves, and allspice, a pound of the hog's fat cut small, some parsley finely minced, sage, sweet herbs, a pint of bread crumbs, salt, and pepper; mix these ingredients well together, put them into well cleaned skins, tie them in links, and prick the skins, that while boiling they may not burst. Let them boil twenty minutes, and cover them with clean straw until they are cold.

WHITE PUDDINGS.

Procure the pig's blood, then add half a pound of half-boiled rice, set it to cool, keeping it stirred, add a little more rice boiled in milk, add it to the blood, cut up about one pound of fat pork into large dice, melt half a pound of lard and pour into the blood and rice, then add your fat, with a few bread crumbs, three shalots, a little parsley, some black pepper, cayenne pepper, and salt; mix all well together, then fill into skins as before; tie them the length you wish them, then boil them a quarter of an hour, take them out and lay them on some new clean straw until cold, then give them another boil for a few minutes, then turn them as before until wanted, put them in the oven when you require them, or fry them or broil them.

LARD.—TO MELT LARD IN A SUPERIOR MANNER.

Take the inner fat of a newly killed pig and strip off the skin completely and carefully, slice it and put it into a jar, and set the jar in a pan of boiling water; let it melt, and when perfectly fluid pour it into dry clean jars, and cover them closelv; it may be kept some time in a dry place, and when used may be mixed with butter for pastry, for frying fish, and many other purposes in cooking.

TO BAKE A HAM.

Put the ham in soak previous to dressing it; if an old one two hours will be required, but if not very old, an hour will suffice. Wipe it very dry, and cover it with a paste about an inch in thickness. The edges being first moistened must be drawn together, and made to adhere, or the gravy will escape. Bake it in a regular, well-heated oven; it will take from three to six hours, according to its weight; when done remove the paste, and then the skin. This must be done while the ham is hot. If well baked and not too salt, it will prove of finer flavour than if boiled.

BACON FRAZE.

Beat eight eggs into a batter, a little cream and flour, fry some thin slices of bacon and dip them in it, lay the bacon in a frying-pan, pour the batter over them; when one side is fried turn and pour more batter over them; when both sides are of a good colour lay them on a dish and serve hot. A nice breakfast dish.

HAM SAUCE.

When a ham is almost done with, pick all the meat that remains from the bone, leaving out any rusty part; beat the meat and bone to a mash with the rolling-pin, put it into a saucepan with three spoonsful of gravy, set it over a slow fire, and keep stirring it all the time to prevent its sticking to the bottom; when it has been on some time put to it a small bundle of sweet herbs, some pepper, and half a pint of veal gravy, cover it up, and let it stew over a gentle fire. When it has a good flavour of the herbs, strain off the gravy. A little of this is an improvement to all gravies.

STEWED VEAL.

Cut the veal as for small cutlets ; put into the bottom of a pie dish a layer of the veal, and sprinkle it with some finely rubbed sweet basil and chopped parsley, the grated rind of one lemon with the juice, half a nutmeg grated, a little salt and pepper, and cut into very small pieces a large spoonful of butter, then another layer of slices of veal with exactly the same seasoning as before, and over this pour one pint of Lisbon wine and half a pint of cold water, then cover it over very thickly with grated stale bread ; put this in the oven and bake slowly for three quarters of an hour, and brown it. Serve it in the pie dish hot.

BEEF STEAK AND OYSTER SAUCE.

Select a good tender rump steak about an inch thick, and broil it carefully. Nothing but experience and attention will serve in broiling a steak ; one thing, however, is always to be remembered, never salt or season broiled meat until cooked. Have the gridiron clean and hot, grease it with either butter or good lard before laying on the meat, to prevent its sticking or marking the meat, have clear bright coals and turn it frequently. When cooked, cover tightly, and have ready nicely stewed oysters ; then lay the steak in a hot dish and pour over some of the oysters. Serve the rest in a tureen. Twenty-five oysters will make a nice sauce for a steak.

VEAL, OLIVES AND OYSTERS.

Take nice cutlets about an inch in thickness ; grate a cup full of uncooked ham, a spoonful of bread crumbs, a little powdered sweet basil, salt, cayenne, and a grated lemon with the juice ; mix this well and lay in three olives, put this mixture into the cutlet, (this is only for one cutlet,) roll this up and tie it, dip it in the beaten yolk of an egg, and then into bread crumbs, and fry a nice brown. As many cutlets as are required may be prepared in this manner ; lay each one on a cloth near the fire to keep hot and free from fat, then fry some large oysters and garnish the cutlets. Lay the cutlets on a trivet in the saucepan, pour in the bottom of the saucepan one pint of the juice of the oysters, a glass of wine, half a nutmeg grated, chopped parsley, and a little salt and cayenne ; set this in a hot place to simmer, cover it very tightly and cook for twenty minutes. Lay the cutlets in a dish and garnish with the fried oysters, and send the sauce very hot in a tureen to serve with the cutlets.

POTTED BEEF OR VEAL.

Take three pounds of rather lean beef or veal ; rub it well with saltpetre and a handful of common salt. Let it lie in salt for two days—rubbing it well each day, then put it into a stew-pan and chop about two pounds of beef suet, not finely, but only shredded, two onions cut up very finely, and put these on the beef, cover it with water, and let it stew very slowly for five hours, keeping the pot tightly covered. When perfectly tender take it out and strain off the liquor, let it stand until cold and remove all the suet, which is nice for frying—better than lard ; then shred the beef and pound it in a mortar with half a pound of fresh butter, until it is a perfect paste ; whilst pounding add a small teaspoonful of good dry mustard, the same of ginger, and moisten it with mushroom catsup , put this into jars, press tightly, and pour over it melted butter—about an inch thick over each jar ; it must be kept in a cool place and will keep for some time. It is a nice relish cut in slices for tea. The broth must be kept for pease soup; veal can be prepared in the same way—it makes nice force-meat for stuffing other meats.

POTTED VEAL AND BACON.

Cut thin slices of veal and the same quantity of nice bacon; then rub together some dried sweet basil or summer savory, very fine, until reduced to a powder, and lay in a stew-pan a layer of bacon, then a layer of veal, and on this sprinkle the powdered herbs, a little grated horse-radish, then again some bacon and veal, and then herbs and horse-radish and a little salt; on this squeeze a lemon and grate the rind, then cover very tightly and put it into the oven to bake for three hours, then take it out and drain off all the gravy, pour over it a little mushroom catsup, and press it down with a heavy weight, then put it away in a pot tightly covered. This is nice for tea.

CROQUETS.

Chop very finely any sort of cold meats with bacon or cold ham, rub a teaspoonful of summer savory very fine, pound twelve allspice finely; boil one egg hard and chop it very fine, and one onion minced fine; mix this all together, then grate a lemon and add a little salt; when well mixed moisten it with walnut catsup, form it into pear-shaped balls, and dredge well with flour; at the blossom ends stick in a whole clove. Then have boiling fat or dripping in the pan, dredge each pear again well with flour, lay them in the boiling fat and fry a nice brown; then take them out and lay on a soft cloth in a hot place to drain. Serve hot.

CALF'S FEET DRESSED AS TERRAPINS.

Boil eight feet until the meat leaves the bones, and then remove all the bones; put them into a pan with half a pint of the rich gravy in which they were boiled, and add two large spoonsful of butter; rub the yolks of three hard boiled eggs with a small teaspoonful of mustard, a very little cayenne, and salt to the taste. When well incorporated with the eggs, stir all together into the feet and gravy, let it simmer ten minutes, and just before dishing add two wine glasses of good cooking wine, and simmer again before serving. The broth is very nice for soup, or will make a good jelly seasoned and cleared with the whites of eggs as directed in the receipt for calves' feet jelly.

SWEETBREADS

Should be soaked in water, put for eight or ten minutes in boiling water, and then into clear cold spring water, to blanch. They may be cut in slices, or in dice, and put into fricassees of meat or ragouts, or they may be served as a separate dish.

SWEETBREADS—ANOTHER WAY.

Two or three good throat sweetbreads will make a dish; blanch as above until fit to eat, take them up and lay them in cold water; when cold dry them well, egg and bread crumb them with or without herbs, put them on a dish and brown them in the oven; garnish them with mushroom sauce, or endives, or spinach, or tomato will do if approved of.

SWEETBREADS FRICASSEED—WHITE.

Blanch and then cut them in slices. To a pint of veal gravy put a thickening of flour and butter, a tablespoonful of cream, grated lemon peel and nutmeg, and white pepper, to flavour. Stew ten minutes, add the sweetbreads, let them simmer twenty minutes.

SWEETBREADS FRICASSEED—BROWN.

Cut them in small pieces, flour, and fry them. When a good brown pour over them a pint of good beef gravy, highly seasoned; stew gently, until the sweetbreads are tender. Add a little flour and butter to thicken; add mushroom catsup to flavour; mushrooms may be substituted, or all may be cooked with the sweetbreads.

TO STEW SWEETBREADS—RIS DE VEAU.

Make a force-meat of the tenderest parts of boiled or roast fowl, some bacon, a little parsley chopped, a little thyme, lemon-peel, the yolks of two eggs, cayenne pepper, and nutmeg. Lay the sweetbreads in a pan, upon a layer of slices of veal, cover them with slices of bacon, put in a bunch of sweet herbs, an onion sliced, a little mace, red pepper and salt. Pour in a quart of good broth, and stew for two hours, remove them, and reduce by boiling the broth to a fourth; heat the sweetbreads in it, garnish with lemon in slices and serve hot.

SWEETBREADS LARDED.

Blanch, and lard them with bacon, put them into a stewpan with a pint of veal broth; add a little browning, with the juice of half a lemon. Stew until tender; thicken the gravy with a little flour and butter. Lay bunches of boiled celery round the dish when you serve. Fresh salad nicely dressed is good with them.

KIDNEYS.

Take four fresh kidneys, parboil them and cut them into good sized pieces for serving at table, season them with a little ginger and salt; sprinkle bread crumbs thinly, and a large spoonful of butter cut fine, over them,and lay them into a pan. Take one pint of cream and the yolk of three eggs well beaten, and add half a pint of good cooking wine; beat well together, and pour over the kidneys; bake this three-quarters of an hour. This is called a Florentine. Serve hot.

DRESSING FOR CHICKEN SALAD.

Take any pieces of cold veal—the white meat only—chop it very fine, and the white meat of any cold chicken, and two heads of celery, chopped; boil an egg hard, throw it into cold water, rub the yolk smoothly; beat the yolk of an egg very light and stir it into the rubbed yolk, a teaspoonful of dry mustard, a tablespoonful of olive oil stirred in well, a little cayenne and salt, and four large spoonsful of good vinegar. Mix the meat into this mixture, and put it into a glass bowl; over this pour one quart of the liquor in which calves' feet have been boiled, with all the fat removed and nicely seasoned; let it be cold, but before it begins to jelly pour it over the mixture; stir it well through, and let it stand until it jellies; then stick all over the top pieces of fringed celery.

TURTLE VEAL.

Make nice force-meat of finely chopped veal, highly seasoned with spice and herbs; cut up two pounds of lean veal into pieces of two inches square; season it with salt and pepper, chop up green parsley, and one large spoonful of sweet marjoram, finely powdered, a little pounded mace, the rind of a lemon grated and the juice; put in first a layer of force-meat balls, the size of a walnut, then the veal, some bits of cut up butter, a thinly sliced onion, then force-meat balls, and then veal, seasoned; pour over this cold water enough just to cover the meat; set the dish in the oven to bake, cover with a plate at first, but afterwards remove it to brown. When done, pour off the gravy, beat up the yolk of an egg, a large spoonful of flour, and a glass of wine; stir it into the gravy, scald it up and pour it over the meat. Send it to table hot.

BOLOGNA SAUSAGES.

Chop very finely ten pounds of lean, juicy beef, two pounds and a half of fat fresh pork cut into very small pieces with a knife—not chopped—a quarter of an ounce of pounded mace, the same of pounded cloves, and two ounces of ground black pepper; mix these well, stuff this mixture lightly into the straight gut of the beef; make each one about twelve inches in length and tie both ends closely. Put them into a ham brine for four or five days, and then press it for a day or two to make it firm, and smoke for a week. They must be kept in a dry place, and improve by age, and when a year old they are excellent.

A RAGOUT OF COLD VEAL.

Either the loin or fillet will make an excellent ragout. Cut the veal into nice slices; put a large piece of butter into a frying pan, and as soon as it is hot, dredge each piece well with flour and fry it a nice brown; take it out and have ready a nice gravy made from the "scrap jar;" put the gravy into the pan, dredge in some flour, stir it over the fire until it thickens, season it with a very little pepper and salt, and a wine glass full of tomato catsup; then cut thin slices of cold ham and lay into the gravy, and add your slices of veal. Serve hot.

VEAL OLIVES.

Cut about six slices from off a fillet, not quite an inch thick, and as long as you can ; flatten them with a chopper, and beat an egg, and dip each slice in the egg ; then cut very thin slices of ham, or bacon, the length of the veal, lay them on each piece of veal and grate a little horse-radish and lemon peel over each slice, and a little salt and pepper; then roll up with care each slice of veal, bacon and seasoning, and tie each one tightly with twine; put a lump of butter in a stew-pan, and sprinkle bread crumbs thickly over each one on the egg-side ; pour over them a wine glass of tomato or walnut catsup, and one pint of hot water ; cover the stew-pan tightly and cook one hour very slowly. Thinly cut rump steaks are nice dressed in this way. Do not unroll them in dishing ; merely take off the twine. For gravy dredge in flour to thicken the liquor in which they were cooked ; simmer it a few minutes and pour over them. Serve hot.

KNUCKLE OF VEAL STEWED WITH RICE.

Break the shank bone, wash it clean, put it into the stew-pan with two quarts of water, an onion peeled, a few blades of mace, and a teaspoonful of salt; set it on a rather quick fire, and remove the scum as it rises ; wash carefully a quarter of a pound of rice, and when the veal has cooked for about an hour, skim it well and throw in the rice ; then let it simmer for three-quarters of an hour very slowly. When done put the meat into a deep dish and the rice around it. Mix a little nice drawn butter and stir in some chopped parsley, and pour it over the veal. Serve hot.

BEEF A LA MODE.

Take a rump of about eight or ten pounds ; then take a spoonful of powdered basil, some finely chopped parsley, half an ounce of powdered allspice, and the same of cloves, and stir these into a wine glass of vinegar. Take some fat corned pork, cut it into thin slices, the length of the beef, and rub them in the spice and herbs; make incisions through the beef, insert these pieces, and rub the remainder of the spices and herbs into the beef; pour over the vinegar and rub in ginger; dredge flour over; and place in the bottom of the stew-pan some thin slices of corn pork; lay on the beef, chop up two onions very finely, and sprinkle over the beef; then pour over half a pint of Claret, and the same of mushroom catsup, half a pint of cold water and a teaspoonful of salt. Cover this tightly and stew very slowly for four hours. Take out the beef, strain off the gravy, remove all the fat, and thicken with browned flour; set the beef over hot water to keep warm, and let the gravy simmer for twenty minutes. Serve it up in a tureen with the beef. This is very good cold.

SPICED ROUND OF BEEF.

Take about three ribs of tender juicy beef and remove the bones; pound half an ounce of cloves, half an ounce of allspice, a teaspoonful of powdered coriander seeds, half a teaspoonful of powdered saltpetre, one teaspoonful of salt, and one teaspoonful of ground ginger. Mix these well together and rub the beef well with them; then tie it up tightly round, as a fillet, let it remain one or two days before cooking, put fat corned bacon cut in thin slices at the bottom of the stew-pan, and on these lay the beef; pour over it half a pint of port wine and a wine glass full of mushroom catsup, and a pint of water. Let it stew slowly for two hours and a half, then remove the beef and keep it warm; skim off the fat and thicken with browned flour, let it simmer ten minutes, and then dust in a very little sugar, and send it in a tureen with the beef. Serve hot.

STEWED CALF'S LIVER.

The liver must be fresh and well washed. Put the heart and haslet on to cook in just enough cold water to cover them. While they are cooking—which must be done in the early part of the morning—lay the liver in cold water and vinegar, with plenty of salt, until ready for cooking; then let the heart and haslet simmer for half an hour, skimming the water well while boiling, and slice two or three onions and boil with them; take out the onions and strain the water in which they were boiled. Then prepare the liver, by making incisions in it, and cutting narrow strips of corned pork, uncooked, and putting into the openings in the liver; the more it is thus larded with pork, the better will be the flavour. Lay a little bundle of summer savory and parsley, with a fresh sliced lemon, into the bottom of the stew-pan, and on this lay the liver; then pour over it the gravy made by the heart and haslet, and put in about a dozen allspice, six or eight whole cloves, and a few pepper corns. Let this only simmer slowly—tightly covered, for an hour and a half, then pour off the gravy, strain it and mix with a little of the gravy a large spoonful of flour; when smooth stir it into the gravy, pour this into a saucepan, and add a wine glass full of Claret wine or mushroom catsup; let it simmer for five minutes. Dish the liver and pour over it plenty of the gravy. Send the rest to the table in a sauce-boat. This is a delicious dish if carefully prepared.

TO STEW DUCKS. No. 1.

Draw and clean your ducks; wash them, and either keep them whole, or cut them up as fricasseed chickens, slice three onion, and lay in the bottom of the stew-pan, slice one fresh lemor add about one dozen allspice, on this lay the ducks and sprinkle salt over them, then pour about one quart of made gravy or broth of any kind over it, and cover them tightly. Let this simmer very slowly for one hour and a half, then pour off the gravy and strain it through a sieve, skim off all the fat, mix a little of the gravy with a large spoonful of flour, stir this into the strained gravy, and keep the ducks covered and hot in the stew-pan. Pour the gravy into a saucepan and let it simmer for ten minutes, then add a wine glass full of good cooking wine and one of mushroom catsup; let this simmer once, then dish your ducks, pour over the hot gravy and send some in a sauce-boat.

TO STEW DUCKS. No. 2.

There is a difference between *a* stewed duck and stewed duck, and it is not the *a* alone; in the one case the duck is stewed whole, and in the other in pieces. To stew a duck or ducks, they should be stuffed and roasted for twenty minutes, and then placed in a stewpan with an onion cut in slices, a little sage and mint, and about a pint of good beef gravy, seasoned with pepper and salt, let it stew gently for about twenty minutes, take out the duck carefully and keep it warm, strain the gravy, pour it into a clean stew-pan, and add to it when well heated the duck and a quart of green peas, let it simmer for half an hour, if not sufficiently thick add a little flour and butter, a glass of good old port wine, and send to table, with the peas in the same dish as the duck.

STEWED DUCK. No. 3.

The ducks should be cut into joints and laid in a stew-pan with a pint of good gravy, let it come to a boil, as the scum rises remove it; season with salt and cayenne, let them stew gently three quarters of an hour, mix smoothly two tea-spoonfuls of fine ground rice, with a glass of port, stir it into the gravy, let it have seven or eight minutes to amalgamate with the gravy, dish and send to table very hot.

BAKED LEG OF MUTTON BONED AND STUFFED.

The principal skill required in accomplishing this dish is the boning, this must be done with a very sharp knife, commence on the underside of the joint, passing the knife under the skin until exactly over the bone, then cut down to it, pass the knife round close to the bone right up to the socket, then remove the large bone of the thickest end of the leg, seeing the meat is clear of the bone ; you may then draw out the remaining bones easily. Put in the orifice a highly seasoned forcemeat, fasten the knuckle end tightly over, replace the bone at the base of the joint, and sew it in. It must be well basted, and should be sent to table with a good gravy ; when dished pour over it a wine glass of wine. Serve hot.

PIGEONS IN JELLY.

Make some jelly of calf's foot, or if you have the liquor in which a knuckle of veal has been boiled, it will answer the same purpose; place in a stew-pan with a bunch of sweet herbs, a blade of mace, white pepper, slices of lean bacon, some lemon peel, and the pigeons, trussed and their necks propped up to make them appear natural, and stuffed with salt oysters. Bake them; when they are done, remove them from the liquor, but keep them covered close, that their colour may be preserved. Remove the fat, boil the whites of a couple of eggs with the jelly to clear it, and strain it ; this is usually done by dipping a cloth into boiling water, and straining it through it, as it prevents anything like scum or dirt sweeping through the strainer. Put the jelly rough over and round the pigeons. Young chickens are nice if done in the same manner. This is a supper dish, as it is served cold.

VEAL CUTLETS FRIED

Procure your cutlets, half an inch thick, coat them with the yolk of eggs well beaten, strew over them bread crumbs, grated lemon peel, and nutmeg, put some fresh lard in the pan, and when boiling put in your cutlets; when the cutlets are cooked take them out and keep them before the fire to keep hot, dredge into the pan a little flour, pour in a little water, squeeze in lemon juice to taste, season with pepper and salt, add mushroom catsup, boil quickly until a light brown, pour it over the cutlets, and serve, the cutlets being laid in a circle round the dish, and the gravy in the centre. Serve hot.

MUTTON CUTLETS.

Loin chops make the best cutlets. Take off the thickest end of each bone and about an inch off the top of the bone; put the chops into a stew-pan in which has been previously melted a little butter seasoned with salt; stew for a short time—but not until they are brown, as that appearance is accomplished in another manner. Chop some parsley very fine add a little thyme, mix it with sufficient yolk of egg to coat the chops, which will have been suffered to cool before this addition to them; then rub them with bread crumbs over which a pinch of cayenne pepper has been sprinkled; broil them upon a gridiron over a clear but not brisk fire, when they are brown dish them; lemon juice may be squeezed over them, or the dish in which they are served may be garnished with some thin slices of lemon in halves and quarters. Serve hot.

STEWED HEART.

Take a fresh beef's heart, clean it and remove the gristle; make a stuffing of two large spoonsful of finely chopped beef suet, three large spoonfuls of bread crumbs, a little finely powdered summer savory and thyme, a little cayenne, then lard the heart well with strips of corn pork, fat only, lay some slices of corn pork in the bottom of a stew-pan, stuff the opening of the heart well, sew it up and lay it in the stew-pan with twelve allspice and twelve pepper corns, pour on one pint and a half of cold water, cover it very closely, and let it simmer very slowly for two hours, then make a rich sauce; rub some flour and butter together, and on it pour from the stew-pan half a pint of the gravy, one large spoonful of mushroom catsup, and let this simmer; pour some over the heart when dished, and send the remainder to the table in a sauce-boat. Serve hot.

RAGOUT OF RABBITS.

Clean with great care, as they require attention in cleaning, and washing through many waters. When perfectly clean, cut them up into nice pieces, lay them in a stew-pan with water to cover them entirely, sprinkle in a teaspoonful of salt, and a few blades of mace; let this simmer for an hour and a half, and remove all the scum as it rises, as they must be kept white; then put on to boil six white onions in salt and water, and boil them until tender. When the rabbits are done pour off some of the broth, rub a large spoonful of butter with a spoonful of flour and stir it into the gravy; put this into a saucepan to simmer, then strain off the onions, put them into the broth gravy, add a cup of cream, and a little grated nutmeg. Dish the rabbits and garnish them with parsley, and pour over some of the gravy and all the onions. Send some of the gravy to the table in a sauce-boat.

8

CURRIED CHICKENS.

Cut up a chicken as for a fricassee, lay it in a saucepan and just cover it with cold water; sprinkle over half a tea-spoonful of salt, and let this simmer for three-quarters of an hour, then slice an onion, put a lump of butter into a pan and fry it a nice brown, take this out and stir into the chicken, rub a spoonful of flour with two spoonsful of butter, and stir this into the broth, then chop up some parsley very finely, let this simmer, then stir two spoonsful of curry powder and a large spoonful of butter well together, and add to it half a pint of the chicken gravy, and when well mixed stir it into the chicken, simmer ten minutes. Serve hot and garnish with rice boiled dry and carefully.

BAKED CALF'S HEAD.

Take a cold calf's head, chop it up—not too fine, and mix with it some bread crumbs, a little powdered sweet basil; should you not have any cold mashed white potatoes, boil and mash about six. Put the head and crumbs, alternately into a deep dish, pour over it two wine glasses of cooking wine, the same of walnut or mushroom catsup; when ready cut up some small pieces of butter and strew over the top, then spread the potatoes thickly on, smooth it down, and dredge it lightly with flour, and with a feather spread all over the top of the flour and potato covering, the yolk of a well beaten egg. Put the dish in the oven, slowly warm it, and brown the top, which will require about three-quarters of an hour. Make a rich gravy of broth or any cold beef gravy, adding some allspice while cooking, then strain it and serve in a sauce-boat with the head

STEWED LEG OF VEAL.

Select a good fat leg with a small portion of the fillet left on, crack it in two or three places, and wash it and lay it in a stew-pan. Slice two lemons very thinly and lay on it, a small blade of mace broken up finely, sprinkle a little salt, and a shake of pepper ; on this pour just enough cold water to cover the leg, set it in an oven and cover the pan tightly. Let it cook slowly for four hours, and skim it occasionally, so as to be entirely free from scum or fat ; if it becomes dry add a very little cold water. When done pour off any gravy in the pan, and rub a small spoonful of flour and half a spoonful of butter well together, and stir it into the gravy. Let it simmer, and just before dishing add a wine glass of good cooking wine. Pour some of the gravy over the leg, and serve the rest in a sauce-boat. This is nice sliced for tea if any is left cold.

TOMATO STEW.

Take eight pounds of the plate of beef, put it on to boil in a gallon of water, with a dozen of tomatoes, the same of okras, six potatoes cut small, two carrots cut lengthwise, two onions; season it to your taste with pepper and salt; let it stew slowly four hours; skim all the fat off the gravy, and garnish the meat with the potatoes and carrots.

CORN FRITTERS.

Grate six ears of corn; add one tablespoonful of flour, and two eggs; pepper and salt to your taste; to be fried like oysters.

CHICKEN SALAD.

Take a pair of fowls and either boil or roast them; when they are entirely cold remove all the skin and fat, and disjoint them; cut the meat from the bones into very small pieces, not exceeding an inch; wash and split two large heads of celery, and cut the white part into pieces also about an inch long, and having mixed the chicken and celery together, put them in a deep china dish; cover it and set it away. Just before the salad is to be eaten, the dressing should be put on, which is made thus: Take the yolks of eight hard boiled eggs, put them into a flat, dish and mash them to a paste with the back of a spoon; add to the egg a small teaspoonful of fine salt, the same quantity of cayenne pepper, half a gill of made mustard, a wine glass and a half of French vinegar, and rather more than two wine glasses of sweet oil; then add the yoke of one raw egg well beaten, or a tablespoonful of cream; mix all these ingredients thoroughly, stirring them a long time, till they are quite smooth. After you pour it on the chicken and celery, mix the whole well together with a silver fork.

ROGNON DE MOUTON A LA FRANCAISE.

The French have a faculty of making a dish recherché out of mere trifles, their receipt for serving up this little dish is no mean evidence of their peculiar skill. Take half a dozen fine mutton kidneys, clear them of fat and skin, and cut them into thin slices; powder them immediately with sweet herbs in fine powder, parsley which has been chopped, dried, and powdered, cayenne, and salt; put into a stew-pan two ounces of clarified butter or fresh lard if the former is not in reach, put in the slices of kidney, fry them, they will brown very quickly, they must be done on both sides, dredge flour over them, moisten with lemon juice, and in five minutes the kidneys will be done; lift them out into a very hot dish, around which are laid slices of bread fried; pour into the gravy two glasses of white wine, give it a boil, pour it over the kidneys, and serve hot.

TURTLE, KILLED AND DRESSED.

Tie a strong cord round the hind fins of the turtle, then hang it up; tie another cord by way of pinion to both fins, that it should not beat about and be troublesome to the person who cuts off the head, then take off the head. All this do the evening before you intend dressing it; then lay the turtle on the back shell on your block, then loosen the shell round the edge by cutting it with your sharp knife, then gently raise the shell clean off from the flesh, then next take out the gall with great care, then cut the fore fins off—all the flesh will come with them, then cut the hind fins off, take the liver as whole as you can from the entrails, likewise the heart and the kidneys; cut the entrails from the back bone, put them in a bucket of water, wash the shell in several waters, and turn it down to drain. In the meantime cut the fins from the lean meat, then cut the white or belly shell in twelve or fourteen pieces, turn up the back shell and take all the fat from it, taking it out as though you were skinning anything, put the fat in a stew-pan by itself, saw a rim off the back shell six inches deep, cut in about twelve pieces, put a large stew-pan full of water on the fire, when it boils dip in a fin for a minute or two, then peal off the shell, and so continue until you have done it all, head and all; then put all the pieces of shell into a stewpan, with about eighteen large onions, and a faggot of sweet herbs, allowing more basil than any other herbs, fill it up with water, let it boil a long time; the next you will cut the fore fins into four pieces, and put them into a stew-pan, cover them with water, the hind ones in two each; cover the stew-pan; let them boil gently until you can take out all the bones, do not mix them, but put them on different dishes, and then put the two liquors in one pan. Cut up the lean meat for small dishes. Put one pound of butter into a large stew-pan, and all the lean next that may be left as useless, cut up three or four fowls, a bunch of cooking herbs, twelve onions, three or four pounds of lean ham, and a bottle of Madeira, simmer it down for one hour, then fill it up with the liquor previously strained from the bones and shells, keep it all boiling gently for several hours, then strain it off, taking care of what lean meat you require for your tureens, put it in your soup pot to keep hot, with a little of the stock, and one pint of mushroom catsup. Have the entrails cleaned and scalded, then cut them into pieces two inches long, and put them on to blanch in cold water, wash them out, line a stew-pan with fat bacon, let them stew very gently for about three hours, then thicken the stock as for mock turtle, and rub it through a sieve, add egg balls, or hard boiled eggs, cut in half, and force-meat balls, the green fat to be boiled by itself in good strong broth, a little to be added to each tureen of soup. If to be sent up in the shell, put a pretty rim of raised pie paste round the top shell; add the juice of lemons and a little more wine before you serve it up. Season with sugar, cayenne pepper, and salt. This is on a large scale, but may be reduced, observing the proportions, or the whole prepared and kept in a cool place for use.

FORCE-MEAT STUFFINGS.

Force-meat meat should be made to cut with a knife, but not dry or heavy; no one flavour should predominate. For veal stuffing, chop some suet fine, a little parsley, a small piece of shalot, rub through a dry sieve a small quantity of basil, some sweet marjoram and thyme, then add these to your suet, a grated lemon, a few grates of nutmeg, a few bread crumbs, and one or two eggs, mix all well up together, and season with pepper and salt. If for game, scrape the raw livers into the stuffing, prepared as above, only in addition pound it all fine.

MEAT CAKES.

Chop any kind of fresh cold meats, very finely, season with salt and pepper, make a nice batter; lay a spoonful of the batter on the griddle, which must be buttered to prevent its sticking, then a spoonful of the chopped meat, and then a spoonful of the batter; when browned on one side turn carefully and brown the other. It makes a palatable breakfast dish. Serve hot.

TERRAPINS STEWED.

Take six live terrapins, have ready a large pot of boiling water with two tablespoonsful of salt thrown in, and while boiling put in the terrapins; let them boil steadily for two hours and a half, then take them out and set to cool. When quite cold separate the shells, remove the heads and the galls with care, chop up the chitterlings, take off the nails from the paws, with the hard skin, put all the edible parts which have been removed from the shells in a stew-pan, then cut up and add a quarter of a pound of butter, a tablespoonful of mixed allspice and cloves pounded very finely, a little salt, and then rub with a little flour the yolk of four hard boiled eggs; stir this into the terrapins, chop up finely and add the whites; set this on a very hot place to warm slowly, stirring it all the time. Let it simmer, or rather cook ten minutes, then add a pint and a half of good cooking wine, and let this simmer five minutes more, and serve hot in a tureen.

TO FRINGE CELERY FOR GARNISHING.

Take the outer thick white and green stalks, cut them about a finger's length, then select a good large new cork, stick it full of coarse needles, and carefully draw each piece of celery over the cork, leaving at the end about an inch of the celery stick to remain unfringed; when all the fibrous parts are separated, lay the celery for a couple of hours in cold water to curl and crisp. This is a beautiful garnish for salads, if laid on thickly.

TO MAKE SAUCE FOR CHICKEN SALAD.

Take the yolk of one hard boiled egg and rub it very finely with a little pepper and salt, and mix this with the yolk of one raw egg, and then stir in gently salad oil enough to make as much sauce as you require, taking care to stir the sauce all one way or it will curdle; when you think you have enough sauce add two tablespoonsful of vinegar, a teaspoonful of mustard, and a little cream, pour this over the chickens (which must be cut into small pieces) with two or three heads of celery cut up; fringe a little of the celery to garnish the dish with. The same sauce may be served with boiled chicken, and is better than any other.

DRESSING FOR CHICKEN SALAD.

Take five teaspoonsful of the best English dry mustard, four yolks of eggs, a teaspoonful of salt, a very little cayenne, beat this well together to a rich froth or cream, then add slowly a large spoonful of fresh olive oil, this must be again beaten. Take the white meat of three boiled chickens, cut it up finely and on it squeeze the juice of three fresh lemons. Mix it well through the meat, and when served add the dressing above. Garnish it with finely fringed celery.

VEAL SALAD.

Cut up any cold veal, finely, and to a pint bowl full of minced veal cut three heads of celery. Rub the yolks of four hard boiled eggs, a tablespoonful of dry mustard, and a large spoonful of olive oil together, then slowly add four large spoonsful of the best wine vinegar, and a little cayenne and salt; when well mixed pour it over the veal and celery, stir it together, and garnish the dish with sprigs of fresh parsley, and celery fringed as directed.

SAUSAGE MEAT.

Chop four pounds of nice clean pork very finely, one pound of good veal also chopped very finely, and season this with a large spoonful of finely rubbed sage, a teaspoonful of sweet marjoram, two dozen pounded allspice, a teaspoonful ot salt, half a teaspoonful of the best cayenne pepper; mix these well together, put it in a tightly covered jar, and set it in a cool place; it is better if standing a few days. Fry it in balls a nice brown. Serve hot and free from fat.

ANOTHER.

To ten pounds finely chopped meat, put four ounces of salt, scant weight, two ounces pepper, good weight, twelve cloves, and one ounce sage.

ENGLISH PIE.

Chop either cold beef, mutton, or veal, very finely, chop up an onion very finely, some thyme, if green chop it with some parsley, and if dried rub it quite fine, the grated rind and juice of one lemon, half grated nutmeg, a saltspoonful of salt, a little cayenne pepper, and a quarter of a pound of butter cut up; mix this well together, altogether making a pint bowl full, and to this add four well beaten eggs. Stir the mixture well, and on it pour one pint of rich gravy, put all into a dish, and cover the top thickly with bread crumbs. Bake slowly to a nice brown. Serve hot.

FORCEMEAT BALLS.

Take one pound of juicy tender lean beef, and half a pound of nice beef suet, chopped very finely, then take the crumb of a stale loaf of bread, about the size of a large tea cup, soak it a few minutes in cold water, and squeeze it very dry, grate the rind of a lemon with the juice, half a teaspoonful of ground ginger, a saltspoonful of salt, half a teaspoonful of finely rubbed summer savory, and a little cayenne. Mix these well together, stir in the yolks of three eggs, well beaten, to make them stick together when cooked, divide this in half, the one-half put into the stew-pan, with a wine glass of wine or mushroom catsup. Cover it tightly and let it stew slowly for thirty minutes. The other half make into small balls, the size of a walnut, roll them in flour, and fry a light brown. When the stew is done, lay it in a nice form on the dish, and place the forcemeat balls around it. Garnish with parsley.

TOASTED CHEESE.

This is one of those dishes rarely well prepared, but when rightly done is very nice. Cut a slice of stale bread about an inch thick, (a day old) pare off the crust and toast it a light brown—without making it hard, then cut a slice of good fat mellow cheese, (English, Gloster or Cheshire is the best,) a quarter of an inch in thickness, but not as large as the bread by half an inch on each side, cut off the rind and lay it on the toast in a cheese toaster, carefully watch it that it does not burn, and stir it with a spoon to prevent a pellicle or thin skin forming, have ready some good mustard, cayenne, and salt. This is a "rare bit." It must be eaten as it is prepared.

OMELETTE.

The great merit of an omelette is, that it should not be greasy, burnt, or overdone; if too much of the white is used it becomes hard. To dress an omelette, the fire should not be too hot, as it is an object to have the whole substance heated without too much browning on the outside; the omelette must not be too thin, therefore it must be thick and have a full, rich, moist flavour. They should be fried in a small pan, with a small quantity of good butter. Five or six eggs will make a good sized omelette. Break them into a basin, separating the whites from the yolks, mince very finely a tablespoonful of fresh parsley, beat up the yolks well, and to it add the parsley and a little salt, and a very little cayenne, then whip the whites to a stiff froth; put about a large spoonful of butter into the hot pan, and while it is melting mix with the yolks two tablespoonsful of good cream, then beat in the whites when well mixed, and pour it into the pan; shake it in the pan until the eggs begin to set, then turn up the edges, and when a nice brown, it is done. Then have a hot dish and lay it on the pan and turn it upside down on the dish. Never make it until it is wanted at table, as it must be eaten as soon as made. They can be flavoured with finely chopped onions, or oysters, or cooked and chopped ham. The above is the basis of all omelettes, only omitting the cream if anything else is used.

OMELET AU NATUREL.

Break eight or ten eggs into a pan, add pepper, salt, and a spoonful of cold water, beat them up with a whisk to a stiff froth; in the mean time put some fresh butter into a frying pan, when it is quite melted, and nearly boiling, put in the eggs. As it is frying, take up the edges, that they may be properly done; when cooked double it. Serve very hot.

OMELET SOUFFLE

Break six eggs; leave out the whites, put them in a cold place until required; add to the yolks a little powdered sugar, a little grated lemon, a little nutmeg, a few drops of lemon juice, and beat all together, add a few spoonsful of cream; then beat up the six whites very stiff; put a piece of butter in your omelet-pan upon a slow fire; when hot pour in the omelet, mix in your whites very gently, turn it out on your dish, glaze it with pounded sugar, put it in the oven, sprinkle more sugar, and send it to table very hot.

OMELET SOUFFLE IN A MOULD.

Break six fresh eggs, separate the whites and yolks, put to the latter three spoonsful of powdered sugar, four crushed macaroons, a spoonful of potato flour, a little orange flower water, stir them well together, whip the whites of the eggs to a froth, mix them with the yolks, and pour the whole into a buttered mould, but do not fill it; set it in a moderate oven the same as for biscuits, and when done, turn it out on a dish, and serve it. This omelet should be of a clear colour, and shake like a jelly.

POACHING EGGS.

The eggs must be fresh for poaching—two days laid are the best. Have ready the boiling water in a shallow pan, break the eggs separately in a saucer, as one bad one will spoil the others, then slip the egg gently into the boiling water; when all are in the water, put the pan on a moderate fire until the water boils, and the white is perfectly set, then with a slicer lay the eggs on buttered toast or broiled ham.

A MEAT SAUNDERS.

Wash and put into a saucepan two pounds of potatoes, cover them with warm water and throw in a spoonful of salt, let them just reach boiling, but never actually boil, until they are done, then peel and mash them with a little cream and butter, shake in a little cayenne pepper, lay them in a smooth paste to cover a dish, cut thin slices of underdone meat, either mutton, beef, or veal, lay them in thickly, pour over them rich gravy, and a wine glass of either tomato or mushroom catsup, then cover this with a crust of the mashed potatoes. Bake in a slow oven for about forty minutes. Serve hot. This is very nice.

JELLIED TURKEY.

Take out the breast bone and cut off the legs, not the thigh part, of a small fat hen turkey. Clean it with great care, and fill the inside with large fresh oysters, sew it up, lay it in a floured cloth, and sprinkle it over with salt. Lay it in cold water, and boil it one hour and a half very slowly, then take it out, lay it on a dish, and draw out the thread with which the turkey was sown. Have ready a nice jelly made of calves' feet, without sugar, but flavored with lemon and wine; when cool but not cold pour this over the turkey. This must be set aside to jelly. When dressed with fringed celery it is a very handsome dish.

YORKSHIRE PUDDING FOR MEATS.

This pudding is an especial accompaniment to roast beef, mutton or veal. Take six large spoonsful of sifted flour, one teaspoonful of salt, three well beaten eggs, and one pint of milk, beat this to a stiff batter; be careful that it is not lumpy; put a dish beneath the meat which is roasting to catch the drippings; when well greased pour in the batter, and when the surface is browned and set, turn it, so that both sides may be alike brown. A pudding an inch thick requires two hours at a good fire. Serve with the meat.

Frizzled, Smoked, or Dried Beef.

Shave very thin slices of dried beef, put a teacupful of cold water into a small saucepan, and lay in the slices of beef, let it simmer up, and add a large spoonful of butter, then beat up the yolk of an egg with a teaspoonful of flour, then stir this in slowly to prevent the egg from curdling, add a little salt and cayenne, and let it simmer for five minutes, then stir in half a cup of cream, or new milk. Serve hot. This is nice for tea. Ham dressed in the same manner is equally good.

Soused Calves' Feet.

When cleaned and cracked, boil a set of calves feet, (four) in two quarts of water; let them slowly simmer for three hours, then pour them through a sieve or cullender, take out all the bones, cut up the feet and put them into the liquor in which they were boiled, let it cool, and then remove every particle of fat; to the liquor and chopped feet pour half a pint of good wine vinegar, a teaspoonful of whole allspice, a little salt and cayenne; pour this all into a saucepan and let it simmer for five minutes, keeping it tightly covered, stir it well, then pour all into a pan, and when quite cold slice for tea. It is both pleasant in flavour and pretty in appearance, if rightly made, it being a clear jelly. Pigs feet are prepared exactly in the same manner.

Veal Cutlets.

These should be cut from the thick part of the leg, about an inch thick, lay them for two hours in vinegar before they are cooked, beat up an egg, and have ready some bread crumbs, then dry the cutlets in a cloth, have ready the frying pan with boiling lard, grate some nutmeg over each cutlet, a little salt and cayenne, then dip it into the egg, and strew them with bread crumbs, and lay them in the boiling fat, and let them cook slowly for ten minutes, first on one side and then on the other to a nice brown. They must be well cooked, and when quite done, lay them in a hot dish, and make the gravy; dredge into the pan where they were cooked, some flour, stir it well, pour in some hot water and a little chopped parsley, and pour this over them when dished for the table.

BEEF STEAK BROILED.

The fire must be bright and clear; good coals are requisite for broiling. The gridiron should be clean and made with fluted bars, which form channels to the gutter, and prevent scorching. The gridiron should always be previously heated and rubbed with suet, before placing the steak on to prevent it from marking or adhering to the bars; a constant watch must be kept over it while broiling, and frequent turning; no seasoning should be put on until it is cooked, then have ready a hot dish with butter, salt, and a little pepper, into this lay the steak and serve very hot. Mutton chops are prepared in the same way.

TO MAKE SAUSAGES.

Take eleven pounds of the fillet of nice fresh pork, and ten pounds of chine fat, chop them very finely, and add five ounces of salt, two and a half of black pepper, one and a half ounce of sage, half an ounce of savory, and little thyme; work this well together. If closely covered, it will keep some weeks in a cool place.

WHITE FRICASSEE OF CHICKEN.

Draw and clean one pair of fowls, lay them in water for half an hour, then dry them and lay them in a stew-pan with milk and water, and a little salt, and let them simmer until cooked; put into a saucepan half a pint of cream, a quarter of a pound of butter, and a little grated nutmeg, stir this and set it on the fire to simmer, and stir in a wine glass of white wine; then lay in the cooked chicken, and let it remain in this, covered up, until dished. Chop up parsley and strew it over the chicken.

ANOTHER—BROWN.

Prepare the chickens for cooking, lay them in a stew-par, just covered with water, sprinkle in a little salt, and let them slowly simmer for twenty minutes; then take the pieces out and dry them in a cloth, put a lump of butter into a pan, dredge the chicken well with flour, and lay it into the hot pan to brown; break up the yolk of an egg, a little grated nutmeg, cayenne and salt, take some of the broth in which the chickens were boiled, put it into a stew-pan, and stir in the egg and seasoning, with a little flour for thickening, and when well mixed, lay in the browned chicken until ready for dishing, and garnish with parsley.

HOW TO COOK PIG'S HEAD.

Have ready cleaned the head, feet, and haslet, put them on to boil with plenty of cold water, and a teaspoonful of salt, reserving the liver to cook separately. Let it boil slowly for two hours, skimming it carefully; then take the head and haslet from the water, take out every bone carefully, put the head into a baking dish, sprinkle over it some finely powdered sage, a little cayenne, grate the rind of a lemon, and cover the whole with bread crumbs; then cut up bits of butter and put them on the top, and put it into the oven to brown. Chop up the haslet finely, season it with a finely chopped onion, three or four allspice, and six or eight pepper corns, slice the lemon grated; on this pour half a pint of the broth in which the head was boiled, and let this cook fifteen minutes. Slice and dredge well with flour the liver, and fry it a nice brown. When the head is browned, lay it on a hot dish and lay around it on the dish the fried liver, and feet, split; pour a little of the sauce on the head, and send the rest to the table in a sauce-boat. If the gravy is too thin, rub a spoonful of flour and the same of butter together, and stir it in very smoothly a few minutes before serving; let it simmer for five minutes to cook the flour. This is very nice. The broth is useful for soup.

ALAMODE BEEF.

Select a piece of the round, of ten or twelve pounds, remove the meat around the bone carefully, keeping it as whole as possible; cut strips of half an inch in width, and the depth of the meat, in length of uncooked corn pork, run these strips into the beef from the top to bottom, as in slicing the meat it will cut nicely, and the more introduced the better the flavour. Then mix together one tablespoonful of ground allspice, one teaspoonful of cloves, five blades of mace, one tablespoonful of finely powdered summer savory, one tablespoonful of sweet marjoram, one tablespoonful of ginger, and one tablespoonful of salt, then make incisions in the beef and introduce through it the above articles well mixed together. This must be prepared the day before it is cooked to allow of the flavour being communicated to the beef. Lay in the bottom of the stew-pan some pieces of corned pork, cut in thin slices, on this lay the beef, having tied it tightly around with tape to keep it in a good form, then make a little bunch of thyme and parsley, and lay it on the beef, slice two onions and scatter them over the beef, and then pour over it one quart of cold water, and set this aside to simmer very slowly for four hours. It must be cooked with care, and kept tightly covered. Half an hour before dishing pour off the gravy and skim all the fat off. Strain it and add a wine glass full of mushroom catsup to half a pint of the gravy, and stir in a spoonful of flour to thicken. Let this simmer for a few minutes only, then pour it over the beef, removing the herbs and onions from the top, as they must not be served.

SOUSED CALVES' FEET JELLIED.

Take six feet, wash and put them on to boil in two quarts of cold water and a teaspoonful of salt, and let them slowly simmer for four hours, skimming it carefully, then pour them through a cullender, and set the liquor to cool. When cool skim off the fat, and while it is cooling take out all the bones of the feet, chop up the meat, and put on to simmer one pint of the best vinegar, one teaspoonful of allspice, whole, and the same of pepper corns. When heated stir in the meat, and keep it tightly covered or the heating of the spice and vinegar causes the flavour and strength to evaporate. When the fat is removed from the jelly, pour it into the vinegar and meat. Stir this all well together, and pour it into a pan to cool. It is very nice for tea, cut in slices.

FRIED CHICKEN.

This requires tender chickens. Clean and prepare as for broiling, then quarter the chickens, wipe them dry, and dredge them with flour. Put some pieces of butter into a hot pan, lay in your chickens, and watch them carefully, as the butter scorches very quickly. At the same time have ready some cold mush, made as directed, and when the chicken is well fried, put it in a hot drainer to keep warm, put in more butter, dredge the mush with flour, which must be cut into nice pieces an inch thick and of a finger's length; fry this a nice brown, have ready some chopped parsley, and when the mush is done, take it out and keep warm. Pour into the pan half a pint of good cream, a little salt and cayenne, and the chopped parsley; stir it for two or three minutes, lay the chickens in a dish, and the mush around it, and then pour over it the hot cream. It is a royal dish.

ANOTHER WAY.

Split the young spring chickens down the back, as for broiling; wash and dry them very carefully; then lay in your pan thin slices of uncooked salt pork; dredge the chickens well with flour, and lay them on the pork; cover the pan tightly, and put into rather a hot oven to cook; when one side is nicely browned, turn over the other; and when done take out the chickens, pour off some of the fat gravy, and add chopped parsley and a cup of cream to that which remains in the pan; let it simmer five minutes, stirring all the time; then lay in your chickens until dished.

OMELET.

Take four eggs, beat up with a bowl of milk, seasoned; heat the skillet, then put in a lump of butter; when melted pour in the egg; as it browns at the edge turn it over to the middle, and keep turning each edge; then cover the skillet with a plate and let it steam a little while, then turn it over into the dish.

CHICKEN CROQUETS.

Take a pair of fowls weighing ten pounds; boil them, chop up the meat finely, adding one pint of cream and half pound of butter; pepper and salt to taste; this will form into any shape you choose. Boil in lard.

STEWED AND FRIED FISH, &c

FISH require care in frying. When cleaned and ready for the pan lay them on a soft cloth to dry; if large, score them well; smelts and all little fish do not require it. Sprinkle salt and a little pepper over them, then have ready some bread crumbs and an egg well beaten, dip the fish in the egg and sprinkle thickly over with the bread crumbs; have the pan very clean and hot, put in the clarified dripping or else lard, and when the fat boils lay in the fish; if the fat is not extremely hot it is impossible to fry the fish brown, or have them firm and crisp; turn them with care to have both sides a light brown and crisp. When the fish are done lay them on a soft cloth near the fire, or in the cullender, to drain all the fat from them, turn them two or three times and keep them hot. When all are done send them to the table very hot.

CHOWDER.

Slice thin some fat salt pork, fry them brown and crisp; take out the slices of pork, then slice some white potatoes and lay them in the saucepan in which the pork was browned, then cut into slices some fish, (any kind of rich juicy fish will answer,) flour them and sprinkle with a little salt and pepper. then have ready some fried slices of onions and lay them on the fish, then grated crackers and a fresh lemon thinly sliced then some of the pork, then fish, sliced potatoes, seasoning, a little more onion, and then the rest of the pork; on the top strew very thickly grated or powdered crackers, and over the whole pour a pint of clam or oyster juice—clam is the best. Then mix in a bowl, two tablespoonsful of flour and half a pint of cold water very smoothly, pour it over the whole. It must be covered up and not opened until cooked, which must be done slowly in three-quarters of an hour. Serve very hot.

LOBSTER SALAD.

Extract the fish from the shell, place it in the centre of the dish in which it is to be served, in the form of a pyramid; arrange the salad round tastefully, and add salad mixture. This dish is not infrequently garnished with the smallest claws of the fish. This is a matter of fancy—or thus:—

The first row is formed of cut cucumbers, the second of eggs boiled hard, and each egg split into four pieces, and the points laid round the salad; the third and bottom row is composed of slices of beets and lobsters, garnished with parsley.

SCOLLOPED OYSTERS.

Toast several slices of bread quite brown, and butter them on both sides; take a baking dish, and put the toast around the sides instead of a crust. Pour your oysters into the dish, and season to your taste with butter, pepper, and salt, adding mace or cloves. Crumb bread on the top of the oysters, and bake it with a quick heat about fifteen minutes.

BOILED LOBSTER.

Select a fat live lobster, have ready a pot of boiling water, throw in a handful of salt; a medium sized lobster is the best, put it tail foremost in the pot, and boil it forty minutes. It must be entirely cooked, or it is indigestible. They are not fit to eat more than twelve hours after they are cooked, and should be eaten as soon as cold. When quite cold take it out of the shell, remove the intestine running through the body, and the spongy parts about the head; keep it as whole as possible, crack the large claws and take out the meat, but lay the small ones around the lobster. Garnish it with parsley, and when dressed with fresh green salad, mustard, and other condiments, is highly esteemed.

PICKLED OYSTERS.

Take one hundred good freshly opened oysters, scald them up once in their own juice, skim it while they scald, then take them out and lay them in a dish to cool, strain the liquor, and boil it with half a pint of the best white wine vinegar, and one pint of white wine, one peeled onion chopped very finely, one ounce of white pepper, whole grains, half an ounce of allspice, whole also, a few blades of mace, and a half a teaspoonful of salt; boil this for five minutes, and when quite cool, strain it and pour over the oysters. They will keep for weeks. Be careful to keep the saucepan covered whilst the juice is boiling, or the strength of the vinegar and spice will evaporate. Cover up tightly the jar containing the oysters.

STEWED OYSTERS.

Drain off the juice from one hundred first-rate oysters, put the juice into a saucepan, let it slowly simmer, skim it very carefully, then rub the yolks of three hard boiled eggs and one large spoonful of flour well together, and stir this into the juice, then cut into small pieces a quarter of a pound of butter, and add half a teaspoonful of whole allspice, half a teaspoonful of salt, (if the oysters are not salt,) a very little cayenne, and the juice of a large fresh lemon; let this all simmer ten minutes, and just before dishing add the oysters. Let them cook five minutes and serve hot.

PICKLED OYSTERS.

Take one hundred oysters, strain them from the juice, and wash the oysters in clear cold water, put the juice on to boil and skim it well. Add to it one large teaspoonful of salt, a spoonful of whole allspice, a dozen whole pepper-corns, one wine glass full of white wine, a wine glass full of the best wine vinegar, and a couple of blades of mace. Then throw in the oysters and let them only scald a minute. Serve cold.

TRIPE—STEWED.

This is prepared like stewed oysters, only it must be first well boiled in salt and water, then cut up, and seasoned like the oysters.

POTTED SHAD.

Select fresh melt shad, as they are fatter and better than the roe shad; clean and cut them through in large pieces, leaving off the head and tail, and have ready a clean large mouthed jar, lay a slice of shad first, then sprinkle salt over it, whole pepper-corns, whole allspice, and half an onion very finely chopped, then a slice of fish, salt, pepper corns, allspice, and half an onion, chopped, and so on until the jar is full; then pour over it enough sharp vinegar to cover the fish, tie a stout brown paper tightly over the top, and set the jar into the oven when the bread is drawn; if considerable heat remains, let the jar be in four hours. This will keep, in a cool place, for several weeks, even in hot weather. It is a nice relish for tea. Herring is as good as shad, if prepared in this way.

A Delicate Way of Stewing Oysters

Strain one hundred oysters through a cullender, and put in a clean saucepan one pint of rich cream, then mix a teaspoonful of flour and a tablespoonful of butter together; when mixed and the cream begins to heat, stir in the flour and butter slowly. Let it simmer, add a little salt, and a very little grated nutmeg; when it begins to boil, put in the oysters, and let them cook for two minutes only. Serve hot.

Clams—Stewed.

The small round, thin-edged clam is the best; it is called "Quahog." The best way of preparing them is to wash the clam carefully, then lay them in an iron pot and cover it, set it in an oven and gradually warm, the heat causes the clam to open, and this saves the juice; when they are all opened, but not allowed to cook, put the juice into a saucepan—not the clams, stir in a large spoonful of butter and a spoonful of flour, chop some fresh parsley, and add them; mix this well with the juice, and let it simmer for five minutes; then add a cup of cream, grated nutmeg, salt, and a little pepper; let this simmer again, then add the clams, which like oysters, must not be much cooked as they harden by cooking. Serve hot.

Clam Fritters.

Strain the clams from the juice, chop the clams up, beat up three eggs very light, stir in the clams, chop up some parsley, a little salt and pepper, grate some nutmeg, and add these to the clams, then stir in one pint of cream, and slowly dredge in some flour, until it is of the consistence of fritters; then have the pan hot, and put in half butter and half lard, as in frying oysters, let it boil and drop in a spoonful of the fritter batter. Serve hot. They are very nice for breakfast.

OYSTERS STEWED WITH CELERY.

Strain one hundred oysters, put the juice on the fire, skim it, and cut up an entire stalk of celery, let it simmer for twenty minutes, then skim out the celery carefully, rub a spoonful of flour with a quarter of a pound of butter, a little mace, a few grains of whole pepper, and salt to taste. Add this to the juice, and let it simmer for a few minutes, then add the oysters, let them just scald, and dish hot for table.

STEWED OYSTERS.

Have one hundred freshly opened oysters, strain them, and put the juice in a very clean saucepan on the fire; when simmering, skim it well, then rub together a large spoonful of butter, and a spoonful of flour, pour to it a large cup of cream, a little grated nutmeg, salt, whole white pepper grains, and a few grains of allspice; stir this into the hot juice, let it simmer for five minutes, squeeze over the oysters the juice of a lemon, and just before the oysters are required for table, throw them into the boiling juice; if cooked too much they become hard and indigestible. Serve hot. Oysters are very nice flavoured with celery; this is done by cutting the celery stalks into the juice instead of the spice, then taken out before the oysters are added.

TROUT—STEWED.

This is a delicate dish when nicely stewed. Clean and wash the fish with care, and wipe it perfectly dry; put into a stew-pan two large spoonsful of butter, dredge in as it melts some flour, grate half a nutmeg, or a few blades of mace, a little cayenne, and a teaspoonful of salt; mix all together, then lay in the fish, let it brown slightly, pour over it some nice veal gravy, some chopped parsley, and a lemon thinly sliced; stew very slowly for forty minutes, then take out the fish, and add two wine glasses of Port or Claret wine to the gravy. Lay the fish on a hot dish and pour over it some of the gravy. Serve the rest in a tureen.

FRIED COD FISH.

Cut the fresh cod into slices about an inch in thickness, and dry it in a towel; have ready bread crumbs, and the yolk of an egg beaten, salt and pepper the fish, dip each slice first in the egg and then in the bread crumbs, have ready boiling lard, and lay them in to fry, until a nice brown; drain off all the fat from each slice, and serve hot.

FRIED OR BROILED SHAD.

Select fresh melt shad, clean it, split down the back, and lay it in a deep dish; then mix one tablespoonful of brown sugar, one teaspoonful of cayenne pepper, one tablespoonful of salt, and rub this mixture into the belly of the fish, close it, and sprinkle some salt on the outside, cover tightly, and let it remain so, if required for dinner, three or four hours, and if for breakfast do it over night; then wipe it dry and lay it on a clean board, before the fire to cook, turn it by placing a dish on it, both the sides must be cooked; when done put melted butter over it. Serve hot.

FRIED HALIBUT.

Cut the slices from about the middle, an inch in thickness, wipe it dry, and have ready some bread crumbs; season with salt and pepper, beat up an egg, dip the seasoned slices into the egg, and then sprinkle the crumbs thickly over, have the fat boiling in the pan as directed, and lay the slices in; when quite brown on one side, turn it with a slicer and cook the other, then lay them in a hot place to drain. Serve hot.

BROILED MACKEREL.

Soak a No. 1 salted mackerel—soak it over night, and wipe it dry in the morning; have ready some clear bright coals, heat and grease the gridiron, and lay the mackerel on it with the flesh side down; when cooked turn it by placing a dish on it, and then slipping the skin side on to the gridiron. Butter it and send up hot.

FRIED OYSTERS.

Drain the oysters through a sieve, beat up two or three eggs, have ready some grated crackers or bread crumbs, sprinkle some salt and a little pepper over the oysters, then dip each oyster into the egg, and cover them well with bread crumbs; have the pan clean and hot, and put an equal portion of lard and butter into it, and when it boils lay in the oysters carefully. They require close attention to prevent either burning or too much cooking; as they are cooked lay them near the fire on a soft cloth to drain. Serve very hot. Care must be used that the fat does not burn.

BAKED BLACK FISH.

Chop very fine a small cup full of the fat of ham, a large spoonful of bread crumbs, a spoonful of chopped parsley and thyme mixed, and a little pepper and salt, then mix this all well together, and stuff the fish, then tie or sew it up, flour it well, and lay in the bottom of the saucepan or kettle in which it is to be stewed some very thin slices of fat ham or salt pork, then on them place the fish; cover it tightly and let it slowly cook, and baste it with butter cut up in a little hot water, it will require slow cooking for about half an hour, and when cooked take out the fish carefully, keep it hot, remove the pieces of ham or pork from the kettle, and pour in a wine glass of Claret wine, dredge in a little flour and let it boil up once, then dish the fish, and pour over it some of the gravy, and serve the rest in a sauce-boat.

STEWED ROCK FISH.

Peel and slice into cold water six onions, then put them into a saucepan and stew them with a large spoonful of butter; slice one good sized, or two small fish, then put into a saucepan a layer of onions, and then a layer of fish, sprinkle over the fish ginger, salt, a very little pepper, and some chopped parsley, then more onions, fish, and the same seasoning, with a pint of cold water; cover this very tightly, and let it cook very slowly for half an hour, then squeeze into it the juice of three good sized fresh lemons, beat the yolks of four eggs very light, and mix with them a large spoonful of flour, and half a grated nutmeg, then pour out some of the gravy from the saucepan and stir it to the above mixture, and when well mixed add it to that in the saucepan; after the fish is taken out give the gravy a simmer and pour some over the fish, and the rest send hot to the table in a sauce-boat. This is a delicious way of stewing a fish; any nice fish is equally as good as a rock.

POTTED SHAD.

Clean and cut your shad in pieces, have a new earthen pot, and between every layer of fish put cloves, allspice, cayenne, whole black pepper, salt, and a blade of mace; cover it with strong vinegar, and tie it up very tight; send it to the bake house to be put in the oven when the bread comes out. Herring may be done in the same manner.

VEGETABLES.

There is nothing which shows the skill of a good cook more than in the preparation and cooking of vegetables. The utensils used must be kept expressly for the purpose, and very clean. When properly cooked they are healthful and acceptable to the palate. When freshly gathered they require less cooking, than those purchased in the market. Nothing gives so much effect to a dinner table as a variety of vegetables well dressed, with the salad for the centre. This branch of the culinary department requires the utmost vigilance; if too much done, both flavour and beauty are lost, and if not enough, they are indigestible and more hurtful than underdone meats. The pernicious use of pearlash in vegetables to preserve their colour, should not be tolerated, and copper vessels for their cooking is equally objectionable.

Potatoes.

First in the vegetable kingdom stands the time honoured potato; the most ill-used, notwithstanding its great importance, for rarely is it well prepared. They must be well cooked and served hot. Select them with care, and protect them in the cellar from frost, by laying them in heaps and covering them well, either bury them in holes, or cover them with sand. They must be examined from time to time, as frost destroys vegetable life, and they speedily rot if once frosted.

When required for cooking, boiling particularly, select them as nearly of a size as possible, fill a steamer nearly full with the skins on, but well washed, put them over the pot containing the boiling water, and cover tightly, watch them, and the moment they are cooked by the action of the steam, remove them and cover them up in a hot place, if dinner is not quite ready, but a judicious cook will so time her potatoes as to have all ready at the same time.

HOW TO COOK POTATOES.—TO BOIL POTATOES.

In Ireland potatoes are boiled in perfection; the humblest peasant places his potatoes on his table better cooked than could half the cooks in this country by trying their best. Potatoes should always be boiled in their "jackets;" peeling a potato before boiling is offering a premium for water to run through it, and go to table waxy and unpalatable; they should be thoroughly washed and put into cold water. In Ireland they always nick a piece of the skin off before they place them in the pot; the water is gradually heated, but never allowed to boil; cold water should be added as soon as the water commences boiling, and it should thus be checked until the potatoes are done, the skins will not then be broken or cracked, until the potatoe is thoroughly done; pour the water off completely, uncover the pot, and let the skins be thoroughly dry before peeling.

TO BOIL NEW POTATOES.

The sooner the new potatoes are cooked after being dug, the better they will eat; clear off all the loose skins with a coarse towel and cold water; when they are thoroughly clean put them into scalding water, a quarter of an hour or twenty minutes will be found sufficient to cook them; strain off the water dry, sprinkle a little salt over the potatoes and send them to table. If very young, melted butter should accompany them.

POTATOES A LA MAITRE D'HOTEL.

Boil the potatoes; before they are quite done take them up, place them aside, and let them get cold; cut them in slices of a moderate thickness; place in a stew-pan a lump of fresh butter, and a teaspoonful of flour; let the butter boil, and add a teacupful of broth; let it boil and add the potatoes, which you have covered with parsley chopped fine, and seasoned with pepper and salt, stew them five minutes, remove them from the fire; beat up the yolk of one egg with a tablespoonful of cold water and a little lemon juice. The sauce will set, then dish up the potatoes and serve hot.

ANOTHER MODE.

Select good sized potatoes, wash them but do not pare them; put them in a clean saucepan, but do not drown them with water, as is usually done; let only an inch of cold water be in the pot, and cover up the pot to prevent the steam from escaping: most boiled things are spoiled for want of water, but potatoes require very little; let them come to a good boil, then set them aside to simmer, until they are soft enough to admit a fork, then drain off all the water, uncover the pot, but set it not too near to burn, and all the moisture will then evaporate; moderate sized potatoes will, if attended to, be done in twenty minutes.

FRICASSEED POTATOES.

Pare and slice half an inch in thickness, into cold water, the required quantity of potatoes, wash them well, put them into a clean saucepan, pour over them cold water enough to half cover them, close the pot tightly, and let them cook fifteen minutes; drain off every drop of water; have ready half a pint of cream or new milk, a large spoonful of good butter, a teaspoonful of chopped parsley, and some salt; pour this over the potatoes, shake them around, and just heat up. Serve hot.

Potato Balls for Breakfast.

Pare and boil dry the potatoes as directed, then put them into a hot pan and mash with a lump of butter and a little salt; beat this well, and make it into little cakes or roll it into balls, and dip them into egg and sprinkle with bread crumbs; fry a nice brown.

Potato Snow Balls.

Take the white mealy kind of potatoes—pare them, and put them into just boiling water enough to cover them—add a little salt; when boiled tender drain off the water, and let them steam till they break to pieces; take them up, put two or three together in a strong cloth, and press them tight, in the form of a ball—then lay them carefully in your dish so as not to fall apart.

Potatoes are very nice, and more healthy, roasted in the oven.

Sweet potatoes require, at least, a third more longer time to boil, than the common potato, and should never be pared before cooking. They are better roasted than boiled.

Greens.

Much depends upon boiling greens, and the manner in which it is done. The water should be soft, and a handful of salt thrown into the water, which should boil before the greens are put in; when in, the water should then be made to what by cooks is termed "gallop," the saucepan kept uncovered, and when the greens sink, they are done, take them out quickly and dress for table.

Vegetables are a most useful accessory to our daily food, and should be made the object of greater study in their preparation than they usually receive. Our country affords such a variety, that the cook is provided with every material for the exercise of her skill in serving the dishes, and presenting to the fastidious palate that which is acceptable and nutritious.

CHARTREUSE OF VEGETABLES.

Line a plain mould with bacon or cooked ham, have ready half cooked carrots, turnips, string beans cut long—all the same length, place them prettily round the mould until you get to the top, fill in the middle with mashed potatoes, or spinach nicely cooked and seasoned, or some veal forcemeat; put it on to steam, turn it out, and put asparagus round it, or baked whole tomatoes, as a garnish.

ASPARAGUS FORCED.

Scoop out the crumb of three or four French rolls, preserving the piece cut from the top, which will have to be fitted on to the part it was cut from; put into a pan with some fresh butter, the rolls, and fry them brown, beat up with a pint of cream, the yolks of six eggs, flavour with some grated nutmeg and a little salt, put it into a stew-pan, and over a slow fire, let it gradually thicken, stirring it all the time.

Have ready the tops of a bundle of asparagus, and having boiled them tender put them into the cream and fill the rolls with the mixture, reserving a few tops to stick in each rol. by way of garnish.

ASPARAGUS—ITALIAN FASHION.

Take some asparagus, break them in pieces, then boil them soft and drain the water off, take a little oil, water and vinegar, let it boil, season it with pepper and salt, throw in the asparagus, and thicken with the white of two eggs beaten to a froth.

Endive, done this way, is good; green peas, done as above, are very good, only add a lettuce cut small and two or three onions, and leave out the eggs.

CABBAGE.

The green savoy is best for boiling. Before cooking cut the head in half and pour boiling water on it to prevent the disagreeable odour which arises from cooking. Cabbage is best boiled with the broth from salt meat, and is a nice accompaniment to corned beef. It requires an hour slow simmering, and must be skimmed constantly while cooking. If not cooked with salt meat broth, put some salt in the water.

CAULIFLOWER.

Select those that are close and white and of the middle size; trim off the outside leaves, cut the stalk off flat at the bottom, let them lie in the salt and water an hour before you boil them. Put them into boiling water with a handful of salt in it; skim it well, and let it boil slowly until done, which a small one will be in fifteen or twenty minutes, take it out the moment it is done, as more boiling will spoil it, and pour over it some nice drawn butter. Serve hot. Broccoli is prepared in the same way.

PARSNIPS

Are to be well washed and rubbed, but not scraped. Boil them from an from an hour to two hours, according to their size, and try them with a fork. They are nice with pork. When done split them in half, dredge with flour, and fry a nice brown. Serve hot.

CARROTS.

Are plain boiled and require as much cooking as parsnips; pour drawn butter over them, and serve hot. They are nice with beef.

TURNIPS.

The Ruta Baga or Swedish Turnip, is the best, when they are well boiled and mashed. The white turnip is very nice with boiled mutton.

GREEN PEAS.

Young green peas, well dressed is a delicious dish, and necessary with lamb. To be good, they must be freshly gathered; wash them well, put a peck of shelled peas in a clean saucepan, and on them pour one gallon of boiling water, and a tablespoonful of salt; boil them quickly from twenty to thirty minutes, the test of being done is best known by tasting; when done drain on a hair sieve, cut into small bits some butter, and lay in the peas, return them to the saucepan; stir in a little salt, and some like a little fresh green garden mint, chopped finely, warm this all well, and serve hot.

TO BOIL RICE.

This simple process is seldom well done. Wash a half pint bowl full of rice thoroughly, put it into a very clean tinned or porcelain saucepan, and on this pour one pint of cold water, and half a teaspoonful of table salt; put this in a hot place, covered, but do not stir it; when the grains are soft it is ready for table. If properly done it will be dry and white, and each grain whole; turn it out with care into a hot dish. It is a very nice vegetable served with beef steak.

To Boil Onions.

Peel a dozen white onions, put them into a stew-pan broad enough to hold them without laying one on the other, cover them with hot water, and sprinkle some salt over. Let it simmer slowly for one hour and a half, then drain off all the water, and pour over half a pint of good cream or new milk, and just let it scald. Serve hot.

A Nice and Handsome Salad.

Select two good heads of lettuce, split them in half, then wash them in cold water and shake them dry in a napkin, lay them in the salad bowl, cut lengthwise some well-cooked red beets, and lay them between the heads of lettuce, boil three eggs very hard, remove the whites from the yolks, and cut up the whites into squares, and scatter over the salad, then cut some squares of the beets and scatter over; of the yolks make the sauce, by rubbing very smoothly the yolk with a spoon, add a little cayenne, salt, a large spoonful of dry mustard, and a teaspoonful of pulverized white sugar, mix these well together in a basin, with a spoon, then slowly add two large spoonsful of olive oil, and when a smooth paste, add three spoonsful of the best vinegar. This sauce must be served with the salad.

SPINACH.

Wash and pick it well, then put it into a bag of coarse muslin, pour over it plenty of hot water with a little salt in it, boil fifteen minutes, take it and shake off all the water, chop it finely, and put it into a saucepan with a large spoonful of good butter, a little pepper, and grated nutmeg; stew it five minutes, dish it and garnish with a hard boiled egg sliced and laid on the top.

SUCCOTASH.

Cut off the sugar corn from the cobs, put the cobs into cold water to boil for an hour, then take out the cobs and put into the water some lima beans and the corn, let it boil thirty minutes; there should be at first only water enough to boil the cobs and make the succotash, as too much loses the flavour of the cob, then stir in a spoonful of butter, a cup of cream, and a little salt. Let it stew for five minutes, dish, and serve hot.

SALSIFY OR OYSTER PLANT.

Wash and scrape the salsify, boil it tender, then drain it dry, and mash it; have ready bread crumbs, make the oyster plant into cakes, roll it in the crumbs, and fry them a nice brown.

RICE CROQUETTES FOR MEATS.

Wash and scald a quarter of a pound of rice, put it into a saucepan with half a teaspoonful of salt, some very thinly pared lemon peel, a tablespoonful of butter, on this pour one pint of cold water, half a pint of new milk, and stir it well for a moment only, then set it in a hot place to cook slowly; when the rice becomes quite soft remove it, and stir in the well beaten yolks of four eggs; do not allow this to cook but keep it hot while stirring in,then pour this on a tin shee' or flat surface, spread it out equally, and let it cool, then divide it in portions two inches long and one inch wide, roll these into scrolls or oblong balls, dip each one into bread crumbs, and fry them a nice brown. Serve hot.

CASSEROLE OF RICE.

Use what is called a "well mould," either of tin or earthen ware; cook with care as directed for Croquettes, a quarter of a pound rice, and instead of frying press the rice when cooked into the mould; have the centre free, and into that put some nicely stewed tart apples, then on the top again put some of the prepared rice; this must be done while it is warm, and have the mould quite full; it must have been wet with milk to prevent the rice from sticking; keep this hot until wanted for table, then turn it out on the dish. Serve hot.

COLD SLAW.

Select a white hard head of cabbage, cut it in half, and lay it in water for an hour; when ready, shave it with a cutter or sharp knife, very finely; put half a pint of vinegar on to boil, beat up the yolk of an egg with a little salt and cayenne, pour the boiling vinegar on the yolk, stir it well, and pour it over the shaved cabbage. This is nice with roast beef.

MACCARONI.

Purchase that which is white and clean, as it is liable to insects. Wash it and put it into a saucepan, pour over just enough milk and water to cover the quantity cooked, and let it simmer slowly for half an hour; then put it into a baking dish, sprinkle a little salt and cayenne over it, and a piece of butter; grate old cheese and bread crumbs thickly over, and add some cream or new milk, and put it in the oven to brown. Serve hot.

EGG PLANT.

Slice the egg plant an eighth of an inch in thickness, pare it and sprinkle salt over it an hour before cooking; then drain off all the water, beat up the yoke of an egg, dip the slices first in the egg, and then in crumbs of bread; fry a nice brown. Serve hot and free from fat.

STEWED MUSHROOMS.

Select fresh button mushrooms. The test if they are good is to drop a silver spoon in the saucepan while they are cooking: if they are the right kind the spoon is untarnished, if not it becomes blackened. Put them into a saucepan, with salt and a very little water, and let them simmer slowly; when nearly done, add butter and a little pepper. Serve hot.

HOMONY—BOILED.

Wash and soak the homony over night; early the next morning put it on to cook, in plenty of water with a little salt; it absorbs, like rice, much water, and must be cooked with care, and be perfectly white and soft. When quite done stir in some new milk and butter, and let it stew for ten minutes. Serve hot. It is very nice fried for breakfast, and is a necessary accompaniment to pork.

"SAUER KRAUT" OR FERMENTED CABBAGE.

Wash it well, and lay into the pot a piece of corn pork; on this strew thickly the sauer kraut, and pour over it enough cold water to cover entirely. Boil this very slowly for two hours and a half, according to the quantity of sauer kraut, and weight of pork. Serve hot.

TOMATOES STEWED.

Pour boiling water on as many tomatoes as are required to be cooked; skin them, take out the seeds, put the pulp and juice into a tinned or porcelained saucepan, with a little salt, and set them in a hot place to cook slowly for three hours; when nearly done, stir in butter, and a very little grated cracker or bread crumbs; some persons like them better without either; when very acid, a little sugar is an improvement, but nothing else, as it is important to retain the tomato flavour.

CRANBERRIES STEWED FOR MEATS AND POULTRY.

Pick and wash one quart of cranberries, pour them into a cullender to drain, then put the berries into a tinned or porcelained saucepan, but no water, excepting that which remains on them from washing; mix through when in the saucepan three-quarters of a pound of light brown sugar, then cover tightly, and set them in the oven to cook slowly. When quite done, they will be soft, then put them in a mould to cool, and if prepared as directed, they will be jellied when turned out. They are necessary with poultry, pork and mutton.

STEWED CELERY.

Wash and clean six or eight heads of celery; let them be about three inches long, boil tender, and pour off all the water; beat the yolks of four eggs, and mix with half a pint of cream, mace, and salt; set it over the fire with the celery, and keep shaking until it thickens, then serve hot.

CORN PUDDING.

Take of green corn twelve ears, and grate it. To this add a quart of sweet milk, a quarter of a pound of fresh butter, four eggs well beaten, pepper and salt, as much as sufficient; stir all well together, and bake four hours in a buttered dish. Some add to the other ingredients a quarter of a pound of sugar, and eat the pudding with sauce. It is good, cold or warm, with meat or sauce, but epicures of the most exquisite taste declare for it hot, and with the first service.

SPINACH A LA FRANCAISE.

Cut and wash, place it in a saucepan with a little salt and boiling water; when tender strain off the liquor, and throw the spinach into clear cold spring water, take small portions of it, and having pressed the water from it, chop it finely. Lay in a stew-pan a piece of butter, add the spinach to it, keeping it stirred until the butter is absorbed by the vegetable, dredge in a spoonful of flour, until it is commingled with the spinach, add three large spoonsful of rich veal gravy, let it boil quickly, keep it stirred; it may be served up plainly or with sliced hard boiled egg round it. The dish is sometimes dressed by pouring boiling cream sweetened with white sugar to the spinach instead of the veal gravy.

SPINACH RAGOUT.

Having well picked and cleaned the spinach, put it into plenty of boiling water, throw in a small handful of salt; as soon as it readily separates it is done enough; strain off the liquor; put it into fresh water for ten minutes; strain off the water completely, chop the spinach, lay it in a stew-pan with a piece of fresh butter, keep it stirred; when the butter has been absorbed, as much well seasoned gravy soup as will make the consistence of cream may be added, with a little grated nutmeg. Serve hot.

WHITE HARICOT BEANS—SPANISH RECEIPT.

Take a pint of beans, pour a quart of boiling water upon them and let them remain in soak until the next day; cut a lettuce in four pieces and put it with the beans in some fresh hot water, throw in a small bunch of parsley, and a slice of ham, boil them until the whole are tender. Chop up some onions, with a clove of garlic, fry them and then put them into a stewpan, put the beans to them, with a well beaten egg and some spice. Send them to table hot.

ENDIVE AU JUS.

Split some endive in half, blanch and drain them, season each with some pepper, nutmeg, and salt, and tie the endive together and put them into a stew-pan with some bacon sliced over them; in the same way put in some veal and beef sliced, two onions, two carrots, two cloves and a bunch of sweet herbs, moisten the whole with some rich gravy, stew the endive for three hours, then drain and press them in a cloth, trim and dish them up for table.

GREEN PEAS.

A delicious vegetable, a grateful accessory to many dishes of a more substantial nature. Green peas should be sent to the table *green*, no dish looks less tempting than peas if they wear an autumnal aspect. Peas should also be young, and as short a time as possible should be suffered to elapse between the periods of shelling and boiling. If it is a matter of consequence to send them to table in perfection, these rules must be strictly observed. They should be as near of a size as a discriminating eye can arrange them; they should then be put in a cullender, and some cold water suffered to run through them in order to wash them; then having the water in which they are to be boiled slightly salted, and boiling rapidly, pour in the peas; keep the sacepan uncovered, and keep them boiling swiftly until tender; they will take about twenty minutes, barely so long, unless older than they should be; drain completely, pour them into the dish in which they are to be served, and in the centre put a slice of butter, and when it has melted stir round the peas gently, adding pepper and salt; serve as quickly and as hot as possible.

It is commonly a practice to boil mint with the peas, this, however, is very repugnant to many palates, and as it may easily be added if it is thought agreeable, it should not be dressed with the peas although it may accompany them to table for those who may desire the flavour.

TOMATO SAUCE FRANCAISE.

Cut ten tomatoes into quarters and put them into a saucepan with four onions sliced, a little parsley, thyme, one clove, and a quarter of a pound of butter; set the saucepan on the fire, stirring occasionally, for three quarters of an hour; strain the sauce through a hair sieve, and serve with beef steak.

DUTCH SALAD.

Select two fresh heads of salad—lay them in cold water until required; cut thin slices of cooked or uncooked ham, put them into a saucepan to fry a light brown—the fatter the ham the better; on these pour a half pint of best wine vinegar,cover tightly and let it simmer five minutes, drain the salad by shaking quickly in a coarse cloth, put it then into a salad bowl, and cut it just a little, shake a very little cayenne over it, and then pour on the hot vinegar and pieces of ham, and stir it through.

PEAS STEWED IN CREAM.

Put two or three pints of young green peas into a saucepan of boiling water; when they are nearly done and tender, drain them in a cullender quite dry; melt two ounces of butter in a clean stew-pan, thicken it evenly with a little flour, shake it over the fire, but on no account let it brown; mix smoothly with it the fourth of a pint of cream, add half a tea-spoonful of white sugar, bring it to a boil, pour in the peas, and keeping them moving until they are well heated, which will hardly occupy two minutes, send them to table immediately.

PEAS PUDDING FOR CORN BEEF OR SALT PORK.

Wash and pick one quart of split peas; put into a cloth, not tied too closely; put them on in cold water, and let them cook slowly until tender; take them out and rub them through a sieve into a deep dish, mix with them two well beaten eggs, a large spoonful of butter, and a little black pepper, stir these well together, then flour the bag well, put in the mixture, and tie as closely as possible; then put the pudding into the pot which is boiling with the corn pork or beef, and let it cook one hour. Serve hot with the meat.

BEEF AND SAUER-KRAUT.—GERMAN RECEIPT.

Put about eight pounds of beef into cold water. When it comes to a boil, let it boil very fast for eight or ten minutes, not longer. Take it out and lay it in a stew-pan, cover it completely over with sauer-kraut, and pour in a pint of thin gravy. Stew it four hours, and serve with the gravy in a tureen or deep dish.

Asperge a la Pois.—French Receipt.

When asparagus is first in season, and too small to make a handsome appearance, this mode of dressing it is very good. Take the asparagus and cut off only the green heads, none of the white stalk must be retained, put them into clear cold water, and when clean pop them into boiling water, in which salt has been thrown; in ten minutes they will be tender; they may then be taken out and laid upon a white cloth, which must be used to wipe them dry; lay in a stew-pan a slice of butter, when it is melted put in the asparagus, stew them over a quick fire, keep them turning, and when ten minutes have elapsed, dredge a little flour and a small quantity of white sugar in powder over them; beat up the yolks of a couple of eggs, pour over the asparagus just sufficient water to cover them, boil up rapidly, stir in the yolks of eggs, and making a pyramid of the asparagus in the dish, serve it very hot.

Artichoke Salad.—French Receipt.

The artichokes should be very young, the choke having scarcely formed, clean them and let them soak thoroughly, drain them, take off the stalks close and even, and send them to table with the vegetables to form the salad This is a favorite mode in Paris of dressing them.

String Beans.

When very young the ends and stalks only should be removed, and as they are done thrown into cold spring water; when to be dressed put them in boiling water which has been salted with a small quantity of common salt; in a quarter of an hour they will be done, the criterion is when they become tender; the saucepan should be left uncovered, there should not be too much water, and they should be kept boiling rapidly.

When they are at their full growth the ends and strings should be taken off and the bean divided lengthways and across, or according to the present fashion slit diagonally or aslant.

A small piece of best soda, a little larger than a good sized pea, but never saleratus, if put into the boiling water with the beans, or with any vegetables, will preserve that beautiful green which it is so desirable for them to possess when placed upon the table.

TOMATO OMELET.

Select one quart of fine ripe tomatoes, pour over them boiling water to remove the skin, then chop them finely, put them into a saucepan without any water, chop two onions very finely, cover closely, and let them simmer slowly an hour, then add a little salt and cayenne, a large spoonful of bread crumbs, and cover tightly; beat up five eggs to a stiff froth, have ready a heated pan, and a small piece of butter just to grease it, stir the eggs into the tomatoes, beat all together, and pour it into the hot buttered pan, brown it on one side, fold it over, and serve on a hot dish the moment it is done. It is very nice with beef steak.

BAKED EGG PLANT.

Select a good sized plant, free from defects, cut off the top carefully, as it must be replaced, then scoop out with a large spoon all the pulp, mix with it a large spoonful of bread crumbs, a little salt, some finely rubbed thyme and summer savory, a little cayenne, and a spoonful of butter; mix these well together, return it to the hollowed plant, then tie on the top which was cut off, lay it in a stew-pan with some thin slices of fat corned pork laid in the bottom, cover tightly, and let it cook slowly for one hour, take off the string, and send to table hot and whole.

STEWED CARROTS.

Scrape and wash five or six good sized carrots, slice them rather thick, lay them in a saucepan, and just cover with cold water, sprinkle in a little salt, and let it simmer until soft; drain off all the water, then pour over them half a pint of good cream, a little piece of mace, a spoonful of butter, and a little finely chopped parsley; let this simmer ten minutes, and serve hot. The dark colored sweet carrot is the best for stewing.

COLD SLAW.

Take a nice fresh head of cabbage and lay it in cold water for one hour, then cut off all the stalk; shave down the head into very small slips with a cabbage cutter or very sharp knife; it should be done evenly and nicely; then put in a saucepan one teacupful of vinegar and let it give a boil up, then add a teacup nearly full of cream, with the yolks of two eggs well beaten; let these also give one boil, and then pour it immediately over the cabbage, which must be seasoned as soon as cut with a saltspoon of salt, a little cayenne pepper, and some black pepper also.

YEASTS.

HOPS loose their flavour by exposure to the air and damp. They should be kept in a dry close place, and lightly packed. Take a single handful of hops, and boil them well, then put half a pint of flour into a basin or pan, pour the hops through a strainer on to the flour, whilst boiling hot; stir this well, to about the consistency of pancake batter, and add a teaspoonful of salt, then pour it into a jug to ferment; after it has perfectly fermented add just yeast enough to cause it to rise: say to one quart of this preparation a cup of yeast; after it is entirely done fermenting cork it up tightly, and keep it in a cool place.

POTATO YEAST.

Take one quart of medium sized good Irish potatoes, boil them, pare and mash them with a wooden spoon, then pour boiling water over them until they are of the consistency of paste; strain this through a cullender, and to one quart of this add a wine glass and a half of good yeast, and three large spoonsful of brown sugar; stir this well together, and put it into a perfectly clean stone jug; if kept moderately warm it can be used in twenty-four hours. In summer this will keep four or five days, and in winter a week or ten days.

ANOTHER GOOD YEAST.

Take four quarts and a pint of water, and into it put two handsful of hops; let it boil away to a pint, then strain it through a sieve, and thicken with some nice corn meal to the consistency of mush; when this is done, set it to rise; when quite light add one pint of good yeast, and let it rise a second time; when risen again, rub in dry corn meal until it will not stick to your hands; spread this on a clean table in the sun, and as it drys sift it and put it into a very clean bag for use. Keep it in a dry place.

ANOTHER.

To half a peck of corn meal, add two handsful of flour and a handful of salt; boil three handsful of good hops in a quart of water, strain it boiling hot through a sieve on the meal and flour; stir this well, and when cool, put on sufficient yeast to raise it; let it stand twenty-four hours, then make it into cakes, and dry them. Keep them in a dry place.

ANOTHER YEAST.

Take a good handful of fresh hops and boil them in one quart of water until they settle to the bottom of the kettle; skim this liquor, and after cooling pour it upon a pint of sifted wheat flour; stir this well, break up all lumps, and make a smooth batter; put this into a stone jar, and when cool add half a pint of good fresh baker's yeast—brewer's yeast will not answer, then cover it tightly and set it to raise; in eight hours it will have risen; it must rise to the top of the jar, therefore the jar at first should only be half full; after it has risen stir in good corn meal until it becomes stiff. This dough must then be rolled out on a table, and formed into a cake a quarter of an inch thick, and cut into pieces three inches square, and placed on boards in a dry and airy room; they must be turned over every day until thoroughly dried, after which they can be put into bags, and hung up in a dry place.

One of these cakes will make a common sized loaf. The cake must be put into a bowl, and a gill of warm water for each cake poured on; they will dissolve in half an hour, then use them in the usual way of yeast in flour. For bread always measure your water; one pint of water will make a moderate sized loaf. For four loaves, take in cold weather, one quart of tepid water; make a stiff batter, and add a little salt, and four cakes softened in water as directed. Let this stand over night, when it will have risen it will sink in the middle, if not, keep it warm until it does. This is setting the spunge. When risen in the morning, take a quart of warm water, put into it a small handful of fine salt, mix it well and pour it into the "spunge" risen as above; then make the dough, working it until it becomes fine and silky; let the dough rise until it becomes very light; have the oven hot, knead well your dough again, and immediately form it into loaves; let them stand until the oven is hot, then bake them.

One cause of the clamminess of bread, is that in general it is removed too soon from the oven. It should be allowed to soak well after it is apparently cooked, and the loaves are better done and the bread more healthy if baked on large tin sheets, instead of pans; the vapour or steam arising from cooking passes off instead of being absorbed as is the case if enclosed in a pan. This most important article of diet is not sufficiently well attended to.

SWEET POTATO LOAF.

Grate four good sized uncooked potatoes, stir half a spoonful of good lard, and half a spoonful of butter, mix it well in and stir in one pint of flour; add a cup of new milk, a little salt, and a wine glass full of good yeast; mix this all well together, and set it to rise in the pan in which it is to be baked; when quite light bake one hour.

PATENT YEAST.

Make a strong decoction of hops—of three handsful and a half gallon of water; when well boiled strain and stir into the hop water as much rye flour as will make it a thick batter, let it stand until cool, then add a handful of salt, and a cup full of good yeast; stir this well and let it stand until risen, then mix in as much corn meal as will make a stiff paste to roll out into cakes; put them to dry and keep them in a cool place in bags.

A CAPITAL YEAST.

Take three good sized white potatoes and skin them, then boil them with a large handful of hops; mash the potatoes, and strain the water in which the hops and potatoes were boiled, then stir in whilst the water is hot, a cup of coarse Indian meal, then stir in the mashed potatoes, and thicken the whole with flour; it must be kept on the stove during the mixing, and stirred all the while; add to the above mixture a teaspoonful of molasses, a teaspoonful of Jamaica ginger, and a teaspoonful of salt; when quite cool, add half a pint of good brewer's yeast, then set it to rise, and add a spoonful of saleratus; after rising set it away to cool, and keep it in the same vessel in which it was made.

BREAD AND RISEN CAKES

Directions for Making Cake.

Flour used for making cake must always be dried and sifted; always break the eggs used for cake separately in a saucer; it is a good plan to lay the eggs to be used for a few hours in very cold water before breaking; they whip into a much better froth for being cold, and in hot weather they are better for being in the ice over night; always beat separately the whites and yolks. When soda* is used always dissolve it before adding it to the general mixture, and be careful not to use the hands in mixing, but a knife or wooden spoon which is kept for that purpose alone is the best. In winter soften, but do not melt the butter in the milk used. Cake not raised with yeast should be baked as soon as made. Never use strong butter for cakes or cooking. When the butter is washed, which is necessary in even good firkin butter, drain it well or the cake will be heavy. Fresh eggs are necessary for nice white cakes; those kept in lime or in other ways, will answer for ordinary cakes, or for those which are raised. Never add the fruits until ready for baking, and for raised cakes spread them on the top, and only stirred a little below the surface, or they will settle at the bottom. Currants require much and careful cleaning before using; wash them first in warm water, rubbing them well between the hands, the water drained off, and then spread on a cloth and rubbed dry, pick them over, dry and lay them then aside for use.

In baking cake which requires long baking, take white paper and lay on the sides and bottom and top; it is easily removed when the cake is done. Experience and attention alone will teach when cake is sufficiently baked; to ascertain when a loaf or dry soft cake is done take a clean stiff straw, double it

* By soda is meant the best quality of "Sub Carbonate of Soda" obtained at the Druggists.

and insert it in the thickest part of the cake or loaf, if it does not stick to the straw the baking is finished.

In breaking eggs be careful that none of the yolk escapes with the white, as the least particle will prevent a stiff froth; always whip the white in a very clean large shallow dish; strike a sharp quick stroke the whole length of the dish; they will come sooner for being whipped in a cool place. Never stop when you commence until they are light, and whip them until you can turn the dish over without their slipping.

For creaming butter and sugar a wooden spaddle or flat mush stick is the best, two inches wide and two feet long, of cedar or hickory.

A LIGHT CAKE.

Take three pints of sifted flour, a pint and a half of milk, and a spoonful of lard; stir into the flour three teaspoonsful of cream tartar, dissolve one teaspoonful of soda in a cup of milk, and a little salt; mix this all well together, and beat very lightly with a wooden spoon; roll this out rather thin and cut into cakes, or bake in two small pans. Serve hot, and split open and butter.

STEAM BAKED BREAD, A LA VIENNA.

It has been known for some time at Vienna, that if the hearth of an oven be cleansed with a moistened wisp of straw, bread baked therein immediately afterwards presents a much better appearance, the crust having a beautiful tint. It was thence inferred that this peculiarity must be attributed to the vapor, which being condensed on the roof of the oven, fell back on the bread. At Paris, in order to secure with certainty so desirable an appearance, the following arrangement is practised: the hearth of the oven is laid so as to form an inclined plane, with a rise of about eleven inches in three feet, and the arched roof is built lower at the end nearest the door, as compared with the farthest extremity. When the oven is charged, the entrance is closed with a wet bundle of straw.

By this arrangement the steam is driven down on the bread, and a golden yellow crust is given to the bread, as if it had been previously covered with the yolk of an egg.

Another Light Cake.

Take two pounds of sifted flour, and cut into this a quarter pound of butter, or very nice sweet lard, a small cup of powdered sugar, and milk enough to mix it into a good dough; add a little salt, and raise it with a wine glass full of good yeast, add two well beaten eggs, and form it into rolls.

Velvet Cakes.

Make a batter of one quart of flour and one quart of milk, three eggs well beaten, and a wine glass full of yeast; beat all together, and add a little salt, then let it rise, and cut into the flour a large spoonful of butter, beat this thoroughly, and when risen put into muffin rings, and bake on the griddle.

Flannel Cakes.

Beat two eggs, and cut into a quart of milk a large spoon ful of butter, stir in as much flour as will make it to the consistency of muffins, then add a little salt, and a large spoonful of yeast, and beat this well together; this must be set to rise in the morning, and bake on a griddle.

Potato Rolls.

Boil four good sized potatoes with their skins on, squeeze them in a towel to have them dry and mealy, then remove the skin and mash them perfectly smooth with a spoonful of butter, and a little salt; beat the yolks of three eggs, (the whites not to be used) and stir into the potatoes, then add one pint and a half of milk, and a large spoonful of yeast, beat in the flour until it is a stiff dough, set it to rise, and when risen, make it into cakes the size of an egg, then let it rise again, and bake a nice brown.

RISING BREAD.

From 6 pints of flour, take out nine spoonsful of flour, and add three spoonsful of yeast for the rising; make this up with milk-warm water, make it into a soft paste, then cover it with the rest of the flour; set it to rise in a warm place, and when quite light take the flour and add it to the rising, with milk enough to make it into stiff dough; work this well, and set it to rise again, adding a little salt. Bake it in tins.

POTATO BREAD.

Sift four pounds of flour into a pan, boil one pound of potatoes, skin and mash them very carefully through the cullender; mix this with a small quantity of milk and water, stir the flour with a knife, add salt, and beat it well, then add a wine glass of good yeast; make the dough into a good consistency and set it to rise. Bake in pans.

TO MAKE BREAD CHEESE-CAKES.

Slice a loaf as thin as possible, pour on it a pint of boiling cream, let it stand two hours; then take eight eggs, half a pound butter, and a nutmeg grated, beat them well together, put in a half a pound of currants well washed, and dried before the fire, and bake them in raised crusts, or patty pans.

MUSH OR HASTY PUDDING.

Stir into a half pint of cold water, enough sifted Indian meal to make a thick batter. Have on the fire a pot containing three or four quarts of water, when it boils, pour in the batter, stirring it fast; let it boil a few minutes, then add sifted meal by the handful, till it is quite thick, and a spoonful of salt. Keep it boiling slowly, and stir it frequently, the more it is stirred, and the longer it is boiled, the better the mush. To be wholesome, it must be boiled at least two hours. This is a good receipt.

FRIED MUSH.

Mush to be fried, should be boiled an hour longer to evaporate the water, and have half a pint of wheat flour stirred into it about half an hour before it is done. Take it out of the pot, and put it in an earthen dish and let it stand until perfectly cold, then cut it in slices half an inch thick, and fry them brown.

CRUMPETS.

Take one quart of dough from the bread, at an early hour in the morning; break three eggs, separating the yolks from the white, both must be whipped to a light froth, mix them into the dough, and gradually add milk-warm water, until it becomes to a batter the consistency of buckwheat cakes; beat all well together, and set it to rise until breakfast time; have the griddle clean and hot, and nicely greased, pour on the batter in small round cakes, and bake a light brown. Serve hot.

SOUFLE BISCUITS.

Cut up four ounces of butter into a quart of flour; make it into a smooth paste with new milk, knead it well, add a little salt, and roll it out as thin as paper; cut out the cakes with a tumbler, and bake quickly. Serve hot.

WHEAT MUFFINS.

Beat one egg very lightly, warm one quart of milk; cut up into it a spoonful of lard and one of butter; add half a pound of good spunge from the bread, and a little salt; let it be of the consistency of rather a thick batter, set it to rise, and bake in rings. Serve hot.

CORN MEAL BREAD.

Pour over a pint of nice corn meal, one pint of hot new milk; beat this well, and add a little salt, then stir in a large spoonful of nice sweet lard, beat two eggs very light and stir in also; this must be well beaten, and of the consistency of rather thin batter, add more milk should it be too thick, then mix in a large spoonful of yeast, butter the pans, and set it to rise in them; when risen, have the oven of a moderate heat, and put them in; bake two hours and a half, to a light brown. Serve hot.

CORN BREAD RUSK.

Take six cupsful of corn meal, four cupsful of wheat flour, two cupsful of molasses, two teaspoonsful of soda, and a little salt; mix this well together, knead it into dough, then make two cakes of it, and put into the tin or iron pans, and bake one hour.

ANOTHER NICE CORN BREAD.

Thicken one pint and a half of rich butter-milk with corn meal to the consistency of batter; dissolve one teaspoonful of soda in a cup of new milk, add a little salt, and beat very light; pour this into buttered pans, and bake two hours. Serve hot.

BUTTER-MILK CAKES.

Make a smooth batter of flour and one quart of butter-milk, then add two large spoonsful of corn meal, two well beaten eggs, a little salt, and one teaspoonful of soda dissolved in a cup of new milk; beat this well and bake on the griddle. Serve hot.

INDIAN LOAF.

To one quart of skimmed sweet milk, put one teacup of molasses, one teaspoonful of soda dissolved in a cup of new milk, a pint of corn meal, a large handful of flour, and a little salt; this must be well beaten, then pour it into pans to bake, which requires five hours. Serve hot, and mixed just as baked.

DELICIOUS BROWN BREAD.

Take three pints of rye, and the same of corn meal of the best quality, a few tablespoonsful of mashed pumpkin, half a tea cup of molasses, two teaspoonsful of salt, a teaspoonful of soda dissolved in warm water, and half a cup of yeast; mix all with warm water, make it as stiff as can be conveniently stirred with the hand, grease two earthen or iron pans which are preferable, put the bread in them, have a bowl of cold water at hand, to smooth over the top, dipping your hand into the water; it rises faster than other bread, and, therefore should not be made over night in summer, and in winter should stand in a cool place, until after the fire is in the oven. It requires a hot oven, and long baking—at least four hours.

RICE BREAD.

Allow half a pint of well boiled rice, and one quart of milk; put the milk over the fire to boil, reserving enough to wet the rice; stir the rice smoothly, add a large teaspoonful of salt, and when the milk boils, stir in the rice as when you make gruel; boil three minutes, stirring constantly, then pour it into a pan, and stir in as much flour as you can with a spoon; after it is cool enough, (which it must be to prevent the bread from becoming sour) add one gill of yeast, and let it stand until morning; then knead in flour until it ceases to stick to the hands. It is necessary to make this kind of bread stiffer on account of the rice, or else it will be heavy. The milk does not sour on account of being boiled. Put this into the pans, and bake as for common bread.

FAMILY BREAD—DIRECTIONS FOR SETTING THE SPUNGE.

Much depends on the yeast and flour, and judgment in compounding. For five common sized loaves, make one pint of thin water gruel; use but a little more than half a teacup full of fine corn meal, salt it a little more than if it were to be eaten as gruel, and boil ten or fifteen minutes. This is of importance, as, if the meal is only scalded, the bread will have a coarse taste; add enough milk to make two quarts of the whole, if the milk is new the gruel may be poured into the pan, if not it should be scalded in the kettle with the gruel. This is important in summer, as it will become sour in the dough in a few hours. When the mixture is cool, so that it will not scald the yeast, add a teacup full of yeast, then stir in sifted flour enough to make a thick batter. This is the "spunge." When prepared in summer, make it in the evening and let it stand in a cool place, and if in the winter, in a warm place. Then add flour enough to make it easy to mould, and knead it thoroughly. The kneading is most important for having good bread, and requires skill and strength; the hands must be tightly closed, and the fists pressed hard and quickly upon the dough, dipping them into a pan of flour to prevent sticking. It requires at least half an hour for the kneading. Attention to bread making is most important for the health of a family. After this is ended, divide it into five parts, and mould each according to the form of the pan in which they are usually baked, but as suggested, tins are preferable, grease them well before placing in the dough, then set the dough in rather a warm place to rise. Loaves of this size require an hour for baking. If the bread rises slowly, take some warm water and wet the top with your nand; the loaves should always be wet before baking to prevent its hardening. Saleratus should never be used, unless the dough has become sour, then a teaspoonful of "soda" for every quart of milk which was used in preparing the bread will be sufficient for correcting it.

There is positive economy in using the best of flour, and sweet new milk for bread; it being the most important article of diet, and for the preservation of health, it should always be made of good materials. When bread becomes stale it may be made fresh, by plunging it into a pan of cold water, and laying it in a stove to steam for ten or fifteen minutes.

BREAD WITHOUT SPUNGE.

If the weather is cool the milk must be warmed, a little more yeast is required than for spunge bread, and must bo made up over night; in the morning knead and mould it, and raise it again in the pans in which it is to be baked. If brewer's yeast is used, one tablespoonful is enough for every quart of setting. In warm weather, it is well to pour the milk (or water if used) boiling hot upon the flour, stirring it all that you can with a spoon, add the yeast when it has become quite cool. Such bread does not readily become sour, and keeps moist.

WATER BREAD.

Take two quarts of warm water, two tablespoonsful of salt, a gill of yeast, and flour enough for the spunge as directed, and in the morning stir in a teaspoonful of soda. It will render the bread tender, as bread without milk is liable to be tough. Water bread requires more kneading than milk bread. Bake as other bread.

DRIED BREAD FOR CRUMBS.

Save all the crusts and pieces, put them into an oven to dry, but not brown, then roll them on the paste board, and keep the crumbs in a jar or box, in a dry place, and then they are ready for cooking purposes.

VERY SUPERIOR BREAD.

Take an earthen vessel, larger at the top than the bottom, and in it put one pint of milk warm water, one and a half pounds of flour, and half a pint of malt yeast; mix them well together, and set it away (in winter it should be in a warm place) until it rises and falls again, which will be in from three to five hours; (it may be set at night if it be wanted in the morning;) then put two large spoonsful of salt into two quarts of water, and mix it well with the above rising; then put it in about nine pounds of flour and work your dough well, and set it by until it becomes light. Then make it out into loaves. The above will make four loaves.

As some flour is dry, and other runny, the above quantity, however, will be a guide. The person making the bread will observe that runny and new flour will require one-fourth more salt than old dry flour. The water also should be tempered according to the weather—in spring and fall it should be only milk warm; in hot weather cold, and in winter warm.

WHIGS.

Cream half a pound of butter and the same of sugar; when well mixed stir in six well beaten eggs, sift in two pounds of flour, a little salt, and add one pint of new milk; mix this well together, then lastly add one gill of good yeast, bake in small tins, or in muffin rings in the stove ; small sized rings are the best for cakes.

CORN CAKE.

Thicken one quart of sour milk with sifted corn meal, one teaspoonful of salt, one and a half teaspoonsful of soda dissolved in a cup of new milk, a teacup of good molasses, and one large spoonful of good lard or butter ; beat these ingredients well together, pour it into a well greased iron baking pan, with an iron cover, place it in the fire-place when the fire is raked for the night, and put fire and hot ashes over and around it. In the morning you will have a nice hot brown loaf for breakfast.

SWEET JOURNEY CAKE.

Stir together two large spoonsful of brown sugar, and two large spoonsful of good butter, beat the yolks of three eggs, and add it to the sugar and butter, then grate half a nutmeg, add an equal proportion of corn meal and flour to knead it, then spread it on a board, and glaze it with the white of an egg. Bake before the fire as other journey cake.

MILK BISCUIT.

Take one pound of sifted flour, cut a quarter pound of good butter into small pieces, half a pint of new milk, warmed, then a little salt ; stir this into the flour, mix well, and add a wine glass of good yeast, three eggs beaten, and a little grated nutmeg ; set it to rise, and when risen, sift on the board half a pound of flour, pour the above into the flour and make it into cakes, then let them rise again until perfectly light, then bake.

DIET BREAD.

Sift one pound of flour and one pound of sugar, a little mace, grated nutmeg, and a little rose water, stir this well together, and beat six eggs very lightly; stir this all together until light, add a little salt, and slowly bake in a pan.

INDIAN CAKES.

Pour one pint of scalding milk on a quart of sifted corn meal, and when cool stir in a spoonful of good lard, three well beaten eggs, one teaspoonful of salt, stir this well, then add two tablespoonsful of good yeast, and well beaten, set it to rise, and when risen bake in tins

ANOTHER.

Boil two cups of rice very soft, then stir in while hot a large spoonful of good butter, and a little salt, three cups of sifted corn meal, two spoonsful of good yeast, and three spoonsful of sifted flour; beat this well together, and make it into a thin batter with water, and set it in rather a warm place to rise, and bake on the griddle.

NICE BUNS.

Take three-quarters of a pound of sifted flour, two large spoonsful of good brown sugar, two large spoonsful of good yeast, and a little salt, stir this well together, and when risen work in two large spoonsful of butter, make into buns, set it to rise again, and bake on tins.

MILK BISCUIT.

Mix one pint milk and six ounces butter, half teacupful pulverised sugar, one teaspoonful of salt, one and a half tea-cup of yeast; add flour enough to make a sponge. Let it rise till perfectly light. Then knead into a loaf, and return to the pan to rise. When very light, make in small cakes, and let them rise once more before putting in the oven. Bake about fifteen minutes—letting them remain in the pans till ready for use, to prevent the under crust being hard. The following *yeast* to make them with may be made the day before :

YEAST FOR THEM.

Boil four large potatoes in one quart of water : pour off the water, and strain them through a collander. Then add enough water to thin them, with one teaspoonful of salt and one tablespoonful of brown sugar; let it cool, then pour in nearly one teacupful of hop or baker's yeast.

CAKE WITHOUT EGGS.

Pour sufficient boiling milk over stale bread to soften it, mash it through a cullender, add as much wheat flour and as much more milk as to make it the consistency of buckwheat batter, add an yeast powder and bake immediately.

DELICIOUS BREAD CAKE.

Two tea cups of risen dough, half tea cup of sugar, half cup butter, two eggs, and raisins, mix these and add a mite of soda and cream of tartar; mix the cream of tartar with the dough, and dissolve the soda in a little milk and add lastly.

DELICIOUS JOHNNY CAKE.

Take one quart of sour milk, or buttermilk; stir in as much corn-meal as will make a pancake batter; take one teacup of flour, and one teaspoonful of saleratus—beat well together, then add three eggs well beaten, and one-half teaspoonful of salt; thoroughly mix all together, pour into well buttered pans, and bake quickly in a hot oven. Small-sized pans should be used for this kind of bread. Eat hot, with good butter.

BANNOCK CAKE.

1½ pint of Indian meal, scalded; four eggs, well beaten; one quart of milk, warmed, with two tablespoonfuls of butter stirred in; salt to your taste; bake in a square or round tin pan, and cut it up in slices. The lightness of this depends on the beating

HOE CAKE.

Scald one quart of corn-meal, with just hot water enough to make a thick batter; stir in two large spoonfuls of good butter, beat this a little; add one-half teaspoonful of salt. Bake in buttered pans three-fourths of an hour. Serve hot.

GRAHAM BREAD.

Three quarts of unbolted wheat flour, one quart of warm water, one gill of molasses, one teaspoonful of soda, dissolved in a little cold water; mix these well together; add a small teaspoonful of salt, and one gill of good fresh yeast. Make this into two loaves, and bake one hour, and cool gradually. No bread, or cake, should be put in an oven that is too hot, as it prevents them rising as they should.

DELICIOUS ROLLS.

Sift two pounds of flour into a pan with a little salt; add four spoons of good butter cut up; two eggs well beaten; one large pint of new milk; two spoonfuls of nice sifted sugar; mix these well together; then take a good "sponge," prepared as directed, which has risen over night, (about half a pound) and mix into this; form them into small rolls and bake a nice brown. Let them rise again after mixing and forming into rolls, or else bake them in a slow oven.

DOUGH NUTS.

Take one pint of warm milk, cut into it one-fourth of a pound of butter; four eggs well beaten; one pound and a half of brown sugar. Stir the sugar into the eggs; grate half a nutmeg, add the rind of a lemon grated in. Mix these all together well; thicken this into a good soft batter with sifted flour; add a little salt; beat this well, then add a wine glass half full of good brewer's yeast. When quite light, have ready some boiling lard, and drop in the dough nuts. Fry a nice light brown, put them into a colander while hot to drain; then sift sugar over them

CORN-MEAL MUFFINS.

Three cups of corn-meal, one half cup of sifted wheat flour, three eggs well beaten, two large spoonfuls of butter, and one teaspoonful of soda dissolved in one pint of buttermilk, and a little salt. Beat these well together, pour into rings, and bake a nice brown in the oven.

RYE CAKE.

Three cups of rye-meal, three of corn-meal, a little salt, one small teaspoonful of soda dissolved in a cup of milk, a teaspoonful of grated nutmeg and ground cinnamon, mixed; then add as much milk as will make a thin batter; bake on the griddle. Serve hot.

POTATOE CAKES.

Boil four potatoes, skin and peal them, mash smootnly, ana beat in a spoonful of good sweet lard; then pour in one pint of new milk; stir this well; add a very little salt, and as much flour as will make it the consistency of muffins—this is to drop from the spoon; then add two large spoonfuls of yeast. Set it to rise. Bake in rings in the oven. Serve hot.

CORN CAKES.

Two pounds of sifted meal; pour on this one pint of sour milk or cream; cut up one spoonful of good butter; beat three eggs, and stir in a little salt, with one teaspoonful of soda dissolved in a little milk. This must be very lightly beaten; then pour into tins and bake quickly.

BUTTERMILK MUFFINS.

Stir into one quart of buttermilk one teaspoonful of soda, and into one quart of flour one teaspoonful of cream of tartar; add them, and beat them well together, and pour into the muffin rings, and bake on a griddle. Serve hot.

POTATOE MUFFINS.

Boil three good sized potatoes, skin and mash them, beat in a teaspoonful of salt, and a piece of good butter the size of an egg; make this perfectly smooth, and about the consistency of starch by adding a little warm water; beat up two eggs, dissolve one teaspoonful of soda in a little water, with a teacup of yeast; then add three pints of sifted flour; mix these well together, and add one pint of milk-warm water; stir in the soda, and set it to rise over night for breakfast. Bake in rings on the griddle.

BISCUIT CAKES.

Take twelve stale biscuits, or water crackers; pour over them boiling milk; let them stand until perfectly soft; then stir in a large spoonful of good lard, a little salt, with two eggs well beaten Make it the consistency of waffles, and make into cakes, and bake in tins or in a pan.

SODA CAKES.

Stir three large spoonfuls of brown sugar, with one of good butter; beat three eggs very light; stir a teaspoonful of soda into a pint of milk, either sour or not; then mix all together well, thicken this with flour, so as to make into small cakes. Bake on tins, a nice brown.

A NICE TEA CAKE.

Cut into two cups of sifted flour one large spoonful of butter, a little salt, two eggs well beaten; mix this together, and stir in half a pint of new milk. Bake in pans in a quick oven.

WAFFLES.

To two teacups of hot hominy, add a spoonful of good butter; when cold, add one teacup of wheat flour, a little salt, as much milk as will make it a stiff batter, and three eggs, well beaten; mix these well together, and bake in waffle irons.

LIGHT BREAD, VERY GOOD.

Warm one quart of milk; add in small pieces one-fourth of a pound of good butter; when cool, beat two eggs very light, and stir in flour enough to knead it to a light bread; mix in half a cup of yeast, knead it over night, and bake in pans as bread.

SODA BISCUIT.

Stir into one quart of flour two teaspoonfuls of cream of tarter, and one teaspoonful of salt; dissolve in three gills of new milk one teaspoonful of soda; stir it into the flour quickly; pour all on the board, and roll out and cut into little cakes; bake them in a quick oven.

TEA CAKE.

Boil twelve good sized potatoes, skin and mash them very smoothly; when cold, rub in a little sifted flour just to make them stick; beat seven eggs very lightly, separating the yolks from the white, beat with the yolks half a pound of good brown sugar, grate with care the rind or oily part of one lemon; mix these well together; when light add the whites of the eggs; either make into little cakes or bake in tin pans. Serve hot and buttered.

OLECOKES, OR KNICKERBOCKERS.

Warm one pint of new milk, cut up in it three quarters of a pound of good butter, beat up eight eggs very light and stir into the milk, add a little salt, then sift in as much flour as will make it a stiff dough, and add one wine glass of yeast; mix well and set it to rise; when light sift in half a pound of good dry brown sugar; mix well, and make into balls the size of a walnut, in each of them put two or three stoned raisins, fry a nice brown in boiling lard, as crullers; drain them from all fat in a hot colander.

YORKSHIRE MUFFINS.

Sift two pounds of wheat flour into a pan, warm one pint and a half of new milk, and cut up in it two large spoonsful of butter, and stir it into the flour; beat three eggs very lightly; add half a small teaspoonful of salt; beat these all well together until thoroughly mixed; then add three spoonsful of good yeast; set it to rise, and when risen bake in muffin rings in an oven.

WAFFLES.

Sift one pound and three quarters of flour into a pan, beat very lightly six eggs, separating the white from the yolks, warm one quart of new milk and cut into it half a pound of butter and a little salt; stir the milk into the flour, mix well, then add the yolks, and then the whites, which must have been beaten to a stiff froth; beat all together, and then add one wine glass full of good yeast; set it to rise, and when risen bake in waffle irons a nice brown; have ready pulverized cinnamon and loaf sugar, as they are done sift over them the sugar and cinnamon. Serve hot.

NICE TEA BUNS.

Sift into a pan two pounds of flour, warm one pint of new milk, and cut into it three-fourths of a pound of good butter; stir this if not too warm into the flour, beat eight eggs very light, separating the yolks from the whites, half a grated nutmeg, teaspoonful of best ground cinnamon; beat these well together, adding lastly the whites of eggs, then a wine glassfull and a half of good yeast, set them to rise; when risen, stir in one pound of powdered sugar to be sifted in and mixed through, then set them to rise in the pans in which they are to be baked. Bake a nice brown.

FRENCH ROLLS.

Warm one pint of new milk, cut up into it two large spoonsful of good butter, add a little salt; when cool sift in one pound of flour, one egg well beaten, one spoonful of yeast; beat these well together, but avoid kneading; when risen form it into rolls, handling as little as possible. Bake on tins.

CROSS BUNS.

Put two and a half pounds of sifted flour into a wooden bowl before the fire to warm, then stir in half a pound of sifted sugar, and a little salt, some coriander seed; pounded cinnamon, of each one-half teaspoonful, a little grated nutmeg, cut into one-half pint of new milk, one-half pound of butter, then mix with the other ingredients, three teaspoonsful of yeast; stir this all well together, set it to rise, when risen form it into buns, handle it as little as possible; on each bun cut a cross with the back of a knife. Bake on tins.

WAFERS.

Cut up one-quarter pound of butter into one pound of flour, add two eggs well beaten, one wine glass of wine and brandy mixed, spices to taste; nutmeg and cinnamon mixed is the best; mix these well together, and bake in the irons.

RICE WAFFLES.

Beat three eggs very light, stir them in one pint and a half of flour, adding by degrees as you mix in the flour two pints of milk; then add a pint of boiled rice, with a tablespoonful of butter stirred in whilst the rice is hot; salt to the taste, and add one tablespoonful of good yeast; if they are made at noon they will be fit for baking at tea time.

SUPERIOR RICE BREAD.

One quart of rice flour moistened with warm water; when well moistened, to prevent its being lumpy, pour in two quarts of boiling water, and stir it while it boils; when quite cool add half a pint of good yeast, and one pint of new milk; if in summer the milk is always better boiled, to prevent it becoming sour; add a half teaspoonful of salt, then as much wheat flour as will make it the consistency for bread; set it to rise, when risen add a small quantity of sifted wheat flour. Bake in ordinary sized loaves; but be careful it is not too soft, as the bread will then be hollow.

POTATOE CAKES.

Boil with care four good potatoes, press them dry in a towel, peel and mash them smoothly whilst hot, when milk-warm stir in a spoonful of butter and a little salt, knead in as much flour as will make a dough like rolls, add a wine glass of good yeast; set it to rise, then make them into small cakes and lay on tins. Bake a nice brown.

SWEET POTATOE BUNS.

Boil and mash two nice potatoes, rub in as much flour as will make it like bread, add a little nutmeg and sugar to your taste, with a table spoonful of good yeast. When it has risen work in two table spoonsful of butter cut finely, then form it into small rolls, and bake on tins, a nice brown. Serve hot, split open and butter; either good for tea or breakfast.

ON THE USE OF A GRIDDLE IN BAKING CAKES.

A griddle should be well scoured with a cloth and sand, then washed with hot soap suds, wiped dry, and just before baking rubbed with a coarse cloth and salt. If this is attended to no greasing is required, which always affects the flavour of the cakes. Between each baking rub the griddle with the dry cloth and salt.

BUCKWHEAT CAKES.

Take as much warm water as you will require for the size of the family, thicken this with good buckwheat to a fritter batter, add a teaspoonful of salt if two quarts is made, two handsful of corn meal, and one wine glass of good yeast; it is much better made with boiled milk; but be careful to let the milk be only warm, not to scald the yeast, or they will be heavy.

RICE JOURNEY CAKES.

Boil a tea cup of rice dry, then stir in half a pint of new milk, and corn meal enough to make it stick together; whilst the rice is hot stir in a spoonful of good lard or butter, and salt to taste; mix these well and spread on a board before the fire. When nicely browned on the side exposed to the fire, take a clean piece of twine and pass between the board and cake carefully; in this way turn it and brown the other side. Serve hot, split open and buttered.

BATTER CAKES.

Boil two cups of small hominy very soft, add an equal quantity of corn meal with salt to taste, and a large spoonful of butter while the hominy is hot. Make it into a thin batter with three eggs and a sufficient quantity of milk; beat all together some time, and bake them on a griddle or in waffle irons. When eggs cannot be procured yeast makes a good substitute, a tablespoonful stirred into the batter, and let it stand an hour and a half to rise.

NICE BUNS.

Four ounces of sugar stirred with three quarters of a pound of flour; make it up with two teaspoonsful of yeast and half a pint of milk; when well risen work into it four ounces of butter, and bake them in a quick oven a nice brown.

SMEAR CAKES.

One-half pint of smearcase, beat this smooth with a little cream; cut up one-fourth pound of butter in a half pint of warm milk; when cool, add a teaspoonful of soda; stir this until it effervesces, then add flour until it is the consistency of bread; add a little salt, roll this out, and cut into cakes with a tumbler. Bake rather quickly.

A NICE CREAM CAKE.

Beat very lightly two eggs; stir them into one pint of sour cream; sift in as much flour as will make a stiff batter; dissolve one teaspoonful of soda in a cup of new milk; add this, and a little salt; mix these well, and pour into rather a shallow pan. Bake quickly, a nice brown. Serve hot.

DELICIOUS BREAD.

One tumbler full of good rice flour, one teacupful of wheat flour, one teaspoonful and a half of cream of tartar stirred in, one large spoonful of butter cut up very finely, a little salt, one egg well beaten, and one teaspoonful of soda dissolved in a large teacup of new milk; mix these well together, and bake in a pan, like pound cake. Serve hot for tea or breakfast.

INDIAN POUND CAKES.

To one pint of corn-meal add one half pound of flour; cream one-half pound of butter with three-fourths pound of sugar; beat eight eggs very light, and stir into the butter and sugar with one teaspoonful of ground cinnamon, half a nutmeg grated, one wine glass of wine, one of brandy; these must be added slowly, and well stirred in; then add slowly, with a knife, the meal and flour.

NICE ROLLS.

Two pounds of flour, a little salt, two large spoonsful of good brown sugar dried and sifted; three spoonsful of butter, cut up into one pint of good new milk; set the sponge to rise over night. If you have any bread sponge, mix the above ingredients into it, adding two well beaten eggs; make this into rolls, and set them to rise early in the morning, if for breakfast, and bake on the tins, without disturbing after having risen. Never put sugar into any cake before rising, but add it afterwards.

CORN-MEAL CAKES.

One quart of meal, one pint of boiling milk, a teaspoonful of salt, a large spoonful of soda; set it to rise in a warm place; when risen, add as much flour and corn-meal as will make a stiff batter; then let it stand half an hour, then pour into the tins. Bake two hours. This requires beating until very light.

SUPERIOR CORN-BREAD.

Beat very lightly two eggs; mix with them, alternately, one pint of sour milk, and one pint of sifted corn-meal; warm one table-spoonful of good butter, and a small quantity of salt; stir these well together. Dissolve one table-spoonful of soda in a small cup of milk; add this just before they are put into the oven; beat these all well together—on that depends the lightness of the cake. Pour into a greased pan, and bake in a quick oven.

INDIAN MUFFINS.

Stir into one quart of boiling water as much corn-meal as will make a nice batter; when just warm, stir in as much flour as will make a stiff batter; add half a tea-spoonful of salt, and half a wine glass of yeast. Set it to rise, and when risen, pour into muffin rings, and bake rather slowly in an oven. To be eaten hot.

BUTTERMILK ROLLS.

Mix one tea-spoonful of cream of tartar into a quart of flour; one quart of buttermilk, with one large spoonful of soda dissolved in it; stir it well and quickly—a little salt added lastly. Pour into tins, or make into rolls. Bake quickly.

FEDERAL BREAD.

To one pint of cream, or new milk warmed, add a large spoonful of good butter; then take a large dining plate of sifted flour, and stir in with a knife; add two eggs well beaten, a little salt, and two table-spoonsful of good yeast; stir these well together, then put it into the tins to rise. Do not disturb it after it has risen. Bake in the same tins three-fourths of an hour.

RICE WAFFLES.

Stir into two pints of well boiled rice, a large spoonful of butter, and a little salt; when cool, add two eggs well beaten, one pint of milk, and stir in one pint of sifted flour, with one teaspoonful of good yeast; mix all well together, and let it stand two hours before baking. Bake in waffle irons.

MARYLAND BISCUIT.

Take any quantity of flour you think the size of the family may require; put in salt, and a lump or table-spoonful of good lard to a half pound of flour—rub it well in the flour; then moisten it with new milk, work it well, and beat it with a rolling-pin until perfectly light. On the lightness depends the goodness of the biscuit. Bake rather slowly, a light brown.

BACHELOR'S LOAF.

Pour on three-fourths of a pound of sifted corn-meal one pint of boiling hot new milk; stir well together; then beat the white and yolk of three eggs separately, reserving the white for the last ingredient added; add a little salt, and a spoonful of lard; the whole to be beaten quite light. Grease the pans, pour in the above, and bake one hour.

WASHINGTON BREAKFAST CAKE.

Cut up in warm milk one spoonful of good butter; when cool, stir in one pound and one-fourth of sifted flour, two eggs well beaten, a little salt, and a large spoonful of good yeast. Mix these well together; put it into buttered tins to rise; when risen, bake three fourths of an hour.

FLANNEL CAKES.

One quart of new milk, thickened with flour to the consistency of fritter batter, one tablespoonful of butter, two eggs well beaten, one large spoonful of yeast, and a little salt. Mix this all well together; set it to rise at night for breakfast. They must not be stirred in the morning. Bake on the griddle, as buckwheat cakes.

BREAKFAST BREAD.

Three pints of flour stirred into one pint of new milk; or, if necessary to make a stiff batter, more flour; two eggs well beaten, one cup of yeast, and a little salt. Beat this well together; set it to rise, and in the morning, bake it in tins.

SWEET POTATOE PONE.

One and three-fourths of a pound sweet potatoes boiled and mashed, stir in while warm two table-spoonsful of butter, beat these well, add a little salt, three table-spoonsful of good brown sugar, then one table-spoonful of ground ginger, and beat three gills of milk, when quite light from beating pour into a buttered pan, and bake three-fourths of an hour; serve hot.

BREAKFAST RICE CAKE.

Take one quart of cold rice well boiled, make it perfectly smooth with hot water, then stir in two table-spoonsful of good butter, two eggs well beaten, sift in two table-spoonsful of flour, a little salt, then pour in just enough new milk to make a consistency of rather thick batter; pour this into pans to make it an inch in thickness, bake one hour, a light brown on the top.

SALLY LUNN.

Cut into warmed milk a large spoonful of good butter, when quite cool add one quart of sifted flour, three eggs well beaten, one teaspoonful of soda dissolved in a little milk; beat this all together well, and add a little salt; when quite light pour into pans and bake in a quick oven.

COCOANUT CAKES.

Grate one cocoanut; mix the milk with it; sweeten to taste. Form into little balls, put on white paper, and dry in some warm place twenty-four hours.

BURLINGTON BUNS.

Rub half pound sugar, and one-fourth and one-eighth pound butter into two pounds flour, add one gill of bakers' yeast and one pint warmed milk. Let the dough be soft as possible to mould. Make this at six o'clock, P. M. Let it rise near a fire till ten, then mould it over again. Next morning it will be light. Make up into cakes and rise awhile. Bake twenty minutes.

TO MAKE BRAN BREAD.

Take a pound of fresh Indian meal, add a handful of salt, and make into thin mush. When sufficiently cool, mix in two pounds bran flour, a tablespoonful of sugar or molasses, and a cup of yeast; mix all together, and form a loaf without kneading. Bake in a pan ready greased, longer than the same quantity of wheat bread.

QUICK WAFFLES.

Take a pint of milk, and beat into it three eggs, and enough wheat flour to make a thick batter; add a tablespoonful of melted butter, and a little salt; bake them immediately. Some persons add two tablespoonsful of sugar, and a little cinnamon; others dust loaf-sugar and cinnamon, or nutmeg over each waffle as it is baked.

CHILDRENS' CAKE.

Two cups flour, one cup cream, one cup sugar, one egg, one teaspoonful of soda, two of cream of tartar; mix the cream of tartar and flour well, and dissolve the soda in the cream, and add last. This is nice for children at tea.

COCOANUT POUND CAKE.

Three cups flour, one cup butter, two cups sugar, whites of six eggs, one spoonful cream of tartar, half spoonful of soda, one cup milk. Grate one small cocoanut, and put in two-thirds of it last.

SPONGE CAKE.

This requires very fresh eggs; to the yolks of twelve eggs, beaten very lightly with a broad bladed knife, add one pound of sugar; grate in one large sized fresh lemon, (only the oily part of the rind, avoid the bitter white skin,) and stir this well. Whip the whites to a froth; stir in half a pound of sifted flour; add the whites last. Bake one hour. Sponge cake is much lighter if the eggs are beaten separately, and the flour and sugar sifted together, and the eggs added lastly; it is liable to be sticky in inexperienced hands if the yolks and sugar are mixed together.

SPONGE CAKE.

Take sixteen eggs; separate the whites from the yolks; beat them very lightly; sift into the yolks one pound of flour, adding a few drops of essence of almond, or lemon, to flavour with; then add one pound and a quarter of pulverized loaf sugar; beat this well with a knife; then add the whites whipped to a stiff froth. Have ready the pans, and bake.

ALMOND CAKE.

Take ten eggs, beaten separately, the yolks from the whites; beat the yolks with half a pound of white sugar; blanch a quarter of a pound of almonds by pouring hot water on them, and remove the skins; pound them in a mortar smooth; add three drops of oil of bitter almonds; and rosewater to prevent the oiling of the almonds. Stir this also into the eggs. Half a pound of sifted flour stirred very slowly into the eggs; lastly stir in the whites, which must have been whipped to a stiff froth. Pour this into the pans, and bake immediately three-quarters of an hour

SPANISH BUNS.

Five eggs well beaten; cut up in a cup of warm new milk half a pound of good butter; one pound of sifted flour, and a wine-glassful of good yeast; stir these well together; set it to rise for an hour, in rather a warm place; when risen, sift in half a pound of white sugar, and half a grated nutmeg; add one wine-glass of wine and brandy, mixed, one wine glass of rose-water, and one cupful of currants, which have been cleaned as directed; mix these well, pour it into pans, and set it to rise again for half an hour. Then bake one hour. Icing is a great improvement to their appearance.

ICING FOR CAKES.

Take ten whites of eggs, whipped to a stiff froth, with twenty large spoonsful of sifted loaf sugar whipped in slowly; then a tea-spoonful of orange-flower water. This is to be laid smoothly on the cakes after they are baked. Then return them to the oven for fifteen minutes to harden the icing.

COCOA-NUT CAKE.

Whip the whites of ten eggs, grate two nice cocoanuts, and add them; sift one pound of white sugar into half a pound of sifted flour; stir this well; add a little rose-water to flavour; pour into pans, and bake three-fourths of an hour.

SEED CAKE.

Take half a pound of butter and three-fourths of a pound of sugar, creamed; three eggs beaten lightly, and two tablespoonsful of picked and bruised carraway seeds; dissolve half a tea-spoonful of soda in a cup of new milk; mix these well together until they are about the consistency of cream; then sift in two pounds of flour, mix well with a knife, and roll them out into thin cakes, about an inch in thickness. Bake in a quick oven.

CUP CAKE.

Cream half a cup of butter, and four cups of sugar by beating; stir in five well beaten eggs; dissolve one tea-spoonful of soda in a cup of good milk or cream, and six cups of sifted flour; stir all well together, and bake in tins.

FRUIT CAKE.

Take four pounds of brown sugar, four pounds of good butter, beaten to cream; put four pounds of sifted flour into a pan; whip thirty-two eggs to a fine froth, and add to the creamed butter and sugar; then take six pounds of cleaned currants, four pounds of stoned raisins, two pounds of cut citron, one pound of blanched almonds, crushed, but not pounded, to a paste—a large cup of molasses, two large spoonsful of ground ginger, half an ounce of pounded mace, half an ounce of grated nutmeg, half an ounce of pounded and sifted cloves, and one ounce of cinnamon; mix these well together; then add four large wine-glasses of good French brandy, and lastly, stir in the flour; beat this well, put it all into a stone jar, covered very closely, for twelve hours; then make into six loaves, and bake in iron pans. These cakes will keep a year, if attention is paid to their being put in a tin case, and covered tightly in an airy place. They improve by keeping.

A DELICIOUS SWISS CAKE.

Beat the yolks of five eggs and one pound of sifted loaf sugar well together; then sift in one pound of best flour, and a large spoonful of anise seed; beat these together for twenty minutes; then whip to a stiff froth the five whites, and add them; beat all well; then roll out the paste an inch thick and cut them with a moulded cutter rather small; set them aside until the next morning to bake.

Rub the tins on which they are baked with yellow wax; it is necessary to warm the tins to receive the wax; then let them become cool, wipe them, and lay on the cakes, bake a light brown.

JUMBLES.

Sift four cups of flour into a pan; cream two cups of nice brown sugar and half a pound of butter; beat two eggs very light; grate a little nutmeg; mix all together with a knife—if too stiff, a very little cream may be added. Sift a little flour and sugar on the pasteboard, and roll them into cakes; handle as little as possible. Bake in tins quickly.

SOFT JUMBLES.

Take one cup of butter, two cups of sugar, three eggs, one cup of sour cream, three cups of flour, the rind of one lemon grated and half the juice, and a large half tea-spoonful of carbonate of soda dissolved in the cream. Rub the butter and sugar together, and add the rest. Bake in two square pans; do not heap the flour too much.

BATH BUNS.

Rub with the hand one pound of fine flour and half a pound of butter; beat six eggs and add them to the flour, with a table-spoonful of good yeast; mix these together with half a tea-cupful of milk; set it on a warm place for an hour; mix in six ounces of sifted sugar, and a few carraway seeds; mould them into buns with a table-spoon on a baking plate, throw six or eight carraway comfits on each, and bake them in a hot oven about ten minutes. These quantities should make eighteen buns.

QUEEN CAKE.

Cream one pound of sugar and half a pound of butter; then stir in five eggs well beaten, one wine-glass of brandy and wine mixed, a little pounded cinnamon and grated nutmeg, five spoonsful of cream, and sift in three-fourths of a pound of flour. Stir this all together, pour into your little tins, and bake.

ALBANY CAKE.

Cream one pound of sugar and half a pound of butter; take three eggs well beaten, one tea-spoonful of soda dissolved in a small cup of cream; add one pound and a half of sifted flour; mix this well, roll it out, cut it into small cakes, and bake immediately.

FAMILY CAKE.

Take one pound and a quarter of butter and the same of sugar, twelve eggs lightly beaten, one glass of wine and brandy mixed, and a little grated nutmeg; cut the butter into one pint of warm milk; sift in when cold three pounds of flour; add one wine-glass of good yeast; set it to rise, and when risen, sift in the sugar; mix in the other ingredients quickly. Put it into pans, and set it to rise one-fourth of an hour before baking.

KISSES—A CAKE.

Whip the whites only of four eggs to a stiff froth; then add one pound of sifted crushed sugar, and one wine-glass of orange-flower water. Mix these well, and drop on tins; sprinkle coloured nonpareils over them. Bake, or rather dry them in the oven. They must be watched not to become brown.

SHREWSBURY CAKE.

To one pound of butter, add one pound of sifted crushed sugar; stir this to a cream; then add four well beaten eggs, a little ground cinnamon and pounded mace; beat these until it looks curdled, then sift in one pound and a half of flour; stir this, then roll out and cut into small cakes. Bake on tins.

COMPOSITION CAKE.

Mix together half a pound of brown sugar and the same of butter until creamed; then take four eggs well whipped, a little grated nutmeg and ground cinnamon, one-fourth of a pound of citron cut into thin slices, three-fourths of a pound of good raisins stoned, the same of currants; one teaspoonful of soda dissolved in one pint of milk added last just before putting into the oven; stir in one pound and one-fourth of sifted flour; mix all together, and put into two pans. Bake in a moderately heated oven.

CYMBALLS.

Stir one-fourth of a pound of butter and half a pound of brown sugar to a cream; add six eggs beaten, one wine-glass of rose water, a little grated nutmeg, and sift in two pounds of flour; stir these together, and bake on tins in small cakes.

NAPLES BISCUIT.

Stir together half a pound of sugar and one-fourth of a pound of butter to a cream, add six drops of good essence of lemon, half a wine-glass of brandy and rose water mixed, and a little grated nutmeg; stir in half a pound of sifted flour. Bake in small cakes on tins.

ITALIAN MACAROONS.

Take one pound of blanched almonds rubbed fine in a mortar; whip to a stiff froth the whites of four eggs; add two pounds and a half of sifted loaf sugar; rub these all well together; add the whites of ten more eggs; whip these well until all is very light, then drop them with a spoon on stiff, white paper, and lay the papers on baking plates in a slow oven; before putting them in the oven, have ready blanched and dry almonds cut into thin slips, and lay on each macaroon four or five slips.

ALMONDS.

Almonds should be kept blanched and dried ready for use. The peach kernels should be saved in peach season and dried. They are, when mixed with almonds, nice for cake. In pounding them always use rose water, or orange flower water, to prevent the oiling of the almonds. Sugar must be used in pounding, if no flavouring is wanted.

BUNS.

Sift four pounds of flour, add to it one pound of good brown sugar; make a cavity in the centre of the pan, and stir in slowly one gill of good yeast with one pint of lukewarm new milk, using just flour enough to make the yeast and milk into a paste the consistency of rich cream. Cover this over, and let it stand two hours; then cut up one pound of good butter into one pint of warm milk, with a little salt; then mix all the ingredients together, dust the top with flour, and let them stand one hour; then make them into buns about the size of a large egg; butter the pans, and lay them in rows three inches apart; bake them in a hot oven, a nice brown color; when done, as soon as they are drawn from the oven, wipe them on the top with a soft brush dipped in milk.

CRULLERS.

To six heaping spoonsful of sugar, add six spoonsful of warmed not melted butter, and six well beaten eggs; beat these well together; grate half a nutmeg, add a very little pounded mace, and the grated rind of two lemons; beat them well together, and sift in as much flour as will make a soft dough; have ready some boiling lard, and cut the dough into any shape; fry them brown, and dry them in a hot colander free from fat. Serve hot. Sift over them pulverized white sugar.

BALTIMORE GINGER-BREAD.

Sift two pounds of flour into a pan, beat eight eggs very light, stir into the flour, cut up very finely one pound of good butter, and add one large cupful of ground ginger, one whole grated nutmeg, the rind of one lemon grated, half a pound of currants, one pound of good brown sugar, one pint of molasses, and one tea-spoonful of soda dissolved in a cup of cream. Mix these all well together, and bake in small cake-pans in rather a quick oven.

ORANGE GINGER-BREAD.

Sift into a pan two pounds and a quarter of fine flour, add one quart of good molasses, three-fourths of a pound of good brown sugar, one ounce of best ground ginger, one ounce of ground alspice; then cut up three-fourths of a pound of good butter, and six ounces of candied orange peel, cut very small; mix these well together; lay it by for ten hours; then roll it out with as little flour as possible, about half an inch thick, and cut into any form; put them on baking tins; rub them over before baking with a brush dipped in the yolk of an egg beaten up with a teacup of milk; bake in a moderately heated oven in about 20 minutes.

GINGER-BREAD.

Stir into one pound of good brown sugar one quart of good molasses, cut up one and a half pounds of good butter; mix them well together and heat them; when cool stir in four pounds of sifted flour, four tea-spoonsful of ground ginger of the best quality and strong, four teaspoonsful of carraway seeds, two carefully grated lemons, and a little salt. Mix these well; then make the cakes, and bake on tins. They are better for keeping awhile.

ANOTHER.

Take half a pint of molasses, three-fourths of a pound of butter cut small, one pound of good brown sugar, two table-spoonsful of good ground ginger, and one gill of cream; beat these well together with a spoon; then add as much sifted flour as will make it stiff enough to roll out; bake in cakes an inch thick on tins.

SOFT GINGER-BREAD.

Take one cup of molasses, one cup of brown sugar, one cup of butter cut up into small pieces, three eggs well beaten, three tea-cups of flour, two table-spoonsful of ground ginger, one tea-spoonful of ground cloves, two table-spoonsful of brandy, and one tea-spoonful of dissolved saleratus. Mix well, and bake in pans.

ANOTHER.

Take one pint of molasses, one pound of butter cut up finely, one pound of sugar, six eggs well beaten, one-quarter of a pound of ground ginger, half of a grated nutmeg, half a pound of cleaned currants, and two pounds of flour; mix all together, and add one tea-spoonful of saleratus, dissolved in a very little water, and stir in well. Bake in a buttered pan.

SCOTCH SHORT BREAD.

Mix two pounds of flour, dried and well sifted, with a pound of powdered sugar, three ounces of candied citron and orange-peel cut into dice, and half a pound of carraway comfits; mix these with half a pound of butter melted in a saucepan; then make the paste, roll it out the thickness of half an inch, cut it into cakes, place them on white paper, prick, and bake them of a pale colour.

DOVER CAKE.

Sift one pound of best rice flour into a pan; beat ten eggs very lightly to a stiff froth, and stir into the flour; cream one pound of powdered white sugar and half a pound of butter together; to the sugar and butter add one wine-glass of wine and brandy mixed, and a large spoonful of orange-flower water; then add these to the flour and eggs; beat them all together until perfectly light, then pour into a pan, and bake like a pound cake. The iceing must be flavored with orange-flour water. It is better than pound cake.

A VERY SUPERIOR POUND CAKE.

Beat the yolks of ten eggs very light, and sift in one pound of best flour; cream one pound of crushed and sifted white sugar with one pound of good butter; and then take half a glass of wine and half a glass of brandy, two table-spoonsful of orange-flower water, one-half a grated nutmeg, stir these into the butter and sugar; then whip to a stiff froth the ten whites, and add to the flour and yolks; lastly, add the seasoned butter and sugar; stir them well together with a broad bladed knife. Have ready a cake-pan well buttered, pour in the mixture, and bake in a moderate oven. Iceing to be flavoured with orange-flower water.

BUNS.

Cut half a pound of good butter into four tea-cups of milk, warm it, and when cool, stir in half a pound of good brown sugar, four eggs well beaten, one pound of sifted flour, half a nutmeg grated, one wine-glass of brandy and wine mixed, and one wine-glass of good yeast; mix well, and set it to rise for five hours, then make it into buns and bake on tins.

BLACK CAKE.

To one pound of butter and one pound of crushed sugar beaten to a cream, stir in twelve eggs whipped to a froth; sift in one pound of flour, and add three pounds of stoned raisins, three pounds of cleaned currants, five grated nutmegs, half an ounce of pounded cinnamon, one tea-spoonful of ground cloves sifted, one pound of citron cut into thin slices; these must be well mixed; bake in a buttered pan in rather a moderately heated oven. This improves by keeping.

TWELFTH CAKE.

Cream two pounds of butter and two pounds of sifted loaf sugar; take one large nutmeg grated, half an ounce of ground alspice, one tea-spoonful of ground cinnamon, the same of ginger, the same of coriander seeds, and one wine-glass of brandy; mix these well, then beat very light eighteen eggs; cut into thin slices half a pound of citron, and the grated rind of two lemons; beat this for at least half an hour until perfectly light; line the pan with buttered white paper, and bake in rather slow heat for four hours: when nearly cold, ice it as directed.

MACAROONES.

Take twelve whites of eggs, beaten to a froth with one pound of sifted sugar; add half a pound of blanched and pounded sweet almonds, and a little rose water; this must all be beaten to a stiff froth; when done, with a spoon place this mixture on a paper in a circular form, or as fancy may dictate; if too soft add more sugar. Put them on the baking tins, in a moderately heated oven; avoid opening the oven until they are done. A few nonpareils sprinkled over them improve their appearance; it must be done before putting them into the oven; when a light brown they are done.

ALMOND MACAROONES.

Blanch and pound three-fourths of a pound of sweet almonds, and one-fourth of a pound of bitter almonds; rub into this paste one pound of pulverized white sugar, the whites of four eggs beaten to a froth, and a table-spoonful of orange-flower water;

beat these well together, and drop a spoonful on paper; when the oven is nearly cool lay the paper on a board, and place it in the oven; a short time will cook them.

JUMBLES.

Beat one pound of butter with half a pound of white sugar to a cream, reserving the other half pound of sugar to roll them with; beat to a froth the whites of three eggs, with a little grated nutmeg and rose water; then stir in with a knife as much flour as will thicken them to the consistency of smooth soft dough; then turn them out and roll in the reserved sugar. Either cut round with a wine-glass or roll them long, and unite the ends in about eight inches in circumference.

NICE ICEING FOR CAKES.

Whip the whites of three eggs; add half a pound of good crushed sugar sifted in; beat this until quite white and cream-like; add a little orange-flower water, or a few drops of essence of lemon; then lay it thickly over the cakes with a knife when the cake is cold; harden it by returning the cake a few minutes near the oven or fire.

MERINGUES.

Beat the whites of ten eggs to a stiff froth; adding slowly ten table-spoonsful of sifted crushed sugar, but which must be very finely powdered; when well beaten and quite stiff, put it in the form of a large egg on paper; then glaze with the glazing sugar, and lay the paper on a tin in a moderately warmed oven; when of a light brown take them out, and remove from beneath all that which is not cooked with a spoon; this must be done with care, placing them in the oven when cold to dry; then put any kind of delicate preserves in each, and flavour with anything fancied, and put two together; either quince, calves foot, apple, or wine jelly is very nice in them.

ALMOND CROQUETS.

Break twelve eggs into a basin, add one pound of blanched and pounded almonds, one pound of white sifted sugar, beat these all well together very lightly; add a few drops of essence of lemon; then stir in slowly half a pound of sifted sugar; then form them into any shape, and lay on paper and brush them with the yolk of a beaten egg, put them in the baking pans, and place in an oven; bake slowly, a very light brown.

SPICE BREAD OF LORRAINE.

Take one pound and a half of flour, one pound of sugar, two table-spoonsful of carefully grated lemon peel, one table-spoonful of very thinly cut citron, one teaspoonful of coriander seed, half a teaspoonful of ground cloves, one teaspoonful of canelle, half a pound of well pounded sweet almonds carefully blanched. Put these into a pan, then pour into a nice pot such as is used for stewing, one porcelained inside, one quart of good honey, and when simmered add a wine-glass of wine; then stir in the above mixture; then remove from the fire, and beat all for half an hour with a wooden spoon; when well amalgamated and light, have ready your pasteboard and dust it with sugar as for jumbles; form the paste into any shape you may desire; then flour some stiff paper and lay the cakes on it; then place them in the oven, which must be of a very moderate heat, and let them cook for twenty minutes, and when cold brush each cake with sugar for glazing when dry; these cakes will be found delicious.

SUGAR FOR GLAZING CAKES.

Put into a vessel with a little water the white of one egg well beaten, and stirred well into the water; let it boil, and whilst boiling throw in a few drops of cold water, then stir in a cup of pounded sugar; this must boil to a foam, then used.

DERBY CAKE.

Cut into two pounds of sifted flour one pound of butter, one pound of cleaned currants, one pound of good brown sugar, beat one egg very lightly; mix all together with half a pint of new milk; roll it out thin, and cut into round cakes; lay them on baking tins in a moderately heated oven for ten minutes.

SAVOY BISCUITS.

Take twelve eggs and their weight of good crushed sugar, also take the weight of seven eggs of flour; beat the whites and yolks separate, add in the flour and sugar, stir them lightly with the juice of two nice lemons, and the rind of one lemon carefully grated, or four spoonsful of rose-water, if you have no lemons; this stirred together, and baked on tins, in not too hot an oven.

POUND CAKE.

Cream one pound of butter with one pound of crushed loaf sugar; whip eleven eggs, leave out four whites, sift in one pound of flour, add one wine-glass of brandy and wine mixed, grate in one nutmeg; mix these well; butter a pan and bake three-quarters of an hour.

SPONGE GINGER-BREAD.

Warm a pint of molasses; stir in while warm a piece of butter the size of an egg, then stir in a large spoonful of best white ginger; dissolve one large teaspoonful of soda in a pint of new milk; strain this into the mixture; when cool, sift in as much flour as will make it stiff; then roll it out in cakes and bake on tins.

CAROLINA GINGER CAKE.

To one pint of molasses warmed, cut up into it while warm one table-spoonful of butter, and stir in one pound of brown sugar, half a grated nutmeg, or the grated rinds of two lemons, but not both, one large spoonful of best white grated or ground ginger; mix these well together, and add as much flour as will enable you to roll it out into a thin cake; while in the pan and nearly done, mark it out in small squares; bake it very crisp and brown.

YANKEE CAKE.

One egg, a piece of butter the size of an egg, a tea-cup and a half of sugar, a tea-cup of milk, a pint of flour, nutmeg and rose water, or other flavor to the taste. In the tea-cup of milk dissolve one teaspoonful of super carbonate of soda. Into the pint of flour rub thoroughly two teaspoonsful of cream of tartar. Beat the egg, butter, and sugar together until it is light, then pour in it at the same instant the flour and milk, having strained the milk. Beat it thoroughly together, then pour the mixture into the turk's head well greased. Bake about three-quarters of an hour in a moderate oven. An excellent cake, requiring very little expense or time to make it.

QUEEN CAKE.

One pound of flour, three-quarters of a pound of sugar, half pound of butter, four eggs; spice to your taste. This makes a batter. Beat smooth, and bake in small tins.

CRELLS.

Two and a quarter pounds flour, rub in a lump of butter the size of a walnut, beat three eggs to a froth, and put in one pound sugar, nutmeg, a spoonful of soda dissolved in milk, cream of tartar, do. This makes a dough which you may roll out into the form of twists. Fry them in fresh goose drippings. They are excellent, and made in a very short time.

1, 2, 3, 4 CAKE.

One cup butter, two cups sugar, three cups flour, four eggs, nutmeg.

KISSES.

To six whites of eggs, one pound finest powdered sugar. Beat the eggs to a solid froth, and add the sugar by degrees, adding at times the juice of one lemon, and a very few drops oil of lemon. Before all the sugar is mixed, try one in the oven on a piece of paper. If frothy and soft to the touch, they require more sugar, but be sure not to add too much, or they will be hard and creamy. Bake in a tolerably quick oven, dropped on paper.

NEW YEARS COOKIES.

Sift four pounds of flour into a pan, and one pound of sifted sugar and half pound of butter well creamed together; stir them into the flour; dissolve in a cup of milk a tablespoonful of soda, stir this in, and four ounces of the best caraway seed. Mix all well together, and roll out the cakes about half an inch in thickness; bake in a moderate oven.

KISSES.

Take the whites of eggs, beat them very light, and mix with them enough sifted sugar to make them very stiff, then drop them on white paper half the size you want them, and let them remain in a slow oven twenty minutes; four eggs will make a cake basket full.

GINGER CUP-CAKE.

Three cups of flour, one of sugar, one of molasses, one of butter, a tablespoonful of ginger, one teaspoonful of soda, and three eggs; bake in pans. A pound of stoned and chopped raisins is an improvement.

SPONGE CAKE.

Six eggs, same weight of sugar, half weight of flour, half a lemon squeezed and put in, the whole of a lemon grated; beat the yellow to a froth, then add the sugar; when well beaten, add the white, which must be perfectly light; then put in the juice, then grating, then last, flour; also salt in sufficient quantity.

FEDERAL CAKE.

One pound of flour, half pound of butter, half pound of sugar, two eggs beaten to a froth, a glass of brandy, quarter of a pound of currants; roll them in thickish cakes, and bake them on tins in a moderate oven; nutmeg or mace to your taste.

SALLY LUNN.

Warm a quart of milk with a quarter of a pound of butter, and a heaped spoonful of sugar; beat up three eggs, and put in, with a little salt, and flour enough to make it stiffer than pound cake; beat it well; put in a tea-cup of yeast, and let it rise; butter a fluted pan and pour it in; bake it in a quick oven, slice and butter it. If you wish tea at six o'clock, set it to rise at ten in the morning. Bake it an hour.

SUPERIOR HOUSEHOLD BREAD.

Wash and pare half a pail of potatoes, taking great care to remove all dark specks as you pare them; throw them into a pan of clean, cold water, which prevents them from becoming brown or dark-colored, which destroys the delicate whiteness of the bread. Boil the potatoes with a large handful of salt, till reduced to a fine gruel, bruising any lump with a wooden potato pounder; pass it through a colander or coarse hair sieve. When cool enough to bear your hand in it, work in as much flour as will make the mixture into a thick batter; to this sponge add a large cupful and a half, or three parts cf a pint of good hop-rising yeast. A deep earthen pot or covered pail, or a trough, is the very best vessel to mix the sponge in. In winter, it is better made over night—but as it rises very light, and is apt to run over the pot or pail, it is as well to set the vessel in a large shallow pan. Work it up early in the morning. This quantity of potato sponge will make a large batch of bread; upwards of twenty pounds of flour may be worked into it. Knead the dough well and thoroughly after you have added the flour, score it on the top, cover it with a cloth, and set it to rise. In about two or three hours, or sooner, your bread will have swelled, and you will find it out like a honey-comb. Knead into loaves, let it stand about five minutes in the pans, and then bake in a well heated oven. When the loaves are done, wet them over with a little skimmed milk (or water will do), and wrap in a clean cloth, setting them up on one side. Wrapping the bread up in the steam till cold prevents it from becoming hard and dry.

BUENA VISTA CAKE, OR BUNS.

Half pound white sugar, half pound butter, four eggs, three-quarters of a pound flour, a wine-glass of rose water, one yeast powder; dissolve each powder in half a teacup of cream or rich milk, and put in separately when the cake is mixed. You may add a nutmeg.

SPANISH BUNS.

Mix a quarter and half a quarter of butter with one cup of cream, warmed, add half pound of sifted sugar, beat four eggs, and stir them alternately with three-quarters of a pound of flour. Dissolve the yeast powders in rose water, put the contents of the blue paper in first, and then that of the white. Nutmeg and brandy improve them, also a cup of currants. They must be baked as soon as made, about half an hour.

PATENT FLOUR.

Pulverise six pounds flour, mix five teaspoonsful of dry soda all through it, then six teaspoonsful cream of tartar, and six teaspoonsful of salt. Incorporate all these, and you have risen cakes at hand, to which add either milk or flour, and a little shortening; make into a soft dough, and bake in tins.

HOT CAKES FOR TEA.

Take half a pint of Indian meal, pour on it a pint of boiling milk, then add a pint more cold milk, beat three eggs a little, and put in salt sufficient to season it, then thicken it with wheat flour to a stiff batter (stiffer than you do buckwheat cakes), add yeast sufficient to rise them; when risen, bake them just as you do buckwheat cakes; butter them, and send them hot to table.

SALERATUS CAKE.

Quarter of a pound of butter, one pound good sugar, four eggs, the rind and juice of one lemon, half a pint of sour milk, in which mix a teaspoonful of saleratus, when mixed with the milk pour it to the butter, sugar, &c.; add flour enough to make it as thick as pound cake; bake in small cups; eight or ten currants in each cup is a pretty addition.

GERMAN DOUGHNUTS.

One pound and a quarter of flour, three-quarters of sugar, two ounces butter, half a tea-cup of cream, half a teaspoonful of soda, with the same quantity of cream of tartar; then add three eggs well beaten.

NONPAREIL DOUGHNUTS.

One pint and a half of milk, three-quarters of a pound sugar, half a pound butter, and one nutmeg. Make a sponge of these over night. They are good as possible. Fry in hot lard.

QUICK DOUGHNUTS.

One teaspoonful of soda, two cups of sugar, three spoonsful cream of tartar, one pint of milk, and flour enough to roll them out in. Fry in hot lard, as also the preceding.

GOLDEN CAKE.

Half pound flour, half pound sugar, one-fourth to one-eighth butter, yolks of seven eggs, yellow of one lemon, and the juice. Beat the butter and sugar together (it may be warmed in the stove a few minutes), add yolks, lemon, flour, half a teaspoonful of soda, with the same quantity of cream of tartar. Bake in flat pans, and ice.

SILVER CAKE.

Half pound sugar, half pound flour, a quarter pound butter, and the whites of seven eggs. Flavor this with peach or almond water, then bake as above. Ice this also, placing alternately gold and silver cake in a silver cake basket, for the tea table. This is a very desirable company cake. It costs but thirty-seven cents.

ICEING.

This elegant finish to rich cake is made by beating the whites of two eggs to a very stiff froth, and adding, little by little, fine white pulverized sugar till quite thick. Lay it on immediately after the cake is baked, with a broad knife, returning it to the oven for a few minutes, leaving the oven door open.

BRIDGET CAKE.

Three cups of dough very light, three cups of sugar, one cup of butter, three eggs, one nutmeg, raisins, one teaspoonful of saleratus; rub the butter and sugar together, add the eggs and spice, and mix all thoroughly with the dough; beat it well and pour into the pans. It will do to bake it immediately, but it will be lighter if left a short time to rise before baking. It is very important that the ingredients should be thoroughly mixed with the dough.

LOAF CAKE.

Three pounds of flour, one and a half pounds sugar, one and a half pounds butter, four eggs, one pint milk, two pounds fruit, half tumbler wine; raise with yeast.

LOAF CAKE WITHOUT EGGS.

Three pounds of flour, one and a half pounds sugar, one and a half pounds butter, one and a half pounds raisins, one nutmeg, one tablespoonful cinnamon, two gills wine, one half pint yeast, one pint milk; put the milk, butter and yeast into the flour and let it rise.

CINNAMON LOAF.

Sift into a pan one pound of flour—cut into half pint of warm milk a half pound of good butter—stir the milk and butter into the flour, and a wine glass full of good yeast and a little salt. Mix these well together, and set it in a warm place to rise; not *too* warm, however. Let it rise a full hour, then add half a pound of sifted sugar, and half a grated nutmeg, one large spoonful of ground cinnamon, and a wine glass of rose water; mix these well into the sponge, pour it into the pans, and set it again to rise for half an hour, then bake in rather a slow oven one hour.

GRAFTON CAKE.

One pint of flour, half pint of sugar, two teaspoonsful cream of tartar, one of soda, one egg, one heaping tablespoonful of butter, and milk enough to make a thin batter.

PASTRY.

THIS requires care and good materials. The flour must always be dried and sifted before using; the butter which is employed washed, and all the water worked out; the best paste is made with beef suet. Render six pounds of nice beef suet; strain it through a hair sieve into a clean pan; to this add a bottle of the best olive oil; stir it well, and then put into jars, each containing about three pounds; cover tightly, and keep in a very cool place. Not more than two jars should be prepared at a time for a small family, as the suet is liable to become musty, and will not keep long.

In making the pastry for pies, when you require it flaky and particularly good, sift one pound of best flour into a pan, then cut into it three-fourths of a pound of the prepared suet; be careful to use the hands as little as possible, and the less worked the better; when all the required suet is cut up add salt to the taste, moisten it with cold water, (in summer ice water,) then flour your pasteboard, which must be always very clean, and never used twice without scouring; roll it as little as possible, and add another quarter of a pound of the suet in thin slices; between each rolling add the suet in thin slices, and dust in with flour; the more thinly it is rolled the lighter the paste. Have ready the pie plates, or pudding; be careful in rolling that you always roll from you, and make it as quickly as possible. For meat pies, the nicest paste is made by sifting into a pan one pound of flour, make a hole in the centre of the dry flour, cut into this hole some suet three-fourths of a pound not prepared, but strip off all the skin, then pour over this suet half a pint of boiling water; sprinkle some flour over it, and let it stand for an hour to become cold; then stir the whole with a knife, add a little salt, turn it out on the board, dust it well with flour, and roll as little as possible.

A NICE PUFF PASTE.

Sift into a pan one pound of best flour; cut into this three-quarters of a pound of best butter, then moisten it with one pint of very cold water; mix it with a knife, then dust your pie-board well with flour and turn out your paste, then cut up into small thin slices a quarter of a pound more of butter, and add this in three rollings, using a quarter of a pound of sifted flour for the rollings; handle it as little as possible, and use a knife for mixing the paste; paste should be made in a cool place, and in summer laid on the ice for an hour before using.

OYSTER PIE.

Pour boiling water on the oysters, a few at a time; open them carefully, strain the juice so as to be free from all particles of shells; then lay the oysters thickly in the bottom of the pie dish; put the juice on the fire; while simmering, skim it well, throwing in a spoonful of whole alspice, and a few whole pepper grains; grate some nutmeg in, and salt to the taste; then stir into a cup of cream a large spoonful of flour; when quite smooth stir it into the juice while boiling; then cut up into small pieces a quarter of a pound of good butter and stir in; pour this over the oysters, in the dish; fill it nearly full of oysters and juice. While this is cooling make a nice puff paste, and when the oysters are cold lay a margin of paste all around the edge of the dish; then roll out the covering for the top, and lay on; pass a knife around the edge and make it smooth; ornament the top covering with a rose of paste; beat up the yolk of an egg with a very little water, and spread it thickly over with a feather—this gives a pretty glazed appearance to the paste; bake half an hour, and serve hot.

ANOTHER.

Take one hundred good oysters, strain the juice, and put it on to boil; add a teaspoonful of celery seed, (if the stalks cannot be obtained,) a very small piece of mace, and some whole pepper grains; take out a cup of the juice, and when cool mix to a smooth paste a spoonful of flour, then add that to the juice, salt to the taste, let this boil for ten minutes, then pour it through a sieve, and cut up one-quarter of a pound of good butter into the juice, adding a wine-glass of white wine; put the oysters into the juice, let them stand, until wanted for the paste, in a cool place. Then make a good puff paste and cut it the shape of the dish, line the sides and bottom, lay the top on so as to be removed after baking; bake this paste in the dish; and before serving scald the oysters and juice, raise the top, and pour all in. Serve hot.

BEEF STEAK PIE WITH OYSTER SAUCE.

Strain off the juice of twenty-five oysters, simmer this with a blade of mace, and some whole pepper grains; mix a table-spoonful of flour in a cup of cream; have two thin tender rump steaks, lay one of the steaks at the bottom of your dish, then the oysters, and then the other steak; add some salt to the taste, and one-quarter of a pound of butter cut up in the juice, and pour it hot over the steaks; whilst cooling prepare a paste and cover it over as the oyster pie. Bake three-quarters of an hour.

A BIRD PIE.

Take squabs, or pigeons either, clean and put into each one a small quantity of bread crumbs mixed with butter, a little nutmeg grated, and chopped fresh parsley; tie them up. Then cut very thin slices of fat salt pork, and lay a thick layer in the bottom of the stew pan, on these place your birds, over them pour just water enough to cover them; then cover the pot very tightly and stew for nearly twenty minutes; whilst they are cooking make your paste. Bottom paste to pies is seldom cooked enough unless baked separately. When the birds have cooked until nearly done, take them out carefully and lay in your dish, which should not be deep; pour over the juice, and mix a spoonful of flour to a smooth paste, and add a wine-glass of white wine; pour this also over. None of the pork must be put into the pie, as the birds have become sufficiently flavoured in stewing. Lay on the margin of the dish strips of paste, and then cover it all with a good rich paste, as for oyster pie; bake half an hour. Any kind of delicate birds can be prepared in the same manner. Reed birds are delicious done in this way.

CHICKEN PIE.

Take a pair of fowls, clean and cut them up as for a fricassee. Cut thin slices of salt fat pork; put a thick layer of pork slices in the bottom of a stew pan, on these lay the fowls; add a small bunch of summer savory tied, so as to take it out easily, and a very little salt; just cover the fowls with water and close the pan tightly; let them stew very slowly for half an hour, then take out the pieces of fowl very nicely, and put them into the pie dish. Take some of the gravy and stir in a large spoonful of flour, and mix with the gravy; grate some nutmeg in and then pour over the fowls, so as to have plenty of rich gravy; cut a piece of butter in thin slices and lay it on the top of the fowls; then cover over with a good paste; bake half an hour, serve hot. Ornament the top with roses or leaves cut out of the paste and baked separately.

PYRAMID OF PASTE.

Roll out some nicely prepared puff paste, an inch in thickness, and cut the paste into any shape you may fancy; make each smaller until the top one is not larger than a cent; between each piece of paste spread some nice preserve or jam; then turn up the edges of the paste, and brush the sides and top with the yolk of a beaten egg. Lay the pyramid on a baking tin, and bake a nice light brown: serve hot.

BRUNSWICK TART.

Make a crust as for vol au vent; pare and core ten pippin apples; put them into a stew-pan with some very thinly pared rind of a lemon, four table-spoonsful of crushed sugar, and one wine-glass full of sweet wine; cover them closely and stew until the apples are perfectly tender; then set them aside to cool; put the paste into a rather deep dish to bake, and make a rich boiled custard; let it get quite cold; and when the paste is done and cool, put the apples into it, and then pour over the custard; this is a delightful dessert.

PASTE FOR CROQUANTS.

Sift half a pound of flour, and quarter of a pound of loaf sugar together; mix these well with a knife; then stir in as many yolks of eggs as will make it into a stiff paste; this must be well stirred; then roll it on a floured board, and cut in the shape of leaves with a cutter; they are a very pretty ornament for tarts, or puddings; bake a light brown, as other paste.

RABBIT PIE.

Wash very carefully two freshly killed rabbits, that have been killed the day before; great care must be used in the washing, and let them remain in cold water for two hours, to whiten; then cut them up nicely; lay some very thin slices of corned fat pork in the bottom of a stew-pan; on these place the rabbits; pour over this one quart of cold water, and let it simmer slowly for half an hour; while it is cooking, prepare a nice puff paste, line the sides of a baking dish with it, reserving a top. Take out the rabbits, and put the pieces of rabbit and pork into the dish with a few blades of broken-up mace; chop up a little fresh parsley and scatter through as the pieces of rabbit are laid in; take about a pint of the water in which the rabbits were cooked, and having rubbed a spoonful of flour and two spoonsful of butter together, stir it into the water, a very little cayenne to be added; when the butter and flour are smoothly stirred into the water, pour it over the rabbits; cover them over with a nice paste, and bake half an hour; serve hot.

VEAL POT PIE.

Take a shank bone, the neck, or any nice piece of veal; wash them and joint well, and crack the bones; put the piece into a stew pan, and on the top lay a bunch of summer savoury and parsley tied together with an eschalot, add a little salt; on this pour cold water enough just to cover it; let it simmer for twenty minutes—then line a stew pot with good potatoe crust; put in a layer of the separated parts of veal, and cut very thin slices of corned fat pork, and thin slices of white potatoes; then another layer of veal, pork, and potatoes; so on until all is in; then take a pint of the water in which the veal was cooked, and stir into it two large spoonsful of flour; when smoothly mixed add a little pepper, and pour it over the meat; cover the top with paste, close tightly, and bake three-quarters of an hour; should it become dry make a small hole in the top, and add more of the broth; it must be baked a nice brown, but care taken that the paste does not scorch; before lining the pot grease it to prevent the paste sticking. Serve hot.

CREAM CRUST.

This is the least objectionable kind of crust which is made; take either sour or sweet cream, and stir in as much sifted flour as will make a stiff paste, and add a little salt; if the cream used is sour dissolve in it some soda in the proportion of a teaspoonful to one pint of cream; if sweet cream one half as much soda; mould this as little as possible.

APPLE PIE.

Fill a pudding dish with pared and cored apples—the tart baking apple; fill each hole of the apple with good brown sugar; cut very thinly the oily part of the rind of two lemons; then cut it into narrow strips, and lay on the top of the apples; squeeze the juice of the lemons into a cup and add a little cold water; pour this over the apples, and sprinkle over more sugar, quite thickly; then cover the whole with a nice puff paste, and bake it rather slowly one hour; serve hot. Peaches are very nice done in the same way, with the stones left in and only pared, but no lemon, and very little water as they make their own juice.

BAKED APPLE DUMPLINGS.

Prepare a paste as for boiled dumplings; only instead of one large one, make several small ones; avoid lapping the paste, as much as possible, after the fruit is introduced; butter the pan in which they are baked, to prevent their sticking; lay the folded side down; bake three-quarters of an hour; serve hot; eaten with cream.

BAKED BLACKBERRY DUMPLINGS.

They are prepared precisely as the apple; cranberries are also very nice, only the cranberries must be partially stewed and cooled before putting into the paste. Peaches are very nice, prepared as the apples.

POTATOE CRUST.

Boil six good sized mealy white potatoes, pare and mash them through a colander; add a tea-cup of sweet cream, and a little salt; sift in just flour enough to make them stick and to roll out; work it as little as possible; if properly made this is an excellent paste; it must be rolled rather thicker than ordinary paste; it is excellent for pot pie, or any kind of boiled dumplings. In boiling dumplings great care is necessary, first to have a nice stout cloth, which must be kept exclusively for the purpose, washed and well floured before the dumpling is put in, and tied tightly. The pot of water boiling when the pudding is put in, and a kettle of boiling water ready to renew it as the water evaporates, and not allowed to remain in the water a moment after it is cooked; served hot.

Vol au Vent.

Roll off a nice puff paste, about the eighth of an inch in thickness; then with a tin cutter, the size of the dish intended to lay the pastry on, cut out an oblong shape; lay this on a baking plate with a sheet of white paper beneath the paste; rub the paste over with the yolk of an egg; then roll out another piece of paste an inch in thickness; cut this also with the cutter the same size as the other; lay this on the other piece of paste, then with a cutter two sizes smaller, press nearly through the two pieces of paste in the centre; be careful not to cut entirely through the bottom of the paste; rub the top with the yolk of an egg; bake it in a quick oven twenty minutes, a light brown color; when cooked take out very carefully the centre piece marked by the small cutter; keep the paste warm until ready for table; then fill in the centre with nicely fricasseed chicken hot, or stewed oysters, or nicely minced seasoned veal; then lay on the top piece, and serve hot.

A French Chicken Pie.

Cut up two nice chickens, as for a fricassee; stew them for twenty minutes, with a little pepper and salt, and half a pound of nice veal, and a bunch of thyme and parsley; take the veal out and chop it finely, rub the livers of the chickens with the yolks of two hard boiled eggs; grate one nutmeg and add a little salt; make this into small balls the size of marbles; make a rich puff paste; lay a very thin piece in the bottom of a pie dish; then put in some of the chicken, some of the balls, and four or five very thin slices of lemon, then more chicken, more balls, a few slices of lemon; then the rest of the chicken; cut up half a quarter of a pound of butter, on the top pour on some of the broth in which the chicken was boiled, cover this with a nice puff paste, bake half an hour.

BEEF STEAK PUDDING.

Select nice rump steaks, tender and juicy, half an inch in thickness; beat them with a pounder to break the fibres; trim off all skin and sinew; peel and chop very finely one onion; slice three white potatoes very thinly; rub the sides and bottom of the baking dish with butter, and line the sides only with good paste; then lay in the steak, sprinkle over a little salt, cayenne and the chopped onion, some of the sliced potatoe, and then lay on the other steak; on this sprinkle the same seasoning with the rest of the onion and potatoe; when all is in pour over a wine-glassful of mushroom catsup, and one pint of veal, or any nice broth; cover it up with a nice paste, dip a feather in the yolk of a beaten egg, and brush over the top; bake one hour; serve hot.

MINCE MEAT FOR PIES.

Boil five pounds of lean and juicy beef until tender, and whilst boiling keep closely covered; when cool, chop it very fine; chop very finely three pounds of nice beef suet; seed three pounds of raisins, and chop; three pounds of well washed and dried currants; two pounds of citron cut into thin slices; grate only the oily part of the rind of six fresh lemons; two table-spoonsful of ground cinnamon; six good sized nutmegs grated; one tea-spoonful of salt; one tea-spoonful of ground white ginger; chop finely fourteen good sized pippin apples; mix these well together; then put it into a stone jar; cover it with good French brandy, and wine; three parts brandy, and the rest wine; this must be kept in a cool, dry place, and improves by keeping. A little good cider is quite an improvement added just as it is baked.

APPLE CHARLOTTE.

Pare eighteen or twenty tart apples, slice them thinly, put them into a saucepan, with just enough water to moisten them; let them stew slowly; pare the rind of two lemons very thinly, and cut into small pieces, and put in; let them cook until quite soft, keeping tightly covered; when done, stir in some finely powdered sugar, and a spoonful of butter; pass them through the colander; set them aside to cool; cut thin slices of bread, and butter both sides; line a pudding dish with these, bottom and sides; then pour in the apples; cover the top with bread crumbs, and bake it a nice brown; then turn it out on a dish; serve with cream.

FRUIT CHARLOTTE.

Take six or eight sound tart apples, pare and grate them; quarter of a pound of stale bread grated; half a pound of well washed currants; half a pound of stoned raisins; strew the bottom of a pudding dish thickly with some of the grated apple; then scatter on some brown sugar, on this scatter ground cinnamon and grated lemon peel, and some pieces of butter cut very thinly; then strew on some raisins and currants; then some grated bread; then the remainder of the apples; more sugar, cinnamon, and a little grated nutmeg, the rest of the raisins and currants; on this pour one wine-glass of brandy, and one of wine, mixed; then scatter more bread crumbs, and strew over it thickly, thin slices of butter; bake in a slow oven three-quarters of an hour.

PEACH POT PIE.

Cover the sides of a Dutch oven with thin potatoe pie-crust; lay in as many pared peaches as will cover the bottom, or more if you please; spread over them a thin covering of pie-crust; then put on another layer of pared peaches, and so on, putting peaches and crust alternately, until you have put in all you wish. Stir together three parts of water and one of molasses; make a cross cut in the middle of the pie as you would for pot-pie; pour the molasses and water into the opening, cover the Dutch oven, and bake it with a brisk heat—not fierce enough to scorch. I should think three-quarters of an hour would be about right. The quantity of molasses must be judged by the acidity of the peaches. For a peck of good peaches of the usual flavour, about half a pint of best molasses would be needed, and three times as much water. This pie is excellent.

BREAD DOUGH PASTE.

This is the best for apple dumplings, peach dumplings, or berry dumplings; and a good pudding is made by rolling out, and spreading it very thickly with any kind of jam, or preserves; then rolling it over carefully, and tie up in a nicely floured square stout cloth; lay the dough spread with jam lengthwise in the cloth; have ready a pot of boiling water and drop in the pudding, and keep it boiling very briskly three-quarters of an hour; keep a kettle of water boiling on the fire, to renew the water as it evaporates, as the lightness of the pudding depends much on the pot being kept full, and boiling until served.

RIPE FRUIT TARTS.

These are made of any kind of fruit; for gooseberries, after picking and washing with care, lay them in a deep dish, the centre highest; then sweeten with, to a quart of berries, a quarter of a pound of good brown sugar, and a cupful of nice honey; add a very little water; and cover with a nice paste, at the edge of the dish a long piece of paste an inch in width and half an inch in thickness before putting on the top; press the thumb around the edge of the paste to close it well to prevent the juice escaping; then pass a sharp knife carefully around the rim to remove the uneven edges of pastry. Bake it in a moderately heated oven; currants ripe, damsons, or blackberries are nice done in the same way, only no honey must be used with them; only sugar and the least possible water, as they are juicy; serve hot. If it is necessary to be very inviting in appearance, a great improvement is to ice the pie; thus,

ICEING FOR PASTRY.

Beat up the whites of two eggs to a very stiff froth; lay some of the froth with a feather on the pie, when cooked; over this thickly sift pulverized loaf sugar; smooth it down with a broad bladed knife; then sprinkle a little cold water over it to dissolve the sugar; set the pie again in the oven to dry; when the sugar is crusted, which will be in a few minutes, remove it and serve cold.

RHUBARB PIES.

Peel with care the tender stalks of the pie plant; cut them about an inch in length; lay them in the baking dish, alternately a layer of the plant and thickly scattered good brown sugar and very thin slices of fresh lemon, until the dish is filled; but no water as the plant is very juicy; then cover with a nice paste; bake three-quarters of an hour; another nice way is to stew the plant to a rich jam, and fill puffs after it is cold, like cranberry tarts.

APPLE PIE.

Prepare nice tart apples by paring and coring, and stew them until tender; whilst stewing, grate in the oily part of the rind of a fresh lemon; when done, stir in a large spoonful of either rich cream or good butter, and grate in a little nutmeg; sweeten to the taste; mix it well together; lay on the margin of the dish a thin piece of pastry, then put in the apples; cover it over with a rich puff paste; turn the edge with a knife; bake in a quick oven, as the paste is the only thing to cook. This is nice iced in the summer when eaten cold. When dried apples or peaches are used, they must be put to soak the night before using, and well washed; for peaches, orange peel must be used while they are stewing; for juicy fruit pies, such as cherries, blackberries, &c., it is a good plan to invert a small teacup in the centre of the dish; it prevents a loss of the juice, as the juice is drawn beneath the cup. Also in oyster pies.

To Neutralize the Acid in Fruit Pies and Puddings.

A large quantity of the free acid which exists in rhubarb, gooseberries, currants, and other fruits, may be judiciously corrected by the use of a small quantity of carbonate of soda without the least affecting their flavour, so long as too much soda is not added. To an ordinary sized pie or pudding as much soda may be added as, piled up, will cover a shilling, or even twice such a quantity, if the fruit is very sour. If this little hint is attended to, many a stomach ache will be prevented, and a vast quantity of sugar saved, because, when the acid is neutralized by the soda, it will not require so much sugar to render the tart sweet.

Cherries, to keep.

Cut the stalks carefully from sound and perfectly dry cherries, and put them into clean and dry bottles; when full, cork them tight, and rosin or seal them; bury them in the ground, with the corks downwards.

Gooseberries, to keep.

When the weather is dry pick the gooseberries that are full grown and not ripe; pick off the tops and tails and put them into open-mouthed bottles; gently cork them with quite new

15

corks; put them in the oven after the bread is drawn, and let them stand until shrunk a quarter part; then take them out of the oven and immediately beat the corks in tight, cut off the tops, and rosin them tightly down, set them in a dry place, and if they are well secured from the air they will keep the year round.

BOILED APPLE DUMPLINGS.

Sift into a pan two pounds of best flour; on this pour from the kettle as much boiling water as will make it a very stiff paste; add half a teaspoonful of salt; when mixed turn it out on the floured paste-board and roll it out rather thin, using a knife to mix and arrange it. Then have ready the pudding cloth, well floured as directed, and put in as many sliced tart apples as the paste will hold; roll it up and put it into the prepared cloth; have the pot of water boiling and drop it in; renew the water with boiling water as it evaporates; boil thirty minutes, then drain and serve.

RICH MINCE PIES.

Take four pounds of beef, boiled and chopped fine; pick and chop three pounds of suet, wash two pounds of currants and one of raisins; grate the peel of two lemons, and put in the juice; pound a spoonful of dried orange peel, slice an ounce of citron, and chop twelve large apples; mix these together with three pounds of sugar, half a pint of wine, and the same of brandy and sweet cider to make it a proper thickness; put in mace and nutmeg to your taste. If the cider is not sweet, you must put in more sugar before the pies are baked; cut several places in the top of each with a pair of scissors.

MINCE PIES.

Take four pounds of beef after it has been boiled and chopped, one of suet, two of sugar, two of raisins, and four of chopped apples; mix these together, with a pint of wine and cider, to make it thin enough; season to your taste with mace, nutmeg and orange peel; if it is not sweet enough, put in more sugar. Warm the pies before they are eaten. Where persons are not fond of suet, put butter instead, and stew the apples instead of so much cider.

CORN PIE.

Take a young tender chicken and cut up as for frying, salt it and let it lay for several hours; then take eight or twelve ears of corn, if large eight will do, grate it off the cob, scrape all that adheres, to this add three or four well beaten eggs, quarter of a pound of butter, seasoned highly with pepper, and one pint of new milk. Put in the chicken and the liquid which is around it. If more salt be required stir it up well before putting in. Put the above in a pan deep enough to allow of its puffing When it first begins to cook stir it well several times, as the richness is apt to settle. When it begins to puff mash it down. Bake it in a moderate oven an hour and a half; brown it before taking it out.

CHICKEN PIE.

Cut up the chickens, and if they are old, boil them fifteen minutes in a little water, which save to put in the pie; make a paste like common pie crust, and put it round your pan or dish; lay in the chicken, dust flour over, and put in butter, pepper and salt; cover them with water, roll out the top crust quite thick, and close the pie round the edge; make an opening in the middle with a knife; let it bake rather more than an hour. If you warm a pie over for the next day, pour off the gravy and warm it separately, and add it to the pie.

PLAIN OYSTER PIE.

Take from the shell as many oysters as you want to put into the pie; strain the liquor, put it with them over the fire and give them one boil; take off the scum, put in, if you wish to make a small pie, a quarter of a pound of butter, as much flour mixed in water as will thicken it when boiled, and mace, pepper, and salt to your taste; lay a paste in a deep dish, put in the oysters and cover them with paste; cut a hole in the middle, ornament it any way you please, and bake it. A shallow pie will bake in three-quarters of an hour.

ANOTHER.

Take fifty oysters—strain the liquor—line a dish with good crust, take two hard-boiled eggs, chop them fine, mix them with a slice of bread crumbled fine; add two ounces of butter; pepper, salt and nutmeg to your taste; then to each layer of oysters sprinkle some of the mixture; it is best to reserve some of the oyster liquor for gravy. To be served in a gravy dish.

A RICH OYSTER PIE.

Strain off the liquor from the oysters, and put it on to boil, with some butter, mace, nutmeg, pepper and salt; just as it boils, stir in a thickening of milk and flour; put in the oysters, and stir them till they are sufficiently stewed; then take them off, and put in the yolks of two eggs, well beaten; do not put this in while it is boiling or it will curdle. Line a dish, not very deep, with puff paste; fill it with white paper, or a clean napkin, to keep the top paste from falling in; put on a lid of paste and bake it. When done take off the lid carefully; take out the paper or napkin, and pour in the oysters. Send it hot to table.

OYSTER SAUCE.

Plump the oysters for a few minutes over the fire; take them out and skim the liquor; stir in some flour and butter mixed together, with a little mace and whole pepper, and salt to your taste; when it has boiled long enough, throw in the oysters, and add a glass of white wine; let all just simmer, and then serve. This is very nice for breakfasts, or for beefsteaks as a sauce.

PASTIES.

Rub a full quarter of a pound of lard into two pounds of flour. Beat the whites of two eggs light, and mix in two half pints of water; wet the flour, leaving out some to work the crust with; take one pound of butter, roll out the crust four times, each time putting in with a knife a quarter of the butter. Use flour freely when rolling out. Cut it round, lay in your preserve or apple, which must be dry; turn over the paste to join a half circle, nip the edge with the thumb and finger to confine the preserve, dip the hand in water, pass it lightly over the paste, then sift sugar thick upon them and bake in a quick oven,

RECEIPT FOR SHELLS.

Take one pound of sifted flour, and one pound of butter; use no salt; make the flour into a stiff paste, with very cold water, touching with the hand as little as possible; then roll thin; cut the butter in small pieces, and lay half of them on the paste; flatten each down by a quick pressure of the hand; dredge flour lightly over the surface, and fold together, first lengthwise, then crosswise into a small lump; roll out again, lay on the remainder of the butter in the same way—sprinkle lightly with flour, fold together, and roll out as thin as possible; dredge again, fold together, and roll out into a wafer-like sheet, which, having dredged, fold lightly into a roll about three inches wide; cut the whole of this into squares, flatten each square with the rolling-pin, and cut out with your shell-cutter; having prepared two of these, take with a small round cutter a circular piece from the centre of one, and lay the rim thus made upon the whole shell. Bake fifteen minutes in a very quick oven; watch them carefully, as much depends on the baking. When properly made they will rise to the height of two and a half or three inches

QUICK PASTRY.

One bowl of lard, one bowl of water, three bowls of flour; mix all well together, and roll out, using patent flour as at page 206

PUDDINGS, FRITTERS, &c.

Preparations of Puddings.

In the preparation of puddings, the best articles, as in all cooking, should be used; there is no economy in employing inferior butter in cooking, as good materials are often spoiled and rendered unpalatable, and in fact unwholesome, by bad butter and stale eggs. The suet which is used for puddings should always be fresh and very finely chopped, all the strings and pieces of skin being carefully removed. The milk for very many puddings should be boiled, and great care observed in the boiling. A porcelained saucepan is the best to use for milk, and should be kept exclusively for the purpose. In beating eggs, always separate the yolks from the whites, it tends to make the pudding lighter; use either an "egg whisk," or a broad bladed knife; break each egg separately in a saucer, as one doubtful egg may spoil the whole. In making batter pudding, add only a part of the flour at first, to prevent lumps; when all the required quantity of flour is sifted and stirred in with the milk, then add the beaten eggs, and the remainder of the milk. All puddings in which berries are used, require more flour than those without; and it must be remembered, to add the berries last in compounding the pudding; whilst it is boiling it requires frequent turning over, or the fruit will settle to one side; it must be kept constantly boiling, and a kettle of boiling water at hand to replace the water which evaporates. Have a pudding cloth kept expressly for the purpose, made of the thickest twilled cotton, and always before using it wash it well in hot water, and flour it well before pouring in the pudding; the seam of the bag must be on the outside, and a strong twine string attached for tying. These details are very necessary to the uninitiated. In baking puddings, always butter the dish well to prevent it sticking.

A LIGHT BATTER PUDDING.

Beat very lightly as directed ten eggs; when light, stir in twelve table-spoonsful of sifted flour with a knife; to this add one quart of good new milk, and a little salt; stir well, and pour into a floured bag; put into boiling water, and boil one hour and a half.

WHITE POTATOE PUDDING.—BAKED.

One pound of potatoes boiled and mashed very smoothly; cream one pound of sugar and one pound of butter well together; beat ten eggs very lightly, and add to the sugar and butter; then mix in the potatoes, if perfectly smooth; one wine-glass of wine and one of brandy, and a large spoonful of orange flower water, with one tea-spoonful of grated nutmeg and cinnamon mixed; beat these well together, and stir in a cup of cream; pour it into a dish, and bake it in a quick oven, a nice brown; serve hot.

WHITE POTATOE PUDDING.

Take six or eight good sized white potatoes, and boil them; skin and mash through a colander; beat to a cream three-quarters of a pound of good butter, and three-quarters of a pound of good brown sugar; when beaten to a cream, whip the yolks of eight eggs very light, and stir into the butter and sugar; grate in half a nutmeg, a wine-glass of rose-water, a wine-glass of brandy and wine mixed; stir this also in; beat it well together, then slowly mix in the mashed potatoes; the lightness of this depends on the beating; have the dishes ready lined with puff paste, and put in the above mixture; bake half an hour.

SWEET POTATOE PUDDING.

Grate three or four good sized raw sweet potatoes; lay some slices of good butter into a dish; on this sprinkle some of the grated potatoes, about one half; grate on the potatoe half a nutmeg and a very little cinnamon, and scatter over two large spoonsful of brown sugar; then the rest of the potatoes; more butter and sugar; and mix one wine-glass of rose water, and a cup of cream together; and one wine-glass of wine and brandy mixed; stir all these ingredients well together; bake very slowly two hours; serve hot as a dessert.

COCOANUT PUDDING.

Grate one pound of cocoanut carefully; beat to a cream one pound of crushed white sugar, and half a pound of good butter; beat the whites of eleven eggs to a stiff froth; stir the cocoanut, butter and sugar, well together; add one wine-glass of rose water, one wine-glass of wine and brandy mixed; beat these well; grate in half a nutmeg; and add lastly the froth of the eggs; have the dishes ready lined with puff paste, and bake half an hour.

LEMON PUDDING.

Stir to a cream, one pound of butter, and one pound of sugar, grate in the oily rind of three fresh lemons, and squeeze in the juice; mix this in with the butter and sugar; beat very lightly the yolks of eleven eggs; add to the butter and sugar one wine-glass of wine and brandy mixed, with one wine-glass of rose water; beat these in well; lastly, stir in the eggs. Line the dishes with puff paste, and bake half an hour. It is most economical to make lemon and cocoanut puddings on the same day, as the yolks can be used for the lemon pudding, and they will keep for several days if kept in a cool dry place.

ANOTHER LEMON PUDDING.

One pound of good butter beaten to a cream with one pound of pulverized loaf sugar; beat the yolks of ten eggs to a froth, and stir into the sugar; grate the rind of two lemons, and squeeze the juice; add then one wine-glass of brandy, one of wine, and one of rose water; mix these in well, grate four water crackers and stir in, and beat all well together; have ready the puff paste in the dishes, put in this mixture, and bake half an hour.

PUMPKIN PUDDING.

Boil and squeeze through a stout cloth the pumpkin which has been nicely stewed, squeeze it very dry; to two pounds of pumpkins thus drained add three-quarters of a pound of good brown sugar, and three-quarters of a pound of butter smoothly creamed; stir them into the pumpkin; a tea-spoonful of pounded mace and grated nutmeg, and a little ground cinnamon to be added; then one wine-glassful of wine and brandy mixed; beat these all together well; lastly add the yolks of eight well beaten eggs. Line the dishes with puff paste, and fill with the above; bake half an hour.

ALMOND PUDDING.

Blanch by pouring hot water on half a pound of best almonds; rub them in a mortar with rose water to prevent their oiling; they must be rubbed to a smooth paste; cream half a pound of good butter, and half a pound of white sugar; when quite smooth and light stir in the almond; then add one wine-glass of wine and brandy mixed, and one wine-glass of rose water; then beat separately the whites from the yolks of seven eggs; first stir in the yolks, and then the whites, beat all well together, line the dishes with puff paste, and bake as long as a custard only.

APPLE PUDDING.

Put four or five good sized pippins in a sauce-pan; on them pour a tea-cup of water, cover tightly, and let them steam over a slow fire until perfectly tender, then mash them carefully through a colander, to remove the cores and skins; stir to a cream four large spoonsful of good brown sugar, and two of butter; mix these with the apples, then stir in one pint of rich cream; grate five hard crackers into the mixture, and half a nutmeg; beat the yolks of eight eggs very light, and stir lastly the whites of four eggs beaten to a stiff froth; this must be well beaten; butter a baking dish and bake as a custard.

AMERICAN PUDDING.

Put on a pint of new milk to scald; while this is heating, stir three large spoonsful of rice flour into a cup of milk; when quite smooth stir it into the boiling milk, add a little salt, and a large spoonful of butter; grate in the oily part of the rind of a lemon, and add also some nutmeg and one wine-glassful of brandy; beat these all together, add three large spoonsful of good brown sugar, beat five eggs very light, and stir in; butter a dish and pour it in; bake as long as custard.

MARLBOROUGH PUDDING.

Grate half a pound of pippins, stir to a cream one-quarter of a pound of sugar, and a quarter of a pound of butter, and add the grated apples; grate the rind of a fresh lemon, whip very light five eggs, and beat all well together; line a dish with puff paste, and put in the above; bake half an hour.

TAPIOCA PUDDING.

Soak over night a tea-cup of the best lump tapioca in milk; the next day boil one pint of new milk, and stir in the tapioca which has been soaked; then stir a large spoonful of butter and a little salt, two large spoonsful of sugar, one wine-glass of rose water, and a little grated nutmeg; then beat four eggs very light and stir in; mix all well together, and bake in a dish half an hour. Sago is very nice prepared in the same way.

RICE PUDDING, OR "RIZ AU LAIT."

This pudding if properly prepared is better without eggs; wash a coffee-cupful of rice well; put it into one quart of new milk over night to soak; in the morning add a large spoonful of butter, a little salt, grated nutmeg, and a little ground cinnamon, then one pint more of new milk; then put it into the oven; and when it has begun to warm stir the pudding without removing from the oven; stone a quarter of a pound of the best raisins, and add at this time; then let it cook until the rice is perfectly done.

BAKED FLOUR PUDDING.

Beat very light six eggs, separating the whites from the yolks; sift into a pan seven large spoonsful of wheat flour; on this pour some milk, just enough to make a smooth batter; then stir in the yolks of the eggs, and a very little salt; then the remainder of the milk, which must be in all a quart; a large spoonful of brandy stirred in; then add the whites beaten to a stiff froth; butter a baking dish, and pour in the batter. The lightness of this pudding depends on the whipping of the eggs. Bake it in rather a quick oven half an hour; send to table the instant it comes from the oven; serve with it "wine sauce."

A RICH WINE SAUCE.

Stir into a table-spoonful of sifted flour, one half pint of cold water; mix it perfectly smooth; put this into a very clean sauce-pan, and put it over the fire; let it simmer until it becomes a starch; then rub to a cream half a pound of good brown sugar, and a quarter of a pound of good butter; when it is well creamed stir it into the starch; then add a wine-glass of wine, and a table-spoonful of orange flower water; just as it is done grate in a little nutmeg; this is a very delightful sauce.

A DELICATE PUDDING.

Put into a clean saucepan one quart of new milk; when boiling stir in slowly one quarter of a pound of rice flour, one quarter of a pound of good brown sugar, and a large spoonful of butter; beat these well together; add some grated nutmeg, and a wine-glass of wine; stir these well; when cold beat three eggs, and stir them in; then pour it into a dish, and bake half an hour a light brown.

COTTAGE PUDDING.

Beat to a cream one cup of good brown sugar, and two large spoonsful and a half of good butter; when well creamed stir in one well whipped egg, a little grated nutmeg, and a large spoonful of orange flower water; sift into a pan one pint of flour, and stir in two tea-spoonsful of cream of tartar; dissolve in a cup of new milk a teaspoonful of best soda; mix the flour and eggs and spice together; then add the milk and soda; beat these well together; butter a baking dish and pour in the pudding; bake half an hour; serve with wine sauce. This makes a delightful cake, by adding two eggs, and when iced, is better than pound cake.

SWISS PUDDING.

Lay alternately in a baking dish slices of nice tart apples; on these sprinkle sugar and the grated oily rind of a lemon, and then crumbs of stale rusks which have been soaked in milk; then more slices of apples, sugar, and crumbs of rusks; cut very thin slices of butter and lay thickly on the top; over this sift thickly pulverized sugar; bake one hour, and send to table in the same dish.

HOMINY PUDDING.

Take from your hominy, when nearly done, a pint of the liquor; put into it while hot a lump of fresh butter, say a quarter of a pound, four eggs, and the juice of half a lemon with the rind grated into it; sweeten to your taste with powdered loaf sugar; bake in a rich paste.

WHORTLEBERRY PUDDING.

Sift one quart of corn meal into a pan, on this pour half a pint of boiling water, and half a tea-spoonful of salt; wash carefully one quart of whortleberries; drain them in the colander; stir them into the meal; then stir in as much good molasses as will make it a very stiff batter; mix these well; then add four table-spoonsful of sifted flour, and dissolve a tea-spoonful of best soda in half a cup of water; add this just as the pudding is put into the bag; have ready a pot of boiling water, and keep it boiling for five hours; tie the bag very closely and tight, as the fruit is juicy, and therefore it requires no space for swelling. Serve hot with wine sauce.

A DELICIOUS PLUM PUDDING.

Take half a pound of stoned raisins, half a pound of currants well washed and dried, four lemons grated and the juice, half a nutmeg grated, half a tea-spoonful of ground cinnamon, half a tea-spoonful of salt, one pound of bread crumbs, half a pound of brown sugar, seven eggs well beaten, three-fourths of a pound of finely chopped beef suet, one-fourth of a pound of thinly cut citron, two glasses of brandy, and two glasses of wine; break the eggs into a large pan; beat them very lightly; then add the spice, salt, lemon peel, and the fruit and bread crumbs; lastly the wine and brandy; put this into a floured bag; have ready a pot of boiling water, and boil four hours. Serve with a rich wine sauce.

SUPERIOR SAUCE FOR PLUM PUDDING.

Beat the yolks of six eggs with four spoonsful of sifted sugar and butter mixed together; have ready a pint of boiling cream to mix with your yolks; afterwards put it on the fire and stir it until it is of the consistency of sauce, then add to it a good wine-glass of brandy.

APPLE CORN MEAL PUDDING.

Pare and core twelve pippin apples; slice them very thinly; then stir into one quart of new milk, one quart of sifted corn meal; add a little salt; then the apples, four spoonsful of chopped suet, and a tea-cup of good molasses; mix these well together; put into a buttered dish, and bake four hours; serve hot, with wine sauce.

BAKED INDIAN PUDDING.

Put on to boil one quart of milk; as soon as it boils, stir in slowly sufficient meal to make a stiff batter, and a little salt; when cool sift in two large spoonsful of flour, and molasses to make it sweet, one tea-spoonful of ground white ginger, and half a grated nutmeg; beat these well together; then add four well beaten eggs, and half a pound of finely chopped beef suet; let this bake five hours in a moderately heated oven; serve hot, with nice wine sauce.

BOILED BATTER PUDDING.

Mix eight large spoonsful of sifted flour into some milk to a smooth paste; then add the remainder of the milk, which must be only a quart in all, including that mixed with the flour; beat very light six fresh eggs, separating the whites from the yolks; stir in first the yolks with the milk and flour, lastly the whites, then a little salt; stir all together well; pour this into the scalded and floured bag, observing the directions already given under the head of "Puddings;" boil this one hour and a half, taking care to tie the bag tightly; serve with wine sauce.

A NICE SUMMER SAUCE.

Beat to a cream four large spoonsful of good brown sugar, with two large spoonsful of good butter; add slowly a wine-glass of wine; beat this to a froth; add one table-spoonful of orange flower water; when quite white and light, set it upon the ice to harden; before sending it to table, grate a little nutmeg over it, and sprinkle a very little ground cinnamon; this is very nice with fritters, pancakes, and puddings.

A RICH WINE SAUCE.

Rub to a cream four large spoonsful of good brown sugar, and two large spoonsful of butter; stir it into a tea-cup of hot water; pour this into a very clean sauce pan, and set it on some coals; stir it steadily until it boils, then add either rose water or lemon juice to flavour it; then give it another quick boil, and add a wine-glass of wine and brandy mixed; if stirred properly a rich foam will be on the top; before sending to table, grate on the sauce a little nutmeg, after it is in the turreen. The reason why the stirring is necessary while cooking, is to prevent the butter becoming oily.

PANCAKES.

Sift into a pan a full half pint of flour; add slowly one pint ot new milk; stir this until quite smooth; then beat four eggs very light, separating the whites from the yolks; add first the yolks, then the whites, beaten to a stiff froth, and a little salt; then if too thick for running freely from the spoon, add a little more milk. Have ready a clean hot frying pan, with a small piece of butter and sweet lard mixed; just enough to grease it, no more; then pour in some of the batter; brown it nicely on one side; then with a broad bladed knife turn skilfully the other side and brown it; they must be brown and crisp; have ready a hot dish; roll each cake twice over on the dish, and lay them lengthwise, until the dish is full; they are very nice if properly prepared; serve hot, with the "summer sauce," made as directed.

GERMAN PUFFS.

Sift eight table-spoonful of flour into a pan, stir in one quart of new milk very slowly; when quite smooth, add the yolks of eight well beaten eggs; a little salt; and then add the eight whites, whipped to a stiff broth; pour into greased cups, and bake twenty minutes; serve hot, with wine sauce.

FRITTERS.

Put on to boil one pint of new milk; mix into a pint of sifted flour, as much new milk as will make it a stiff smooth paste, and add a little salt; then stir this paste slowly into the boiling milk, stirring well to prevent its scorching or being lumpy; remove it from the fire, and stir in a large lump of butter and the grated oily part of the rinds of two fresh lemons; beat this well to prevent the butter becoming oily; set it aside to cool; then beat very lightly four eggs; add the eggs when it is cool; much depends on these being well beaten. Have ready a clean frying pan; put it over a brisk, clear fire, and put into it two large spoonsful of fresh good lard; as soon as it becomes heated, drop in from a spoon the fritters, a spoonful for each one; the batter must be stiff enough just to drop from the spoon; brown one side first, then turn them and brown the other; have the colander hot by the fire, to lay the fritters in as they are cooked, to drain off all fat. Thus continue until all are done; when dished, sift over them pulverized sugar; arrange them on the dish neatly. If these directions are observed, fritters are not unwholesome; it is the miserable fatty, tough articles so called, which have brought fritters into disrepute.

FRITTERS, ANOTHER MODE.

Put a piece of butter the size of an egg into a pint of water; let it boil a few minutes, then thicken it very smoothly with a pint of sifted flour; let it remain on the fire for two or three minutes, stirring well all the time to prevent lumps or scorching; then set it aside to cool; beat six eggs separately to a stiff froth; when the paste is cool beat in the eggs very lightly; on the beating depends the lightness of the fritters; grate in half a nutmeg, and a little ground cinnamon; fry in boiling lard, make out the fritters the size of eggs, have ready a hot colander, drain off the fat as they are fried a nice brown, sift sugar over them, and serve hot, with wine sauce.

SPANISH FRITTERS.

Sift one quart of flour, mix into it as much milk as will make it rather a soft dough, beat up one egg and a little salt, stir these well together, add a large spoonful of yeast, set it to rise early in the morning; when quite light, mix in two large spoonsful of melted butter; then make it into balls the size of a walnut, and fry in boiling lard a nice brown; drain them in a hot colander as the others; serve hot, with wine sauce.

GERMAN FRITTERS.

Cut into nice slices about half an inch in thickness a stale loaf of bread; beat four eggs very light, add three large spoonsful of good brown sugar, a little grated nutmeg, a table-spoonful of orange flour water; and then pour in one quart of new milk; stir these well together; remove the crust from the sides of the bread, cut the slices in half, and lay them in a deep dish; on them pour the above prepared eggs, milk, &c.; let the slices absorb all the custard; then have ready a clean pan, grease it with butter; and when quite hot lay in carefully the slices of prepared bread, brown both sides a nice color; lay them on a hot dish, and sift over them ground cinnamon, and loaf sugar as for waffles; serve hot; this is a very nice dessert.

"SAVE ALL" PUDDING.

Always save carefully pieces of bread, they are useful for many purposes. Put any scraps of stale bread that may be in the "save-all jar" (for every good housekeeper has one) into a clean saucepan, say half a pound of scraps; on these pour one quart of new milk, set it in a warm place covered closely, and let them soak and soften gradually; when perfectly soft, press them through the colander; then add two large spoonsful of good brown sugar; beat these well together; then whip very lightly three eggs and stir in; then three spoonsful of well cleansed currants, some grated nutmeg, a little cinnamon, and one wine-glass of wine and brandy mixed; beat these all well together; butter a baking dish, and put in this compound; on the top just as it is put into the oven, strew two spoonsful of finely chopped beef suet; bake a nice brown three quarters of an hour. Serve hot.

GREEN CORN PUDDING.

Take two quarts of grated corn, one quarter of a pound of butter, one pint of milk, two eggs, and one table-spoonful of flour; salt to your taste; beat these well together. Bake it three quarters of an hour in a slow oven.

CHEESE CAKE.

Four eggs well beaten, stirred into two cups of boiling milk; then put your pan containing the milk and eggs on some coals or a stove; stir them until it curdles; then strain off the whey, and let the curd cool; grate six ounces of sponge cake, or any other light cake that is stale, and mix with the cold curd; cream half a pound of butter, and half a pound of sugar; add a wine-glass of brandy and wine mixed; spices and rose water; then mix all your ingredients together; add the rind and juice of one lemon, just before putting into the paste; have ready a nice puff paste; put in your mixture, and bake in a slow oven.

LEMON CHEESE CAKE.

Grate with care the oily rind of three fresh lemons; rub this with a quarter of a pound of loaf sugar pounded, until perfectly incorporated with the sugar; then add by degrees half a pound of good fresh butter; beat very light the yolks of six eggs, and add; mix these well together; then line a dish with puff paste and put in the above mixture. Bake three quarters of an hour; serve hot.

CHEAP PUDDING, AND GOOD.

Put on one quart of milk to boil; into this stir as much corn meal as will make rather a stiff batter; chop very finely half a pound of beef suet; wash very carefully one pint of dried peaches, and stir in; the meal must cool before the peaches and suet are added; stir in half a tea-spoonful of salt, a tea-spoonful of ground ginger, and a large cup of sifted wheat flour; beat these all well together; have ready the pudding cloth or bag as directed; put in the compound, tie it rather loosely allowing for swelling, and put it into a pot of boiling water. Boil four hours; serve hot with wine sauce.

ENGLISH PUDDING.

Grate four Naples biscuits, pour over them one pint of scalding cream, or rich new milk; cover it closely until cold; then add some grated nutmeg, the yolks of four well beaten eggs, two whites beaten to a froth, and two large spoonsful of powdered sugar; the grated rind of one lemon, and half a table-spoonful of sifted flour; mix these well together and put into a china bowl, tied closely with a cloth, and boil one hour; the water must boil when it is put in; serve hot, with rich wine sauce.

BAKED APPLE PUDDING.

Pare and core nine larged sized tart apples; stew them until quite soft; beat them whilst hot, with a quarter of a pound of good butter; sweeten to taste, grate half a nutmeg, pound or roll one quarter of a pound of water crackers, one wine-glass of wine and brandy mixed, one table-spoonful of rose water or the rind of a lemon grated; mix these well together; when cold add one pint of rich cream, and the yolks of five eggs when well beaten; have ready a nice puff paste; line the dishes and pour in the mixture; bake a light brown.

QUINCE PUDDING.

Take six quinces, pare them, cut them in quarters, and stew them in a little water with lemon peel; cover them and let them cook gently till soft, when mash, or rub them through a sieve; mix them with sugar till very sweet, season with mace and nutmeg; beat up four eggs and stir in with a pint of cream; bake it in paste.

POTATO PUDDING.

Take a pound and a half of well mashed potatoes; while they are warm put in three-quarters of a pound of butter; beat six eggs with three-quarters of a pound of sugar, rolled fine—mix all well together, and put in a glass of brandy; season with nutmeg, mace or essence of lemon, and bake in paste.

COCOANUT PUDDING.

Take three-quarters of a pound of grated cocoanut, with the brown skin taken off, half a pound of sugar, the same of butter, the whites of six eggs, beaten light, half a pint of cream, a glass of brandy, or rose-water, and a quarter of a pound of crackers pounded fine, beat them together and bake in paste. If you wish the pudding rich, take a pound of butter, the same quantity of cocoanut, of sugar and whites of eggs, omitting the crackers and cream. Season as above. This quantity will fill six dessert plates of large size.

COCOANUT PUDDING.

Cut with a pen-knife the rind off three cocoanuts; grate them fine, then add one-quarter of a pound of butter, three-fourths of a pound of sugar to every pound of cocoanut; let the butter and sugar be well incorporated first; then to each pound add the whites of nine eggs beat to a froth; six crackers rolled fine, or the same amount of dry bread wet with a wine glass of rose-water, (a wine-glass of wine is good but not needful,) and all the milk of the nuts; a little variation of the above is to use five eggs, putting in both yolks and whites; the three nuts makes one and a half pounds, or twelve small puddings.

COCOANUT CUSTARD.

One nut grated into one pint of milk and three eggs, sugar to taste, butter the size of a walnut; grate in the outside of a lemon, and add nutmeg.

CUSTARD PUDDING.

Beat together the yolks of five eggs; add one quart of milk; sweeten with white sugar to taste; flavor with French extract of vanilla and nutmeg; if baked in cups let there be cold water poured in a pan, and the cups placed in that for the oven, to prevent injuring the china; if in a basin, cut a little bread very thin, first spreading it with butter, and lay on the top.

DRIED APPLE PUDDINGS.

Stew one quart of dried apples well, sift them through a colander, and add one pound of butter beaten light with an equal weight of sugar; beat seven eggs light, and mix all together, flavoring to the taste; mace, nutmeg and rose-water make them excellent, or squeeze in the juice of four oranges or lemons; cream may be used in place of so much butter. These puddings are delicious, and may be made at mid-winter, when green apples cannot be obtained

APPLE PUDDINGS.

Three-quarters of a peck apples pared, cored and stewed soft; then run through a colander, and while yet hot put in a pound of butter, cut in thin slices, and stir it well to keep it from oiling; when quite cold beat ten eggs to a froth, and put in about a pound of sugar, with one nutmeg, grated; bake in crust.

FLEMISH PUDDING.

Prepared corn boiled as usual, and put in the mould to cool; when cold turn it out in the dish to serve; then beat up the white of an egg and powdered sugar, as for iceing; spread it over the flummery; bake a few minutes; eat with sweetened cream.

ADELAIDE'S PUDDING.

Pare and core six apples, fill up the cores with sugar and cinnamon; make a batter of one egg, patent flour, one teaspoonful of salt; pour round and bake. Serve hot, with sauce.

LEMON PUDDING.

One-fourth and one-eighth of a pound of butter, one-fourth and one-eighth of a pound of sugar, one lemon, one glass rose-water, and four eggs; bake in crust. This quantity makes two puddings.

A BIRD'S NEST PUDDING.

Pare and core some apples, enough to fill a deep dish; they should be ripe, and such as will cook easily. Make a custard of five eggs to a quart of milk, and sugar and nutmeg to taste; pour this over, and bake half an hour.

SODA CRACKER PUDDING.

Four soda crackers, soaked in three tea-cups of cold water, two lemons, and two tea-cups of sugar.

A YANKEE WAY

Five and a half crackers, and a quarter of a pound of butter; sweeten to taste; three lemons, and nutmeg.

ANOTHER.

Three soda crackers, one pint warm water—let them soak awhile; then three tablespoonsful of vinegar, and sugar the same. Make it between two crusts.

APPLE FRITTERS, OR BEIGNET DE POMME.

Sift one pound of flour into a pan, stir in as much new milk as will make it a stiff batter, and one large spoonful of good yeast and a little salt, set it to rise; when risen grate the rind of two lemons carefully, and two well beaten eggs; mix these well into the batter, then set it to rise again until wanted for dessert; then have ready about eight or nine tart apples, pared and sliced half an inch in thickness, then dip each slice of apple into this risen batter and drop them into boiling lard—of which there must be plenty in the pan; as they brown on one side, turn them and brown the other, and lay them in a hot colander to drain; as they are laid on the hot dish for table, sift over each layer ground cinnamon and loaf sugar. These are very nice.

FRITTERS WITH YEAST

Make a batter of one pint of milk and as much flour as will form it, salt and five tablespoonsful of yeast. Put this in a warm place three hours before dinner. Just before boiling them, beat up one egg and add. These fritters are lighter, absorb less fat, and are of course more wholesome than any others

COFFEE, CHOCOLATE, AND TEA.

COFFEE, CHOCOLATE AND TEA.

Of this berry the Mocha is the best esteemed, as much for its flavour, as fine aroma; the best of this kind comes from Oudet, a little province in "Arabia happy." Although the other qualities are, if rightly prepared, very fine; yet this will always hold the first rank. The first requisite in coffee is, to be of a good quality; and when carefully cleansed, to be roasted with the utmost care, as on the roasting the flavour depends. It should be done in a tightly closed cylinder, which should be constantly turned over a moderate heat while the parching is going on, and only roasted until the berries are a dark brown maroon, and the aromatic oil is developed; a small quantity should only be roasted at once, and kept in a tightly covered case; and ground not too finely, and only as required for use. The best method for extracting the aroma and strength is the French, which is to have a "biggin" proportioned in size to the family; scald out the biggin, then to each person allow a table-spoonful of ground coffee; when arranged in the strainer, pour on as much boiling water as will allow to each a cupful of the decoction; let it slowly filter, having either a spirit lamp beneath, or a heated place, until all is filtered through. It should be prepared just before using, then diluted either with boiled milk or cream. Prepared in this manner it is nutritious and agreeable.

Chocolate.

Ot this the best is brought from Caraccas, South America There are a variety of methods of preparing this beverage; so much use is made of it, that they say a Spaniard is reduced to his last misery when he cannot obtain his chocolate. The best or principle articles in the preparation of the chocolate, are the cocoa, sugar, and some aromatiques. The cocoa shells are very nutritious and palatable; they must be roasted with the same care as coffee, turned slowly during the operation, but constantly, and in a tightly covered cylinder. After being carefully roasted a deep brown, when cool it must be triturated smoothly in a mortar, as much as may be required; when reduced to a paste, and all the little husks removed, then pour over a spoonful of the paste a cup of boiling water, thus proportioned to the quantity required; then boil it for twenty minutes, stirring, but kept covered; then serve as coffee, diluting with boiling milk or cream, and sugar to the taste; this forms a very agreeable beverage. There is a very admirable machine which can be obtained to prepare the chocolate for use, and preserve the aroma. The house-furnishing establishments now keep them. A nice preparation of chocolate, is to grate half a cake of the best chocolate, and pour over it a pint of boiling water to dissolve the chocolate; then add a pint of fresh milk; let this all boil for five minutes, then beat up the yolks of two eggs very smoothly, and stir in; sweeten to the taste, and serve hot, with hot, dry toast.

ANOTHER METHOD FOR COCOA.

For invalids, is to boil a tea-cupful of the shells for an hour, being tightly covered, in a quart of water; the water must boil when poured on the cocoa shells; let it stand for several hours; then carefully remove with a spoon every particle of oil; then heat it, and add scalding milk and sugar, as for coffee. This can often be taken when other beverages cannot be retained on the stomach.

TEA.

This plant has become now as much in use in America, as in England and Holland, where it is a national beverage; but the best out of China is only to be obtained in St. Petersburgh, brought overland by caravans; the sea voyage is said by connoisseurs, to affect the fine flavour and odour. To make tea requires skill and experience. Scald the pot with boiling water; then put in a tea-spoonful of tea for each person; on this pour sufficient boiling water to allow a cup for each person; close the pot tightly, and let it stand for five minutes, to infuse well; then pour into each cup some hot water before pouring in the tea, to warm the cup. This is the method for Imperial tea. Souchong, or black tea, is prepared in the same manner, only that the infusion is made by allowing it to remain for twenty minutes, either over a spirit lamp, or in some hot place. It is most important that the water should boil at the moment of using for the tea.

FERMENTED BEVERAGES

AND

DOMESTIC WINES.

FERMENTED BEVERAGES, AND DOMESTIC WINES.

THE quality of fermented liquors depends first on the selection of the fruit, then on the cleanliness and purity of the casks or kegs employed; hot water should be used in cleaning them before putting in the fruit for preparation; to be effectual it is a very good plan to fill the cask half full of water, and then throw in red hot stones; when cool empty them out and rinse the cask well; and then care must be exercised in the fermenting, neither too much nor too little; experience is the best guide.

CIDER AS PREPARED IN NORMANDY.

The apples are gathered in September and October; mix the sweet and sour; throw all into a large vessel to ripen; then mash them quite soft; put the pulp into the press for crushing, adding a little water; when well pressed put the juice into a barrel well cleaned as above directed, wherein will be deposited all the particles contained in the juice; the fermentation is very slow, continuing two months sometimes; then draw it off very carefully into another cask or barrel, leave an opening for the escape of the gas; when settled draw off this carefully into very clean bottles, into each bottle put two large raisins, it is then fit for use and requires no clarifying; this boiled and reduced from a quart to a pint is very nice for sauces or puddings.

CURRANT WINE.

Pick the currants when fully ripe, strain the juice through a cloth, to one quart of juice put one gallon of water, with three pounds of brown sugar to each gallon dissolved in the water before using; the keg used must be new and clean; fill it up with this juice and sugar, thus proportioned, and when it ferments add fresh water every day until it is done fermenting, which will be in six or eight weeks; then rack it off; scald and clean out the keg; put the juice in again and cork up very tightly; in two months it will be fit for use, and of a very superior quality.

DAMSON PLUM WINE.

Cut the plums in half; to a gallon of the plums add one gallon of fresh water which has been rendered aromatic by cloves; this is done by putting two ounces of cloves into a bag and boiling in the water, and then removing the bag; to this proportion of water and fruit, add two pounds of brown sugar; let this ferment four or five days, then clarify with the whites of eggs or isinglass, then bottle up; in two weeks it is fit for use, and if rightly prepared is very palatable.

ELDER WINE.

Put to six gallons and a half of ripe elder berry juice, twenty-two pounds of brown sugar, and nineteen gallons of water; in this water before adding it, boil three ounces of ginger, four ounces of alspice and one ounce of cloves, let it boil until a fine aromatic flavor is imparted to the water; then strain it through a cloth, and add it to the juice; a small quantity of the water can be flavored, it is not necessary to boil the whole; when almost cold add half a pint of good brewer's yeast; let it ferment fourteen days in a clean cask, then bung it up closely; in six months bottle it, and in each bottle put five or six blanched bitter almonds; it is fit for use as soon as bottled, and is a wholesome beverage.

CHERRY WINE.

Take twenty-four pounds of the finest ripe cherries, the black English cherry is the best; remove all that are defective.

press and bruise out all the juice through a cloth; then take the skin and stones, pound them with a mallet, so as to crush the kernel and stones, then put all into the juice again; when this has been fermented twelve hours, strain it through a cloth of flannel and squeeze the bag well; pour this into a pan containing one pound of loaf sugar; when the sugar is entirely dissolved put the liquor into bottles, filling each within an inch of the cork; cork rather loosely for two days, then examine them and cork tightly; keep for three months in a cool place, or buried in sand in the cellar.

TO MAKE A DELICIOUS CHERRY WINE.

Wash and dry one-quarter of a peck of wild-cherries; put them into a demijohn that is perfectly clean; on this pour one gallon of the best cogniac brandy, and two pounds of crushed white sugar; shake this well, and in one week it is fit for use, and will keep for years; the brandy acts on the stones as well as the cherries, and imparts a fine flavor to it; it is a good tonic for invalids, and improves by age. The cherries must be fresh and good.

ANOTHER CURRANT WINE.

Put the currants into a large bowl; mash them with your hands; then strain them through a jelly bag; to each pint of juice add two pints of water; eight pounds of white sugar crushed will be sufficient for six pints of juice, and twelve pints of water; put all into a very clean demijohn, and in a place where it will not be moved; cover with a thin cloth while fermenting; when it has fermented well, then pour it off carefully, and either put it into very clean bottles or a demijohn, and cork tightly.

ORGEAT.

Pound very finely one pound of blanched sweet almonds and one ounce of bitter almonds in a mortar, with half a gill of orange-flower water, to prevent their oiling; then mix with them one pint of rose water, and one pint of spring water; rub them through a hair sieve till the almonds are quite dry, which will reduce the quantity to a quart, then have ready three pints of clarified sugar, which must boil until the watery particles are evaporated; put in the preparations; boil it two minutes, and when quite cold put it into small bottles closely corked; a table-spoonful will flavor most delicately; always shake the bottle before using; it is very nice for cakes.

PEACH CORDIAL.

In preserving there is generally more syrup than is required for the preserves; to every pint of syrup add half a pint of good brandy; stir this well together and bottle and cork tightly; this is very nice diluted with water for summer.

QUINCE CORDIAL.

Take the parings and cores of the quince when preserving, cover them with water, and boil one gallon down to half a gallon, and so proportion any quantity; when reduced in this way to a thick clear mucilage, strain carefully through a hair sieve; whilst hot, to one gallon of this mucilage add two pounds of crushed sugar; stir this well until dissolved; then add two quarts of best white brandy; pour this into very clear wine-bottles, and into each bottle put four or five blanched bitter almonds; shake each bottle well and cork tightly. In a week it is fit for use.

ANOTHER QUINCE CORDIAL.

Cut the specks from the quinces, grate and squeeze them through a cloth; to three pints of juice add one pint of fresh water and one pint of good brandy, and one pound and a half of white crushed sugar; one ounce of alspice, one ounce of peach kernels blanched; let this stand for three weeks, then strain off into very clean bottles.

ANOTHER, VERY FINE.

Grate and squeeze your quinces through a cloth; to two quarts of juice add one pint of French brandy, half a pound of loaf sugar, one ounce of peach kernels, one ounce of cloves and cinnamon mixed; put this into bottles, cork it well, and let it stand two months; then filter it through brown paper placed in a funnel, then wash your bottles very clean and pour it into them; it is then fit for use.

GINGER WINE.

Twenty gallons of water, twenty pounds of crushed sugar, three-quarters of a pound of the best race ginger pounded, the thinly cut rind of eighteen lemons; let these boil slowly one hour, the scum carefully removed; then pour into a very clean tub to cool; when cold add one quart of lemon juice, one gallon of the best French brandy, and half a pint of excellent and fresh yeast; put the whole when mixed into a very clean cask, stop it tightly and shake it well; in ten days it is ready for bottling, and ten days more quite fit for use.

CURRANT SHRUB.

Strip off the currants from the stem, put them in a large jar, and put the jar into a pot of boiling water until all the juice is extracted from them; strain them through a cloth; to three pints of juice add one pint of water, one pound and a half of crushed sugar, and one pint of brandy; put this into a cask, let it stand for two weeks, then bottle it up.

A GOOD CORDIAL.

To three quarts of good apple brandy add one quart of water, two pounds of crushed sugar, one ounce of cloves, and one ounce of cinnamon sticks; boil this briskly for ten minutes, tightly covered; let it stand until quite cool, then strain and bottle it, and it is fit for use; into each bottle put four or five bitter almonds, blanched.

BLACKBERRY CORDIAL

Two quarts of blackberry juice, one pound of loaf sugar, four grated nutmegs, half an ounce of ground cinnamon, quarter of an ounce of ground cloves, and quarter of an ounce of ground alspice; simmer these all together for thirty minutes in the sauce pan tightly covered to prevent evaporation; strain through a cloth, when cold, and then add one pint of the very best French brandy; bottle and cork tightly.

GINGER SYRUP.

Take ten pounds of refined loaf sugar and half a gallon of water, boil gently and skim it until quite clear, then add of tincture of ginger to the taste; while the syrup is hot, which takes off the alcoholic taste, bottle carefully.

TINCTURE OF GINGER.

Three quarters of a pound of the best race ginger steeped in two pints of pure alcohol three weeks, then stir it and bottle for use; the ginger is useful for cooking purposes, as much strength still remains after straining. Shreded green ginger makes the strongest tincture.

CHEAP CHAMPAIGN CIDER.

Clean well a keg in which any kind of liquor has been kept; fill it one-third full of any kind of tart apples; mash them with a mallet, then head up the keg, and fill it with cold water, and lay a piece of muslin over the bung-hole to exclude dust, but allow the gas generated to pass off; keep it in a cool place; in three weeks draw off the juice, and again fill the keg with cold water; pour that drawn off into very clean bottles, and into each bottle put two or three best quality raisins, cork tightly and keep the bottles in a cool place. This quantity of apples will thus afford a superior quality of home-made wine, at a very small expense.

When grapes are abundant, one-half tart apples and one-half ripe grapes is a great improvement. After the second filling the refuse apples make an excellent vinegar, by simply filling the keg with warm water, and setting it in the sun and occasionally stirring; then drain off at the expiration of two weeks.

GINGER BEER.

On three pounds of brown sugar, three tablespoonsful of best ground ginger, and two fresh lemons thinly sliced, pour two gallons of boiling water, and stir in two teaspoonsful of cream of tartar; mix all well together; when cool strain, and when quite cool add one pint of home-made or baker's yeast; then bottle, and in twenty-four hours it is fit for use.

CREAM NECTAR.

Put six pounds of crushed white sugar into a preserving kettle, on it pour two quarts of warm water and add four ounces of tartaric acid; stir well, keeping it in a hot place; when the sugar is dissolved by the heat and water (but do not let it boil), add the whites of four eggs beaten to a stiff froth, stir them well through; then remove the kettle from the fire, and when cool, add enough of essence of lemon to give it a pleasant flavor; then bottle and keep in a cool place. When required for use take two tablespoonsful of this syrup and then fill the tumbler two-thirds full of ice water, stir in a teaspoonful of subcarbonate of soda until it effervesces, and it will prove a most refreshing and delicious drink.

PICKLING AND CATSUPS.

Pickles have been properly termed the "sponges of vinegar;" the Eastern mode of pounding them is the best; we do not approve of their use; in no country are they indulged in to the same extent as in our own; and they are only vehicles for the introduction of vinegar and spices into the stomach, as the flavour of whatever is pickled is lost in the mixture of garlic, spice, &c., used. The best quality of wine or cider vinegar should be used, not the store compound sold under that name; vinegar must not be boiled, as the strength of both spices and vinegar is lost by evaporation. The pickles should be scalded in the brine until parboiled; this saves time and does away with the necessity for soaking six or eight days in brine; take them out of the brine and let them get cold, and cover them in unglazed earthen ware or glass with the prepared pickle here given. Bruise in a mortar half an ounce of black pepper corns, the same of alspice, the same of cloves, one large spoonful of grated horseradish, one tea-spoonful of mustard seed, one table-spoonful of chopped garlic, and one tea-spoonful of table salt; put these into an unglazed jar, on them pour three pints of the best wine or cider vinegar; close the jar tightly, so as to prevent all evaporation; set this by the side of a fire, to heat only, for three days; shake it frequently during that time. Put the pickles prepared by parboiling in the sieve to drain perfectly dry; then to enable them to imbibe thoroughly the pickle, as they are put into a jar run a "larding pin" through them; then lay them into jars, covering them with the above prepared spiced vinegar, which must be warm only, *not hot;* sprinkle in each jar before pouring on the vinegar a small tea-spoonful of finely pulverized alum, this keeps the pickles firm; cover the jars closely, and keep in a dry cool place; almost any kind of fruit or vegetable can be pickled; the best are peaches, cherries, and grapes; eggs are by some an esteemed pickle; they are hard boiled, and then the above pickle poured over them, they do not require any preparation in brine; and nearly the whole vegetable family can be prepared in this way.

WALNUTS.

Be careful to obtain them at the right season, before the shells begin to harden; make a strong brine of salt and cold water in the proportion of one quarter of a pound of coarse salt to one quart of water; let the walnuts soak in this for a week, or if desired to be sooner ready, put the brine in a kettle and perforate each walnut in two or three places with a larding pin; let the walnuts and brine gradually warm, and slowly simmer for five minutes; then take them out and lay on a sieve to drain; let them stand in the air until they turn black; then put them into glass jars, and pour over, covering them entirely with the prepared vinegar; the pickled walnuts improve with age. When all the walnuts are used, take that which is left in the jars, and simmer it, adding some fresh spices and a few pounded anchovies; let it simmer ten minutes, and stand until cold, tightly covered; then strain and bottle for use, it is a delightful catsup for fish or meats.

SWEET PICKLED PLUMS.

Take seven pounds pricked with the "cork" described for preserving; lay them into jars; then prepare the pickle; dissolve in a quart of best vinegar four pounds of good brown sugar, add twelve cloves, ten or twelve alspice, the same of whole pepper corns, and a little salt; let it gradually warm and slowly simmer, not boil; pour this on the plums scalding hot; let it remain on until cold, then pour it off the next day, and repeat it and pour it again on the plums, do this three or four days; then cork closely. Cherries are pickled in the same manner. It is best in spicing pickles, particularly fruits, to make several little thin muslin bags, and after the spices are mixed to sew them into the bags, and lay a bag on each jar before corking up; turn the jars occasionally upside down to allow the flavour to pass through.

SWEET PICKLED PEACHES.

Select firm "morris whites;" rub off the down with a coarse towel; stick the peaches well with a sticking cork; weigh them, and allow to one pound of fruit one pound of good brown sugar and one pint of best vinegar, half an ounce of cloves, one quarter of an ounce of mace; dissolve the sugar in the vinegar; put all cold into a stone jar, and set it in a vessel of boiling water; let it remain in the water on the fire until the peaches are soft; then cork up closely and keep in a dry place.

PEACH MANGOES.

Select large ripe open yellow peaches, but not too ripe; lay them in a strong brine for eight hours; take them out and drain them; remove the stones carefully; close the peach by tying it together and laying four hours more in the brine; then prepare a stuffing of two ounces of celery seeds, two of coriander seeds, two ounces of white mustard seed, two ounces of tumeric, two dozen very small onions chopped small, and one table-spoonful of horse-radish; bruise the coriander seed and the mustard seed in a mortar; then stuff the peaches and tie them; lay them in glass jars, and prepare a spiced vinegar, and when cold pour over the peaches; lay on the top of each jar before closing a small bag of tumeric; cork very closely; for a day or two turn the jars occasionally upside down; this stuffing will do a peck of peaches; they are very fine.

INDIA PICKLE.

To every gallon of vinegar put two ounces of ground tumeric, and half an ounce of the pure cayenne; cut the cabbage into pieces; then lay it in an earthen vessel, unglazed; strew a handful of salt over the cabbage; this must be renewed for three or four days; pour off the water which accumulates, before sprinkling on fresh salt; then spread the cabbage on a dish; set it either in the sun or before a fire until perfectly dry; then put the cabbage into a jar, and strew over each layer a tea-spoonful of grated horse-radish, the same of whole cloves, three heads of chopped garlic, a tea-spoonful of ground ginger, having ready the seasoned vinegar, which must be done by heating the vinegar and covering very tightly to prevent evaporation, and then pour the vinegar over hot; cork up and close tightly, pour off this after three days and heat again, and pour over hot. Beans or any kind of vegetable may be prepared in the same way.

ENGLISH OYSTER CATSUP.

Select fine fresh oysters; drain off the liquor; pound the oysters in a mortar; to a pint of these mashed or rubbed oysters, add a pint of white wine, one ounce of table-salt, one quarter of an ounce of mace, half an ounce of good cayenne pepper; mix these with the oysters and wine; let it simmer only for ten minutes, skim it well; then pour it into a sieve and rub through; when quite cold, bottle it and cork closely and seal; put it into small bottles; this is very fine for seasoning when oysters are not edible, and will keep for months.

MUSHROOM CATSUP.

Mushroom gravy approaches more the nature and flavour of meat than any vegetable production. In soups, and all meat sauces, it is the best flavouring. The usual method of preparing the catsup is such a combination of spices, &c., that the pleasant flavour of the mushroom is lost. Select full grown, fresh gathered mushrooms; be very careful that they are the right sort, for if not "there is death in the pot." Put a layer of the mushrooms at the bottom of a deep pan, then sprinkle on salt thickly; then the mushroom and salt on until all are in the pan; let them remain three hours, by which time the salt has penetrated the mushrooms; then mash them well with the hands, and cover over; let them stand thus for two days, stirring up each day well; then put them into a large stone jar; to each quart of mushrooms allow an ounce and a-half of black pepper corns, and half an ounce of whole alspice; close the jar tightly, and set it in a pot of hot water, and let it boil three hours regularly, then take out the jar, pour the juice clear from the settlings, through a hair sieve, without pressing, into a clean stew pan; let this juice gently simmer half an hour or three-quarters; skim it well whilst cooking, then pour it through a cloth, and add one table-spoonful of good brandy to each pint of catscup; and let it stand as before; then bottle it in half pint bottles, and closely cork it; dip each bottle into cement; keep it in a cool place, and it can be kept for years.

QUINTESSENCE OF MUSHROOM.

This is made by sprinkling a little salt over the fresh button mushrooms for three hours, then mash them; next day strain off the liquor; put it into a stew pan and boil it till it is reduced to one-half; this will not keep long, but can be made during the season; but mushrooms can be obtained throughout the season, by preparing a small, rich bed of guanoed earth, and sprinkling it thickly with the seeds.

TOMATOE CATSUP.

Take one gallon of ripe, fresh tomatoes; mash and simmer them in three quarts of water; boil it half down, strain this through a sieve; let it slowly drip; do not squeeze it; when all is drained, add one large spoonful of cloves, the same of mace, two large spoonsful of salt, one of whole black peppers, one tea-spoonful of best pure cayenne; let these simmer in the juice until it is reduced to one quart; then pour in half a pint of best wine vinegar; then pour the whole through a hair sieve; bottle in half pint bottles, and cork very tightly. This is an excellent catsup.

MUSHROOM CATSUP.

Sprinkle with salt one bushel of mushrooms freshly picked, let them remain three days, stirring daily; then put them into a stone jar tightly covered to prevent evaporation; set them in not too warm an oven for five hours, then strain them through a hair sieve. To every gallon of juice add one quart of mixed wines, one part red cooking wine, one of port wine, and one of brown sherry all mixed, making in all the required quart; salt to the taste; one ounce of blades of mace, one ounce of cloves, half an ounce of black pepper corns, one pod of garden pepper, two table-spoonsful of dry American mustard, one root of green ginger cut up, and the juice of three fresh lemons; let these simmer until reduced to one-third, then strain and put into half pint bottles tightly corked and sealed. This improves with age, and is a very superior catsup.

TO PICKLE WALNUTS.

Take the walnuts about midsummer, when a pin will go through them; then wipe them very tenderly, boil a pickle of salt and water strong enough to bear an egg, let it stand till cold, then pour it over the nuts, tie them down close so that no air can get to them; they must lay two weeks in salt and water, changing it twice in that time; from that let them stand in vinegar a month, then take a gallon of best vinegar, when it is nearly boiled put in an ounce of pepper and cloves, half an ounce of mace and nutmeg, four ounces ginger, cut the ginger and nutmeg in pieces, let it boil a little and stand till cold, close covered; take a pot that will hold them, so that a gallon of vinegar will cover them, and at the bottom put a large head of garlic, then place your nuts, strew as much mustard seed well beaten and sifted as will cover them, pour on your vinegar—it will take five quarts for one hundred nuts.

PEPPER SAUCE.

Take twenty-five peppers, without the seeds, cut them pretty fine, then take more than double the quantity of cabbage, cut like slaw, one root of horseradish grated, a handful of salt, rather more than a tablespoonful of mustard-seed, a tablespoonful of cloves, the same of allspice, ground; simmer a sufficient quantity of vinegar to cover it, and pour over it, mixing it well through.

PICOLLILLY.

Take of cut cucumbers, beans and cabbage each six quarts; of cut peppers and small onions three quarts each; horseradish one quart—green them with vinegar and water, then put them in strong vinegar, seasoned with mustard, mustard-seed and grôund cloves; add of celery and nasturtions each four quarts.

UNIVERSAL PICKLE.

To three quarts of vinegar half a pound of salt, an eighth of ginger, a half ounce of mace, one teaspoonful of cayenne pepper, one ounce mustard-seed; simmer these with the vinegar, and when cold put into a jar. You may put in whatever green fruit or vegetables you choose from time to time.

SPICED PEACHES.

Nine pounds peaches, four of sugar, one pint vinegar; boil peaches in water till tender; then put in vinegar and sugar, with a little whole alspice till done; pare and stone and halve the peaches first.

PICKLED TOMATOES.

One peck of ripe tomatoes, prick them with a fork several times, lay them in a jar, with a thick layer of fine salt, then a layer of tomatoes; let them lay eight days, take them out and soak them in cold water two days; one small bottle of mustard, cloves, alspice, and pepper, (whole) each half an ounce, a layer of tomatoes in the jar you intend keeping them in, and a layer of spices alternately, then vinegar enough to cover them.

TOMATO KETCHUP.

To a half bushel of tomatoes, after they are strained through a sieve, add a quarter of an ounce of ground cloves, a quarter of an ounce of ground mace, the same of ground ginger, half the quantity of cayenne pepper, and a small tea-cup of salt; the juice must boil two-thirds away, and then the above ingredients added, after which it must boil half an hour.

TO PICKLE GREEN TOMATOES.

Slice one peck of green tomatoes, take one gallon of vinegar, six tablespoonsful of whole cloves, four of alspice, two of salt, one of mace, and one of cayenne pepper; boil the vinegar and spices together ten minutes, put in the tomatoes, and let all boil together about a quarter of an hour; when cold put them in jars.

OYSTERS.

Take one hundred and fifty oysters, put them into a saucepan, and add salt to your taste, set it on hot coals, and allow the oysters to simmer till they are heated all through, but not to boil; then take out the oysters and put them into a stone jar, leaving the liquor in the saucepan; add to it a pint of clear strong vinegar, a large teaspoonful of blades of mace, three dozen whole cloves, and three dozen whole pepper corns. Let it come to a boil, and when the oysters are quite cold in the jar pour the liquor upon them.

SALTING, CURING, AND PICKLING

ALL KINDS OF

MEATS, HAMS, TONGUES, ETC.

SALTING MEAT.

This is a most important operation in the culinary preparations; the best pieces for corning are the ends of the rump, the thin end of the sirloin, and the edge bone; if alternate streaks of fat and lean are prepared, the pieces called the brisket and round are very good; the edge bone affords the lean meat; so much for beef. The choice pieces are the shoulder and hams for pork. A brine for beef is made strong enough to bear an egg, with alum salt, and a tea-spoonful of saltpetre to every ten pounds of beef; let it remain in nine days only; the best piece for chipping is the round; hang that up to dry but not to smoke; all the other pieces for boiling must have a little smoking to keep, and for the flavour, two hours for two or three days only in the smoke; if this is strictly followed, it will (the beef being of a good quality) be very fine; smoke to be made of hickory wood; then to be hung in a dry place for use.

Curing Hams.

Pack the hams and shoulders in a cask; a bushel of alum salt to the thousand weight of pork, a tea-spoonful of pounded saltpetre to every pint of salt; let this all be very accurately proportioned; then lay in the pork skin side down, then the salt and saltpetre; another layer of pork, then salt and saltpetre; so on until the cask is full; not a drop of water used with it, as it makes its own pickle: cover it up for six weeks, then hang up and smoke with hickory saw-dust or chips, for four or five days;

this is the experience of one celebrated in Delaware for the fine quality of his salt meats. Legs of good mutton are very nice salted and smoked in the same manner; and beef's liver is very nice also; then frizzled for tea like beef.

ANOTHER FOR CURING HAMS.

To twelve hams of twelve pounds each put three and a half pounds of fine salt, two pounds of good brown sugar, one pound of saltpetre, each piece to be well rubbed with the mixture and packed down in a barrel; at the expiration of a week cover them with pickle made of coarse salt strong enough to bear an egg; if the hams are large it might be well enough to add a little more fine salt to the mixture.

A RECEIPT FOR SALT SPICED HAMS.

This is for six hams only, and is very excellent, and for legs of mutton also: take quarter of a pound of pounded saltpetre, three quarts of fine dairy salt, one pound and a half of good brown sugar, six ounces pounded cloves, six ounces best ground cayenne pepper; mix these well together, divide it into six equal parts accurately, then rub each ham well with the mixture of its own portion, lay them in a firkin or salting tub, the skin side down, closely packed, and any mixture not used sprinkled over; let them remain thus for three days, then change their position by placing the top ones below and those beneath above; do this every third day for six weeks, and on each removal pour over the pickle they have made themselves; if the hams have absorbed the salt, &c., sprinkle some more salt each time they are changed; at the end of six weeks take them out and smoke them with hickory chips or saw dust, but be careful in removing them not to remove any part of the mixture which covers them; the hock should be well rubbed with it.

TONGUES SPICED AND SMOKED.

They are prepared exactly as hams, and are very fine.

TO MAKE MUTTON HAMS.

Take four mutton hams or legs of mutton, good, tender, and rather fat meat, and mix for them a quart of salt, a quarter of a pound of coarse brown sugar, and one ounce of saltpetre; mix these well together, and rub the hams with the mixture for a considerable time; then put them into a tub or tray, rub them with the brine they yield every other day for twelve days; then wipe them carefully, and hang in the smoke house the thick end upwards.

TO PREVENT INSECTS OR WORMS FROM GETTING INTO HAMS OR SHOULDERS.

Take two bottles of cayenne, the best quality, in all about a quarter of a pound to about one thousand weight of the pork, and mix in with the salt and saltpetre, but rubbed freely in before packing; if properly looked after and kept in a dry place, there is no danger of insects; if the weather becomes sultry and damp during the summer, a very little smoke occasionally will prevent any bad consequences. When the hams are hung up, if any apprehension is felt about insects, make a thin paste of one pound of wheat flour and three quarts of water; when cold, add two pounds of good black pepper, and a quarter of a pound of cayenne; with this cover the hams well and no insect will ever touch them.

TO CURE BEEF AND BEEF TONGUES.

To four gallons of water, add eight pounds of rock-salt (Turk's Island), two ounces saltpetre, and one pint of molasses; dissolve them well in water, cold or boiling, as choice may dictate; if the latter, when cold pour it over the meat, which must be kept down with a weight, though not too heavy. Drying pieces to remain in only ten days. This same receipt will apply equally to hams, but they must not be cured together; if of the weight of ten to twelve pounds, keep them in four weeks, larger, five or six weeks. in proportion.

ANOTHER TO CURE BEEF AND TONGUES.

To one hundred pounds of beef, take six gallons of water, six pounds of salt, four ounces of saltpetre, and one pound and a quarter of brown sugar; the beef to remain in eleven days, then hang to dry.

FOR CURING HAMS AND BEEF.

Take as much water as will cover your beef, add clean salt till it will bear an egg, so that the egg will show above the pickle as large as a shilling, half ounce saltpetre to a gallon, and molasses enough to make it the color of good molasses and water, or cider color; let the beef lay in ten days, and then hang to drain in a cool place.

For hams, make the same as for beef, except saltpetre, of which add a tablespoonful for a large ham. Do not pack them too tight, keep them well covered with pickle, and remove all scum. They should lay in pickle about six weeks. Take them out, and hang them up to dry. When dry outside, commence smoking; a light mahogany color is best, and bag before the flies come. Hickory or apple tree chips are best for smoking.

The above are superior to the mode of dry salting and rubbing, as practised by some, also less trouble, and making a more juicy and highly flavored ham.

A PICKLE.

Eight gallons of water to twelve pounds of coarse salt, one pound of sugar, two ounces saltpetre; boil and skim, cool and put over the meat. Beef will be fit for use in ten days; hams, one month. Pork pickle may be boiled again and used Keep a potato in it to test the strength.

CURING HAMS.

Receipt by which the hams were cured, which took the first premium of the Maryland Agricultural Society. To each green ham of eighteen pounds, one dessertspoonful of saltpetre and a quarter pound of brown sugar applied to the fleshy side of the ham, and about the hock: cover the fleshy side with fine salt half an inch thick, and pack away in tubs; to remain from three to six weeks according to size. Before smoking, rub off any salt that may remain on the ham, and cover well with ground black pepper, particularly about the bone and hock. Hang up and drain for two weeks. Smoke with green wood, eight weeks, or until the rind is a light chestnut color. Pepper prevents the fly. No need of bagging these hams.

BRANDIED FRUITS.

THIS requires care and experience, first, in the selection of the fruits, then in the preparation. The fruit must be just matured, free from defects, and wiped with care; and if having any down, that must be removed by immersing in saleratus water, but not allowed to remain in the ley sufficiently long to injure the flavour of the fruits, or become soft, after which each one must be well pierced to the very stone with a sharp needle to prevent the fruit shrivelling; after simmering in the ley only five minutes, they must be put into a pan of clear, cold water, then laid into a large vessel of boiling water, ample room given for each one to be well heated and acted on by the boiling water; the heat of the fire then reduced to let them gradually cool in the water; let them remain for two hours quietly in this water, then place the vessel again on the fire, and only come to a boil; then take the fruit out with great care separately, and lay them in cold water. This second boiling is done to restore the colour, and for thin skinned fruits a small piece of alum must be added, while this second boiling is going on. In this second boiling the water must boil quickly, if that is not attended to the flavour of the fruit is lost, and be careful in putting the fruit into cold water; the fruit must then be laid on a hair sieve to drain perfectly dry; then make a rich syrup of white, broken loaf sugar, the drained fruit dropped into this syrup whilst it is boiling; let the fruit remain in until it becomes soft to the touch, which is easily ascertained by removing one from the syrup. When all are done in the syrup, beat up the whites of two fresh eggs in a little cold water, and stir this into the syrup to clarify it; skim it with care, and when the watery particles are all evaporated, and it is quite clear, pour the syrup in a boiling state over the fruit, (having previously laid them carefully in a deep pan or some vessel;) cover them entirely with the syrup; let it remain on them for twenty-four hours, then remove with care, and put them into good sized jars, the opening not too large for sealing up with corks; then pour your syrup again into the kettle, and boil it up once or twice to evaporate all watery particles left by the fruit. When the syrup becomes quite cold, to one half-pint of the syrup, add half a pint of the best alcohol (obtained from a reliable importer), for on the quality of the alcohol depends the keeping of the fruit; pour this thus proportioned over the fruit, quite covering it; then cork very tightly, being careful to lay a piece of muslin or linen between the cork and the fruit; then dip the jars into the prepared cement to exclude the air; thus prepared, fruit will keep for years. This is the very best French method of brandying fruit, in which they certainly excel.

FRENCH WAY OF BRANDYING PEACHES.

Three-quarters of a peck of peaches, six pounds of loaf sugar, and one quart of white brandy; this is the proportion to be used. The "morris white" peach is the best. Boil your peaches in a strong pearlash water quickly for ten minutes, then rub off the skin with a coarse towel; throw them as the skin is removed into cold water, this preserves their colour and hardens them; then lay them on a dish to drain, and cover them very closely or the air will darken them; take half of the sugar and make a syrup, in this boil the peaches until tender, then take them out carefully to drain, and add the remainder of the sugar to the syrup; make a very clear syrup, skim it carefully, and when quite clear, pour it into a pan, then add the brandy; cover it closely until quite cold; put the peaches into glass jars, and pour over them until covered, the cold syrup and brandy having been well mixed, cork the jars tightly, and seal them; keep them in a dry and cool place.

BRANDIED CHERRIES.

Select large ripe red cherries, let the stems remain on; make a small hole with a large needle at the end opposite the stem; put them into cold water, then drain them, and put them into clean jars; pour over them a rich syrup of boiling sugar; leave them one day in this; drain off this entirely, and boil it again, and add to it a proportion of one pint of syrup to a quart of the best white brandy; then pour this over the fruit, on the top of each jar put a thin muslin bag containing quarter of an ounce of cloves, half an ounce of coriander seed, half an ounce of anise seed; this imparts to the syrup a pleasant aromatic flavour; cork up tightly and expose them to the sun at least a month; then remove the spice bags, cork again tightly, and shake the jar so as to impart to all the syrup the aromatic flavour. In taking out the cherries for use, be careful to cork the mouth of the jars tightly to exclude the air.

COVERING FOR JARS.

For Jellies or preserves, a nice way is after laying on the brandied paper next to the jelly, to cut soft nice paper an inch and a half larger round than the jar, then coat the under side with the white of an egg and whilst moist put it on, pressing down the edges well, which will adhere tightly better than paste, and excludes insects as well as air.

PRESERVING, &c.

An iron kettle lined with porcelain is the best for preserving; the most important thing after the fruit is properly selected and prepared, is to make a rich, clear syrup; this must be well clarified, if brown sugar is used. Preserves require very careful and slow cooking, as the least scorch spoils the flavour; and in fast boiling, the sugar does not penetrate so well as in moderate cooking; too much cooking darkens the fruit, and renders some kind of fruits very hard; a preserving spoon with a drainer is indispensable for preserving, and is easily obtained at a small expense; an apple corer is another important article; a gimlet with a long screw of about half an inch in circumference, and two or three inches long, is a great convenience in preparing many kinds of fruits for preserving, as it removes the cores at the blossom end of the fruit, without removing the stem; a nice sound cork stuck full of large sized needles, is very useful for pricking the fruit, which has the tender skin on. Glass jars are preferable for preserves, as they can be examined from time to time, and the moment a tendency to fermentation is shown the fruit can be attended to; this must be done by first removing all the scum which has risen on the top, and then set the jars into a pot of lukewarm water; if hot, it will break the jars; let the water gradually heat; let the jars remain in the hot water one hour, then remove the pot and let the jars cool in the water; then put on a fresh piece of cotton or linen, and cork tightly. They must be kept in a cool, dry place, as dampness acts injuriously on preserves. If the preserves are in stone jars, they can be set in a moderately heated oven, and kept in for two hours; then put on fresh coverings and cork tightly. The finely pulverized sifted sugar from some cause in the preparation does not answer for either preserves or jellies; the only kind to be used, is the loaf sugar of the best quality; there is economy in using it.

To Clarify Sugar.

Break up two pounds of loaf sugar; put it into a porcelain saucepan; pour on one pint of cold fresh water, when this is perfectly dissolved set the saucepan on a moderate heat; beat the white of one egg, and before the syrup becomes hot stir in the egg well through; watch it very carefully, and when it begins to boil remove the scum as it rises; continue to boil it until no more scum rises; then remove it, and either bottle it for future use, or use it at once for preserving; this is the basis of all syrup; it can be increased to any quantity, only preserving the above proportions in preparing it; this will keep for months in a cool place.

Curaçoa.

To one pint of the strongest rectified spirits of wine or pure alcohol, add two drachms and a half of the sweet "oil of orange peel," obtained at the druggists; shake these well together; then add one pint of the above clarified syrup; shake these well together; this is an admirable liqeur and flavors cake pleasantly.

Orange Syrup.

Select ripe and thin skinned fruit; squeeze the juice of the fruit through a sieve; to every pint of juice add one pound and a half of loaf sugar; simmer this very slowly; remove the scum which rises; continue to do so, as long as any is on the surface; then let it become cool; then bottle it off; cork very tightly; two table-spoonsful of this will flavor sauce for puddings delightfully, and is very nice to flavor custards; fresh lemons can be prepared in the same way, observing the same proportions.

CEMENT FOR JARS.

One third of yellow bees-wax, and two-thirds of finely pounded rosin; put them together into a clean saucepan, and set it near the fire to melt slowly; when all is melted remove it from the fire, and stir in finely powdered red brick dust until it becomes the consistency of sealing wax; then dip the corked jars in twice.

THE COMMON PURPLE DAMSON.

Select those which are just ripe, but not soft; wash them and drain perfectly dry; then stick them well to prevent bursting; put a layer of the plums in a stone jar; then a thick layer of good brown sugar in the proportion of three quarters of a pound of sugar to a pound of plums; alternately layers of sugar and plums until the jar is full; then cover with a cloth and set the jars into a moderately heated oven; put no water in, they will make their own syrup; let the jars remain in the oven six hours; examine them occasionally to see that the heat is not too great, if it is they will become dry; then cork tightly; they are nice for tarts, and will keep well; peaches cooked in the same way are very nice; they must be pared, however, before putting into the jars.

PRESERVED PEARS.

Select sound medium sized preserving pears; pare and halve them, take out the core; or if they are done whole, remove the core with a corer; lay the pears into a saucepan for preserving; cover them with clean cold water with half a pound of green ginger in the water; let them simmer slowly until quite soft; then drain them on a sieve; weigh them and allow as much sugar as they weigh, their equal weight; then pare thinly the oily rind of three fresh lemons, and put into the syrup, also the juice, and very little water; when it boils lay in the pears, and let them cook slowly for twenty minutes; then lay the pears on a dish, and return the syrup to the fire; let all the watery particles evaporate; when the pears are cold put them into the jars, and when the syrup is quite cold pour it over the pears, and let the lemon peel remain in; cork tightly.

PRESERVED PEACHES.

Select the free-stone yellow peach, not too ripe; pare and halve them; weigh them, take their weight in sugar; make a strong ginger tea by putting good ground race ginger in a bag, and boiling it in a pint of water, until the water becomes strongly flavoured; then pour off this water and strain it into the loaf sugar; that will be all the water required; when the syrup is melted lay in the peaches, let them slowly warm, and then simmer until they are quite clear; then take them out and lay in a dish and pour over them some good brandy; return the syrup to the fire and let it simmer fast for twenty minutes; when the peaches become cold drain them, and put them carefully into glass jars, free from the syrup in the dish; when the syrup is quite cold pour it over the peaches; quite fill the jar; cork tightly, and seal.

CRAB APPLES.

Select those free from defects; pour over them boiling water which removes the skin; then core them with a strong goose quill; weigh them, and take their weight in loaf sugar; lay the apples into a preserving kettle; cover them with water; let them slowly simmer until soft; then drain them well on a sieve, and then make a syrup, when it is dissolved and hot, lay in the apples and let them slowly simmer fifteen minutes; it is a great improvement to have nicely scraped green ginger boiled in the syrup, it imparts a fine flavour to the syrup; when the apples look clear, lay them on dishes to cool, and when cold place in the jars; return the syrup to the fire after the apples are taken out, and let it simmer for ten or fifteen minutes; when cold pour it over the apples; cork tightly

TOMATOES TO KEEP FOR COOKING.

Select good ripe tomatoes; scald and skin them; then chop them but not very small; put them into strong pint porter bottles; do not fill up the bottles to the cork with the fruit, or the bottles will burst; put the bottles thus filled and corked into a large boiler of lukewarm (not more) water; let it gradually heat, and be kept boiling seven hours; the boiler must then be removed from the fire, and the bottles allowed to cool in the water; then dip each bottle corked tightly into the cement made as directed; keep them in a cool, airy place.

PRESERVED GREEN ROSE PEPPERS.

Select the green rose pepper, as many as required; cut out with a sharp knife all the seeds; make a strong brine; lay them in this for six days, until they become yellow; then put them in clean cold water for four days; change the water daily to soak out the salt; then place them in a preserving kettle, with alternate layers of green cabbage leaves and peppers; place the kettle containing them over a very moderate heat; let them remain until quite green, then remove them from the kettle and make a strong ginger water, and let them remain in this water four days; then make a syrup as directed of loaf sugar; drain the peppers well and put them in a deep dish or pan, and pour over the warm syrup; let them remain in the pan for two hours; then pour off all this syrup and again heat it, and pour it warm over the peppers; let them lay in the syrup all night; in the morning pour off the syrup and add to it one pound and a half of loaf sugar, to every pound of peppers; shave very thinly the oily part of the rind of four fresh lemons, according to the number of peppers, just to flavor the syrup; boil the rind in the syrup; put the peppers into glass jars; and pour the syrup over them warm; fill up the jar well with the syrup; then lay on a piece of linen and cork lightly, and dip the corks in the cement: in a month they are fit for use; and if this direction is strictly observed they are very delicious.

QUINCES.

They may be prepared if of a small size whole, or in quarters if large; pair and core them, and lay them as they are pared into cold water to prevent their becoming dark; when all are pared and cored, put the cores and parings into a preserving kettle and cover them with cold water; let them simmer four hours, keeping the quinces in the cold water during the time; then strain off the juice from the parings and cores, and into it put the quinces to cook; let the quinces simmer in it until they are perfectly tender, then remove them carefully and lay in a sieve to drain, and make the syrup as directed; when the syrup boils lay in the quinces, and let them cook slowly fifteen minutes and no more, or they will become hard and dark; then take them out of the syrup and lay them on dishes to cool; return the syrup to the fire and evaporate all the watery particles by a smart boil for ten minutes; when the quinces are quite cool put them into small sized glass jars, as when large jars are used the frequent openings to take out preserves injure the fruit; when the syrup is quite cold pour it on the quinces and fill the jars well up; cover with a cloth and cork up tightly; keep them in a cool dry place; then take the juice in which the fruit was cooked and to every pint of juice add one pound of the best brown sugar; let it simmer slowly for thirty minutes and it will become a nice jelly, and is delightful with blanc-mange.

DAMSONS.

Select full-grown ripe but not soft damsons, free from defects· stick each one well; then make a syrup as directed, and put in your fruit; let them only simmer very slowly for one hour; then take them out and lay them on dishes to cool, whilst they are on the dishes pour over them good brandy; this tends to keep them from fermenting; return the syrup to the fire and let it simmer ten minutes; when the fruit is perfectly cold take them carefully from the dishes and place them in small sized jars; when the syrup is quite cold pour it over the fruit, cork tightly, and keep them in a cool dry place.

To Preserve Tomatoes.

Pick off the stems from green tomatoes and weigh them, make a strong tea of green ginger, simmer them slowly in the tea for two hours, and then take them out and spread on dishes; make a syrup, allowing one pound of sugar to one pound of tomatoes; take the pieces of ginger that were in the tea, and put them in the syrup, put in the tomatoes, and let them boil until quite clear; when sufficiently cooked, lay them on dishes to cool; boil the syrup some time longer, leaving enough to cover the tomatoes when poured over them; put the ginger away with the tomatoes.

Preserved Citron.

Take some fine citron melons; pare, core and cut them into long slices; then weigh them; and to every six pounds of melon allow six pounds of the best loaf sugar, and the juice and yellow rind pared off very thin of four large fresh lemons; also a half pound of race ginger. Put the slices of melon into a preserving kettle; cover them with a strong alum-water, and boil them half an hour, or longer, if they do not look quite clear; then drain them, lay them in a broad vessel of cold water, cover them, and let them stand all night; in the morning tie the race-ginger in a thin muslin cloth, and boil it in three pints of clear pump or spring water till the water is highly flavored; then take out the bag of ginger; having broken up the sugar, put it into a clean preserving kettle, and pour the ginger-water over it; when the sugar has all melted, set it over the fire, put in the yellow peel of the lemons, and boil and skim it till no more scum rises; then remove the lemon-peels, put in the sliced citrons, and the juice of the lemons, and boil them in the syrup till the slices are all quite transparent, but not till they break: when done, put the citrons and syrup into a large tureen, set it in a dry, cool, dark place, and leave it uncovered for two or three days till all the watery particles have exhaled; afterwards put the slices carefully into wide-mouthed glass jars, and gently pour in the syrup

Lay inside of each jar upon the surface of the syrup a double white tissue-paper cut exactly to fit, and then close the lids of the jars; this will be found a delicious sweetmeat, equal to any brought from the West Indies, and is well worth doing.

TO PRESERVE PINE APPLES.

Take one pound of sugar to one pound of fruit; make a syrup as directed; slice the apples in it, letting them stand about twenty minutes, then boil twenty minutes, and boil the syrup fifteen minutes after taking out the apples; lay the apples on a dish and let them stand one night before adding the syrup; the thin syrup which comes from the apples in the dish should not be added, as this would cause them to ferment.

TO PRESERVE PINE APPLES WITHOUT COOKING.

Take one pound of sugar, to one pound of fruit, putting into small sized glass jars a layer of fruit and of sugar alternately; to each jar add about half a tumbler of the best white brandy, varying the quantity according to the size of the jar; these must be corked and sealed to make them air tight, and it is a good plan to turn the jars bottom up occasionally for a few days after they are first put up.

TO PRESERVE GAGES GREEN.

Lay in the bottom of a saucepan a thick layer of grape leaves well washed, on these place a layer of gages, each having been pricked with needles to prevent their bursting; then another layer of leaves; again the gages; so on until all the fruit is in; then cover them with spring or soft cold water; place them in a situation to heat but not to cook; keep them covered, let them remain for six hours; then take them out very carefully, they will be yellow, and lay fresh grape leaves alternately with the gages to green them, covered with the same water in which they were yellowed; then keep them in a warm place for four hours;

they must not be allowed to boil; take them out, and make a very clear syrup of one pound of loaf sugar to every pound of gages; lay the fruit in the syrup and cook slowly ten minutes; then lay them on dishes to cool and drain; boil up the syrup ten minutes; put the fruit in glass jars, and pour the syrup on cold; fill the jars up well, cork very tightly, and keep them in a cool dry place.

PRESERVING PEACHES.

To twelve pounds of peaches take six pounds of clean brown sugar, and one pint of the best cider vinegar; simmer the sugar and vinegar together, which will make a clear syrup; pour boiling water upon the peaches, and remove them in two minutes from the water, and wipe them dry without breaking the skin; put them into the syrup and boil gently till the fruit is cooked to the stone. Keep the preserves in jars, which must be kept closely covered and in a cool place; they should be inspected occasionally, and if white mould appears upon the surface of the syrup, it must be carefully skimmed off, and the syrup scalded and returned to the peaches; this is the most economical, and to our taste, the very best preserve we know of.

TO CANDY ANY KIND OF FRUIT.

When cooked in the syrup, lay them in a sieve to drain, a single layer at a time; dip them very quickly into hot water to remove any syrup which may adhere to them; then drain them and lay them on a cloth before the fire to dry; when all the fruit is thus dried, sift thickly over finely pounded loaf sugar while the fruit is warm, then lay the fruit on dishes in a moderately heated oven; turn them and drain all moisture from them; the fruit must not become cold until perfectly dry; if done properly they present a beautiful appearance.

FOR PRESERVING STRAWBERRIES WHOLE.

Pick off the stems carefully; the berries must be the large scarlet kind; to every quart of the stemmed fruit add one quart of finely powdered loaf sugar; sprinkle the sugar through them, let them stand fifteen minutes, then put them in the same vessel over a very slow fire, until the syrup begins to form; then put them over a very hot fire, and let them boil quickly for fifteen minutes, being careful to remove all scum as it rises; then have ready stone jars, and put them boiling hot into the jars; fill them well up; have ready well fitting corks, and place on the side next to the preserves, a piece of linen, then seal up tightly. Put the jars in a box, and fill it with sand, and keep it in the cellar. These if prepared as directed are finely flavoured.

APPLES JELLIED.

Pare and core one dozen sound tart apples; lay them in cold water to prevent their becoming dark; put the parings and cores into a clean saucepan, on them pour one quart of cold water; slice without paring eight or nine tart apples, and add to these parings and cores; let them all simmer very slowly fully three-quarters of an hour; then slice three fresh lemons, and put in with the apple parings; then strain this all through a hair sieve; add one pound of crushed sugar; put the whole apples into a saucepan and on them pour this apple syrup; cover tightly and let them very slowly simmer until the apples are soft; then take them out and lay in a shallow dish; let the syrup simmer twenty minutes uncovered; then pour it over the apples to cool.

A DELICIOUS WAY OF PRESERVING CHERRIES.

The bright red morello is the best, wash the cherries but keep on the stems; drain them in a colander; weigh them, and to one pound of cherries, allow three quarters of a pound of the best brown sugar; put them into wide mouthed bottles; cork them lightly; lay the bottles into a kettle of cold water; place straw between the bottles to keep them from striking; then set the kettle containing the bottles in a hot place, and let it slowly heat, and boil for three hours; renewing the water as it evaporates; then let the bottles cool a little, and cement the corks closely; keep them in a cool dry place.

SYRUP OF ALMONDS.

Bleach one pound of sweet and four ounces of bitter almonds; then rub them to a paste in a mortar, adding one pint of orange flower water, and one pound of loaf sugar while triturating; then dissolve five pounds of loaf sugar moistened with one quart of water; heat it very slowly, and skim with care; when clear, stir in the almond paste, and let it simmer slowly ten minutes, stirring frequently; then strain the syrup and almonds through a fine sieve; bottle the syrup and cork tightly; keep in a cool place. This is very fine, either as a beverage mixed with ice water, or to flavor ice creams. It may be reduced to one-half the quantity, observing the right proportions.

APPLES.

Apples should be preserved in November, and they will keep till June. Take firm pippins, pare them and take out the cores, leaving them whole; or after you have cored them, cut them across in two pieces, they will then be in rings; put them in cold water as fast as they are pared, to keep them from turning dark; make a syrup of a pound of loaf sugar, and half a pint of water to each pound of apples; wipe the apples, and put in as many as will go in, without one laying on another; let them boil swiftly till they look clear, then take them up carefully on dishes, and put in some more; when all are done, if the syrup should seem too thin, boil it up after the apples are taken out; cut the peel of several lemons in thin rings, boil them in a little water till they are soft, and throw them in the syrup after the apples are taken out; put the syrup in a bowl, and set all away till the next day, when put the apples in glass jars or large bowls, spread the lemon peel about them, and put the syrup on the top; paste several thicknesses of paper over, and set them in a dry cool closet.

If you only want the apples to keep a few weeks, they may be done with half a pound of sugar to a pound of apples, and will look and taste quite as well.

LIMES.

Take green limes and put them into salt and water, strong enough to bear an egg, for six weeks; at the end of six weeks make an incision in each one of them the length of the lime, take out all the seeds, and put them into cold water twenty-four hours, changing the water several times; then boil them in soda water till tender enough to put a straw through; say one tea-spoonful to six quarts of water. Put them again in cold water for twenty-four hours, changing the water several times. To each pound of limes, two pounds and a half of crushed sugar, and three pints of water. Boil syrup fifteen minutes, then put in limes; boil them slowly for fifteen minutes. They are then clear. Let the syrup boil fifteen minutes more, and they are all done. One hundred limes make about two pounds weight. These preserves are delicious.

TOMATO FIGS.

Take six pounds of sugar to one peck (or sixteen pounds) of ripe tomatoes—the pear-shaped look best; put them over the fire (*without peeling*) in your preserving kettle, their own juice being sufficient without the addition of water; boil them until the sugar penetrates and they are clarified. They are then taken out, spread on dishes, flattened and dried in the sun, or in a brick-oven after the bread is taken out. A small quantity of the syrup should be occasionally sprinkled over them whilst drying; after which, pack them down in jars, sprinkling each layer with powdered sugar. The syrup is afterwards concentrated and bottled for use. They retain surprisingly their flavor, which is agreeable and somewhat similar to the best figs. Ordinary brown sugar may be used, a large proportion of which is retained in syrup.

CONSERVED PEACHES.

Two pounds of sugar to six pounds of fruit; the syrup should be made of three-fourths of the sugar only, into which drop the halved peaches till clear; take them from the syrup, and spread on dishes to dry in a cool oven or the sun. Have the remainder of the sugar powdered, and strew part of it over them, changing the fruit from time to time; pour off the liquor as it oozes out, get all the sugar on by degrees, and when dry, put away in boxes.

PRESERVED PINE APPLES.

Take pound for pound, cook the slices in water fifteen minutes, a few at a time; then make the syrup with this water and cook the slices fifteen minutes in it. If the syrup is not slightly thick, boil it longer.

PRESERVED PEACHES.

To one pound of peaches half a pound of sugar; cook them five minutes; the syrup some time longer. Hermetically seal these, by inserting a piece of bladder under the cork, and dipping each bottle (at two different times) into a cement made as directed on page 277.

JELLIES, &c.

FOR the preparation of all kinds of jellies the best materials are the most economical, and secure the making of good jellies; always keep the preserving kettle in good order, and pay great attention to it while cooking.

APPLE JELLY.

This if rightly made is one of the best jellies. Select full ripe pippin apples free from defects, wash them carefully; but neither pare or core them, as much of the delicate flavour is lost by so doing; slice the apples thinly and lay them in the kettle with just water enough on them to cover them; let them slowly simmer until the apple is reduced to a soft pulp; pare the thin oily rind of three or four fresh lemons, add the juice to flavour the apples; it will require three or four hours slow simmering to do them well; cover the kettle to prevent evaporation; when quite done pour the whole mass into a fine sieve, and set it on a pan to drip; but do not stir it; when all is dripped through, allow one pint of the juice to one pound of broken loaf sugar; let it boil slowly thirty minutes; then pour the jelly into jars, and cover closely; keep in a cool and dry place.

CURRANT JELLY.

Gather the fruit when fully ripe; remove the stems, and put the currants into a very clean stone jar; cover it closely; then set the jar into a kettle, three parts filled with cold water; put the kettle in a hot place to gradually heat; let it boil (renewing the water as it evaporates) for three hours; then gently pour the currants from the jar into a fine hair sieve; let the juice slowly drip through, and when all has dripped, add to every pint of juice one pound of loaf sugar; then put it into the kettle and let it simmer slowly thirty minutes; then pour the jelly into small jars, and set them in the sun for one day before closing the jars; lay on the top of each jar a piece of white paper dipped into brandy to prevent mould; cover tightly and keep in a coo. place. Raspberry jelly is prepared exactly in the same manner; so is dewberry jelly, which is better than blackberry, as the dewberries are sweeter and better flavoured than the blackberry.

MARMALADES AND JAMS.

This mode of preserving fruit, having more consistency than jelly, requires great care in preparing, to avoid scorching or too much cooking; an iron porcelained kettle as for preserving must be used; a large wooden spoon is necessary for stirring.

CHERRY MARMALADE.

Select ripe, juicy, sour and sweet cherries, an equal quantity of each; stem and stone them with care; to one quart of the pulp and juice, add one pound of the best New Orleans brown sugar; mix these well together and put into the kettle; set it in a warm place to slowly heat, and simmer for one hour and a half; then put it into jars; cover with care and cork tightly.

APRICOT MARMALADE.

Select nice green apricots; put two quarts of water into a preserving kettle, and add two large spoonsful of saleratus; put in as many apricots as this will cover; set it on the fire to heat. and when simmered, have ready a basin of cold water, and put the apricots into the cold water from the saleratus water; when all are removed put in more apricots, if the saleratus is not discoloured, if it is, make fresh; take the apricots out of the cold water and wipe them on a coarse cloth, to remove the down; when all the fruit is ready place them into a preserving kettle, and just cover them with water; let them simmer very slowly, and uncovered to evaporate the water; after they have become soft take out all the stones; break the stones, and blanch the kernels by pouring the water on them; then put the blanched kernels into the kettle with the marmalade as they improve the flavour; let this be thoroughly well cooked; then press the pulp through a colander; to guard against the pulp sticking whilst it is cooking, it is a good plan to lay when it is first put into the kettle a large dining plate in the bottom of the kettle. After the pulp is all strained through, add one pound of crushed white sugar, to one pint of the pulp and juice of the fruit; simmer this only twenty minutes stirring carefully to prevent scorching; then put it into jars and cork tightly; any kind of fruit may be prepared in the same manner; only not requiring the saleratus water; that is done to remove the down.

PINE APPLE JAM.

Select large ripe pine apples; pare them carefully; then grate them; preserve all the juice with the pulp in grating; then weigh the fruit and juice, and put it all into a kettle; let it slowly heat, stirring very carefully, or else placing a plate at the bottom, which is best; having weighed the juice and jam as directed, allow an equal quantity of the best white crushed sugar, put the sugar in, when it has simmered fifteen minutes; great care must be used to guard against the least scorch, or the delicate flavour of the pine apple will be affected; let it simmer thirty minutes after the sugar is added, then add one pint of white brandy to one kettle of jam, stir this through gently, so as to become incorporated with the mass; this prevents fermentation; let it simmer five minutes slowly after the brandy is stirred in, then put it into jars, cork tightly, covered, and keep in a cool place; great care must be observed in this jam that the watery particles are very much evaporated before the brandy is added.

APPLE JAM.

Core and pare any quantity of good tart apples, weigh an equal quantity of good brown sugar, then chop up the apples grate some fresh lemon peel, and shred some white ginger; make a good syrup of the sugar and skim it well; then throw in the apples, lemon peel, and ginger; let it all boil until the fruit looks clear and yellow: this is a delicious jam.

RASPBERRY JAM.

Pick them over very carefully, as this fruit is very liable to worms; weigh equal quantities of berries and sugar, put the fruit into a kettle, and break it with a ladle and stir continually; let it boil quickly; when the watery particles are all evaporated, add the sugar, this is better than adding the sugar at first; let it simmer slowly for twenty minutes, then put in jars and cover.

QUINCE MARMALADE.

Take the poorest of quinces; pare, core, and boil them in as little water as will cover them; when quite soft, put them on a sieve, and when cold weigh them, and break them with a ladle; to a pound of fruit add one pound of good brown sugar; put them on the fire and simmer slowly for one hour, stirring constantly in them; put it into jars for use, covering very tightly; a great improvement is to add one-third of sweet apple to the quince; this requires no addition of sugar.

PEAR MARMALADE.

Select not too ripe pears, wash and parboil them soft, when cold rub them through a colander; to two pounds of pears allow one pound of good brown sugar; simmer slowly for one hour, then put into jars; cork tightly.

GRAPE JAM.

Boil the grapes in just water enough to make them tender, strain them through a colander, then to one pound of pulp put one pound of good brown sugar, boil this half an hour; the common wild grape makes a nice jam.

GELATINE JELLY.

Take three ounces of gelatine, two quarts of water, one pint of wine, three lemons squeezed, one and a half pound of sugar, three eggs and shells; boil twenty minutes without touching; pour all through a flannel cloth into a colander, and cool for use.

RASPBERRY JAM.

Take three pounds of raspberries, mash them and boil them twenty minutes; put one pint of currant juice, and coddle them as for jelly; then add three-quarters of a pound of sugar to each pound of the fruit, and boil it until it will jelly.

TO PRESERVE COCOANUT

Make a hole in the shell and pour off the milk; then break the nut and pare off the brown skin, grate and add the milk after a teacupful of crushed sugar is put into it, and dissolved; after it is put into the preserving kettle stir it constantly, to prevent burning, about fifteen minutes, or perhaps twenty; then turn it out to cool.

DESSERTS, JELLIES, BLANC-MANGES &c.

Lemon Custards.

Beat the yolks of eight eggs until they are quite light, stir in one quart of boiling water, grate the rind of two lemons and their juice in a cup, pour it into the eggs and water; add a cupful of white or brown sugar; mix these together well: then set the pan containing the mixture in a hot place, stir it until it thickens, then remove it and add one wine-glass of wine and one of good brandy; stir it well; when cool put it into jelly glasses for the table; whip the whites to a stiff froth with a knife, with three spoonsful of fine white sugar, put a spoonful on each glass, and sprinkle small coloured nonpareils on the top; this is a beautiful and nice dessert.

Orange Cream.

Take the juice of six oranges, beat to a cream the yolks of nine eggs and a quarter of a pound of white crushed sugar, add the orange juice, and pour on one quart of boiling water; stir it well and set it in a warm place to thicken; when heating stir all the time; as soon as cool put into glasses and ornament as the lemon cream with the froth of the whites, &c.

A Nice Custard.

Put on to boil in a saucepan which is kept for boiling milk, one quart of new milk, stir very smoothly one large spoonful of flour in a cup of cold milk, when quite smooth stir it into the boiling milk, with a little salt; stir these well; beat five eggs, the yolks only, to a cream, then add four large spoonsful of good brown sugar, when well mixed stir it thoroughly into the milk, and be careful that it does not curdle, and do not remove the milk from the fire while adding the eggs; then take it away from the heat, and when nearly cold add a few drops of essence of almond, or when the milk is first put on cut a vanilla bean in half and put it in; if essences are used never add them until nearly cold, or it will curdle the custard.

SPONGE CAKE PUDDING.

Soak a sponge cake in wine, lay it in a glass bowl and pour over the above custard; savoy biscuits are equally nice, with boiled custard poured over and flavoured with vanilla.

CUSTARD ICE.

Beat the yolks of six eggs very light, and add six table-spoonsful of white sugar, stir these well; put over the fire one quart of new milk with a piece of vanilla bean; when it comes to a boil stir in with care the eggs and sugar; let it remain on the fire about one minute, stirring all the time to prevent curdling; then remove it, and add one quart of good cream; take out the vanilla bean; when quite cold put it into the freezer and freeze; this is a nice dessert; it may be flavoured with almond or any other flavouring, but that must be added after boiling, as all essences are liable to curdle the milk, unless pounded almonds are used, which enriches the milk and is a very delicate flavour; cinnamon sticks flavour the milk pleasantly; they must be boiled in the milk and removed before freezing.

CHARLOTTE RUSSE.

To half a pint of milk put one ounce of isinglass, (the French is the best and most economical,) to this add a vanilla bean;

put this to simmer over the fire; beat the whites of four eggs to a stiff froth; stir the yolks thoroughly with three ounces of pulverized sugar and one pint of thick cream, with one wine-glass and a half of white wine to a complete froth; when the isinglass is dissolved strain the milk while lukewarm into the yolks and sugar, add the whites immediately; next the cream, beat all quickly together; then line the mould with strips of sponge cake or savoy biscuit, one side of the cake dip in the white of an egg to make it adhere to the mould; then pour on the mixture and let it stand until firm; then carefully turn it out into a glass dish.

FLOATING ISLAND.

Beat the whites of eight eggs to a stiff froth, then whip in four table-spoonsful of currant jelly, four spoonsful of fine pulverized white sugar, all this beaten to a firm consistency, then pour a small quantity of cream into a glass dish, and drop with a spoon the mixture on the cream; on this sprinkle coloured nonpareils; in serving pour some cream into the saucer, and drop on the island.

ITALIAN SNOW.

The whites of two dozen eggs whipped to a stiff froth, the juice of six lemons, two pounds of white sugar, and two quarts of water; mix the water, juice, and sugar well together, then add the eggs; stir all together, and put into the freezer and stir until it freezes.

ALMOND ICES.

Throw into very hot water five ounces of bitter and ten ounces of sweet almonds, and remove the skin; then pound them in a mortar to a paste, adding slowly a few drops of orange flower water; when quite smooth stir in one quart of milk, mix this well and add two quarts of cream; put over a slow fire one quart of milk to boil, stir in with a wooden spoon slowly while simmering twelve ounces of sugar; then add the almond paste very slowly, stirring all the time with a wooden spoon; when well mixed, set it aside to cool, and put it into the freezer for freezing.

COFFEE ICES.

Roast with care to a dark brown seven ounces of Mocha coffee, then grind to a rather finer state than for ordinary use; cover it in a vessel; put over the fire in a very nice vessel one pint of cream and three pints of milk, when boiling stir in half a pound of sugar; when dissolved pour it over the coffee in a boiling state; stir it quickly; then cover tightly and let it stand until cold; then strain it very carefully through a hair sieve, and put it into the freezer for freezing.

ITALLIENNE ICES.

Boil two quarts of cream, have ready fourteen ounces of ground Mocha coffee, when boiling pour the cream over the coffee, cover very tightly and let it infuse for two hours; then take ten eggs, very fresh, separate the whites from the yolks, whip lightly the whites; then pour the coffee and cream through a very fine sieve and stir in the whites, and add half a pound of sugar; put this on the fire for a few moments, then pour all through a hair sieve; when cold put into the freezer for freezing.

CHOCOLATE ICES.

Boil one quart of milk, grate half a pound of best French vanilla chocolate and stir into the milk, let it boil until thick; add a quarter of a pound of sugar; add one quart of cream, and stir well, then pour into the freezer.

PLUM PUDDING GLACÉ.

Stem and seed one pound and a quarter of best bunch raisins on these pour three pints of good new milk, and add three or four sticks of best cinnamon, and two blades of mace; put these into a saucepan to simmer ten minutes, covering tightly; whilst this is cooking beat up the yolks of five eggs with half a pound of white sugar to a smooth cream; strain the milk through a hair sieve; put it on again to boil; pound in a mortar a quarter of a pound of almonds; when the milk boils, stir in the yolks, and stir it well, as for boiled custard; remove it from the fire, and add the almonds when the custard is nearly cold, or they will curdle the custard; then add the raisins which were boiled in the milk, but not the spice; stir these well together, and cut into very thin slices half a pound of the best citron, stir this in, with half a pound of preserved ginger cut very thinly; when these are well mixed, add one quart of best cream; stir well, and put into a freezer for freezing. A "Turk's head mould" has the best appearance on tables. This is a most delicious dessert, or for an evening party.

RASPBERRY ICES.

Select fresh ripe berries; extract the juice by pressing them in a hair sieve with a wooden spoon; then squeeze gooseberries fully ripe also through a sieve; to one quart of the raspberry juice add one pint of gooseberry juice, and the juice of two lemons; put this on the fire to simmer slowly, and add two pounds of clarified sugar; let this simmer for twenty minutes; then strain it through a hair sieve, and when quite cold freeze it in your freezer; other fruits may be prepared in the same way; currant juice is a good substitute for gooseberries, strawberries are even superior to raspberry with the addition of the currant.

CLOVE ICES.

This is much esteemed in France; pound coarsely two ounces of the best cloves in a mortar; add to it four ounces of white sugar; boil two quarts of milk and throw in the cloves and sugar mixed, let it simmer for ten minutes tightly covered; then add one quart of cream, with half a pound of white sugar, let these only scald; then press all through a hair sieve, and freeze it; a nice after dinner ice. Cinnamon ice is prepared in the same manner; be careful to select the best stick cinnamon and only break it; not pounded as the cloves.

APPLE ICES.

Select good pippins; but do not pare or core them; lay them in a kettle, just cover them with water; set them on the fire and cook slowly, being tightly covered; when reduced to a jam, pour it in a hair sieve or fine colander, then add to one pint of the juice thus obtained three-quarters of a pound of sifted sugar and the juice of two fresh lemons, stir these well, and when quite cold pour it into the freezer.

PEACH ICE.

Pare and cut finely half a peck of very ripe peaches; stir in well two pounds of the best white sugar; let it stand for two or three hours, then stir them well together and put into a preserving kettle to simmer for twenty minutes, stirring all the time to prevent scorching; then pour them into a pan and when quite cold add one quart of cream and one quart of milk; stir them well together; put instantly into the freezer to prevent curdling; this is delicious.

WINE ICE.

Pare with care the rind of twelve fresh lemons; pour over this rind one pint of boiling water, cover tightly for two hours, then add one pound of white sugar crushed; beat very lightly the whites of four eggs, then stir them into the mixture; whip it well and strain through a colander, then add two quarts of good red or white wine, and freeze it; this may be reduced according to the quantity required, but be careful to keep the proportions.

JELLY LEMONADE.

Slice three fresh Seville oranges very thinly, and six fresh lemons; pour on them one quart of boiling water, cover tightly and let them steep; soak three ounces of good isinglass in a cup of cold water, when soft pour on it the lemon, orange and water; let the whole simmer for fifteen minutes; stir in one-fourth of a pound of crushed sugar, one pint of good wine, let it simmer three minutes, and strain through a bag or "jelly strainer," which is the best thing for jelly, and can be obtained at the tin furnishing stores; when it is clear pour into moulds.

CHARLOTTE RUSSE.

One and a half ounces of French isinglass dissolved in a pint of water, let it simmer to half a pint; make a rich custard of six eggs, and one pint of new milk, let it be smooth and then cool it; boil a vanilla bean in the milk, whip a quart of rich cream to a froth, lay it on a sieve as you whip the froth; stir the custard into the isinglass, having strained the custard until thick; then add the whipped cream, beat all together, line a mould with lady fingers or savoy biscuits; pour in the mixture, and when required turn into a glass dish.

APPLE TRIFLE.

Pare and core six good pippins, just cover them with water and simmer them until soft, then mash them through a colander; beat them with four large spoonsful of powdered loaf sugar, whip to a stiff froth the whites of five eggs, beat these with the apples and sugar until perfectly light and white; lay slices of sponge cake in a glass dish, pour over it some wine just to soak the cake, on the cake put raspberry jelly, then put on the apple ana sugar on the top of the jelly and cake; this is very nice.

APPLE PUDDING AND BOILED CUSTARD.

Put five pippin apples, pared and cored carefully, into a baking dish, then fill the holes with sifted loaf sugar and nutmeg, on these pour a rich custard having in it a wine-glass of wine, or French brandy, and bake half an hour. To make the custard, boil one quart of new milk with several pieces of cinnamon stick, let it simmer five minutes; beat up eight eggs with only half the whites; stir in two table-spoonsful of sugar and one wine-glass of good wine; strain the milk and add it to the eggs, and then pour it over the apples, and bake as directed.

PLUM CHARLOTTE.

Stone one quart of ripe plums; stew them in one pound of brown sugar; cut slices of bread and butter; lay them at the bottom and around the sides of a deep dish or bowl, pour in the plums boiling hot, and set it away to cool gradually; to be eaten with cream.

CLOTTED CREAM.

Mix together one gill of rich milk and a wine-glass of rose-water, and four ounces of white sugar, then add the yolks of two eggs well beaten; stir all into a quart of good cream, set it over hot coals, let it just come to a boil, stirring all the time; then take it off, and when cool enough pour it into a glassbowl, set it away to get cool; eat with it any sort of sweetmeats.

WHIPPED SYLLABUB.

Stir into a quart of good cream one pound of crushed sugar, and one pint and a half of good wine; put these into a deep dish; squeeze in the juice of three fresh lemons; whip these half an hour, and as they froth lay the froth on a sieve, until all is whipped; serve in lemonade glasses.

APPLE SOUFFLE WITH RICE.

Blanch half a pound of the best rice in scalding water, strain it clear, boil it in sufficient milk to cover it, to this add a little grated lemon peel, and a small bit of cinnamon, let it boil until the rice has absorbed the milk; then remove the stick of cinnamon, turn it into a dish, and when cool raise a wall with it about three inches high, having first taken the precaution to egg the dish to make it stick firmly, smooth the rise to an even surface, then egg it all over, fill the dish half way up the wall of rice with apple marmalade; beat to a fine froth the whites of four eggs, pour them over the marmalade, then sift powdered white sugar over it, put it into the oven, keep up an even heat to give it a fine colour. Serve hot with wine sauce.

BLANC MANGE OF MOSS.

Take half an ounce of "Carrigean moss," the white; put it into one quart of new milk; reduce it by simmering to one pint, and then flavour it with a few drops of essence of bitter almond, and sweeten it to the taste, add one glass of white wine; pour it into a mould, until cold and firm; serve in a glass dish.

CALVES FEET BLANC MANGE.

Clean and break eight calves feet; pour on them two quarts of cold water, and half a tea-spoonful of salt; let them simmer three hours, skimming carefully; strain off the feet which will make a nice dinner dished with drawn butter and parsley; set the liquor to cool; when cool remove every particle of fat; add one quart of cream; let it simmer ten minutes; then sweeten, and add good essence of lemon to the taste; pour the whole through a hair sieve into moulds; when cold and firm it is ready for table.

COFFEE JELLY, CREAM A LA FRANCAISE.

Infuse a quarter of a pound of ground Mocha coffee in a glass of water boiling; when the coffee is precipitated pour it off clear. Boil a quarter of a pound of sugar to a rich syrup, pour the coffee to it, and then set it on hot ashes that the sugar may dissolve gently, and when it is perfectly melted stir in gradually the yolks of eight eggs, four glasses of boiling milk, and six ounces of sugar, after which put it on a moderate fire, stirring with a wooden spoon; when it begins to simmer pass it through a fine sieve, and let it stand till lukewarm; then mix into it one ounce of clarified isinglass, and finish it by just dissolving the isinglass; pour into moulds to cool.

FRUIT CHARLOTTE.

Grate eight good pippins, free from cores and skin; cut up some pieces of butter, and lay in the bottom of a pudding dish; on this put half of the apples, grated; grate some nutmeg; a little lemon peel grated; sprinkling thickly good brown sugar; a quarter of a pound of currants; the same of stoned raisins; one large spoonful of finely chopped beef suet; three spoonsful of grated or crumbled stale bread; then more apples; a quarter of a pound of currants, the same of stoned raisins, sugar, nutmeg, and lemon peel; lastly strew thickly crumbs of stale bread; cut up pieces of butter, and lay on the top; bake one hour; eat with wine sauce.

BLANC-MANGE.

Boil two ounces of French isinglass in three pints of water twenty minutes; strain this into one pint and a half of good cream, and let it simmer five minutes; add one glass of good peach water; sweeten and strain through a sieve into a mould.

CALVES' FEET JELLY.

Clean six feet; pour on them two quarts and a pint of cold water, and half a tea-spoonful of salt; boil them down one half, strain it, when cold remove all the fat carefully; then put it into a very nice saucepan; add sugar and wine to the taste; the rind of two fresh lemons peeled very thinly, and their juice; one wine-glass of brandy; let these all simmer; then add the whites of four eggs beaten up with their shells; let it boil twenty minutes; then pour it through a sieve, or "jelly strainer," into the moulds; let it stand, however, fifteen minutes before pouring it through the strainer to settle; it is much clearer for so doing.

CALVES' FEET JELLY, SUPERIOR.

Take a set of four calves' feet; wash and clean them; put them into a saucepan, with four quarts of cold water covered closely; let this simmer, skimming carefully, five hours; strain them through a colander; take the broth and set it aside to cool; when cold remove all the fat from the jelly and the settlings; it must be prepared the day before it is required; place this jelly into a clean saucepan with three or four sticks of cinnamon, three whole cloves, and the rind and juice of three lemons; set this on the fire to warm; beat the whites and shells of four eggs in a half pint of cold water; stir these in quickly, also half a pound of white sugar dissolved in one pint of best "Champagne cider," at the same time as the eggs; and one pint of good Sherry or Madeira wine; let this simmer for five minutes; then set it aside to settle for fifteen minutes, after which pour it through a strainer or jelly bag into a mould to cool.

BLANC-MANGE, DUTCH.

Put a pint of cleared calves' foot jelly into a stewpan, mix with it the yolks of six eggs, set it over a fire, and whisk till it begins to boil, then set the pan in cold water, and stir the mixture till nearly cold to prevent it from curdling, and when it begins to thicken fill the moulds. Set it in a cool place.

BLANC-MANGE A LA FRANCAISE.

Blanch one pound of sweet and twenty bitter almonds, drain them on a sieve, and afterwards dry them by rubbing them in a napkin, pound them in a mortar, continually moistening them with half a tea-spoonful of water at a time, to prevent their oiling. When they are pounded as fine as possible take them out of the mortar, and put them into a pan, then with a silver spoon beat up your almonds gradually with five glasses of water; after this spread a napkin over an oval dish, and put your almonds upon it, then gather up the corners of your napkin, and wring it very tight to press out all the milk from the almonds, then put into this milk twelve ounces of crystallized sugar broken into small pieces. When the sugar is dissolved pass the whole through a sieve, and then add to it one ounce of clarified isinglass rather warmer than lukewarm, and when the whole is well incorporated together pour it into your mould; your mould should be previously put into pounded ice; when your blanc-mange is ready to serve, which will be in two hours after it has been put into the mould, you must take it out.

APPLES A LA TURQUE.

Pare and core ten good pippins, put them into a kettle with clarified sugar, cover them closely and simmer very gently, turning often so as to have both sides well cooked; when soft and clear take them out and lay on a dish with wet white paper over them; put around the margin of the dish a rim of puff paste; when the paste is done fill the holes of the apples with raspberry or currant jam, beat the whites of six eggs to a stiff froth, and add to them four large spoonsful of white sifted sugar, beat this in with the whites; put this on the apples; sift some fine white sugar over the whites; set in the oven until baked a light brown.

CURDS AND CREAM.

Turn to curd three or four pints of milk with runnet; before serving drain off the whey, and pour over some cream; then sweeten half a pint of rich cream and grate nutmeg over it; serve this with the curd.

CREAM CHEESE.

TAKE your rennet and cover it with scalding water; let this remain in for two days. Then to a large milk pan of new milk add one quart of rich cream; strain into it as much boiling water as will make the milk warm; then add as much water from the rennet as you think will turn it, say two table-spoonsful; when it is sufficiently turned lay a thin cloth in a sieve, and put in your curd to drain; then put a cloth in your press, lay on something to keep it down; let it remain until the whey is well drained from it; then take out the curd, and put it in a dry place with the hoops over it; salt the side that is up, the next day turn it and salt the other side.

DEVONSHIRE CREAM.

Set the risen cream on a warm place, and as it rises skim it off and set it aside; sweeten it, and grate nutmeg over it; this is very nice for tea, with sweetmeats.

APPLE FLOAT.

Twelve large apples, quartered, cored and boiled in as little water as possible and passed through a sieve; when cold add two whites of eggs, beaten—sweeten to taste; beat all up with a spoon till quite stiff. Have made previously a soft custard, with the two yolks. Flavor and sweeten slightly.

LEMON CREAM.

Pare the rind very thin from four fresh lemons; squeeze the juice and strain it, put them both into a quart of water, sweeten to your taste; add the whites of six eggs beaten to a froth; put it on the fire, and keep stirring it until it thickens; but do not let it boil; pour it in a bowl; when cold, strain it through a sieve; put it on the fire again, and add the yolks of the eggs; stir until quite thick, and when cold serve up in small glasses and on each glass lay a maccaroon.

ALMOND CUSTARD.

Take one pound of shelled and blanched almonds, pounded with rose water; add one quart of boiling water, this then must be strained; add eight well beaten eggs, and a sufficient quantity of sugar to sweeten with; a small quantity of grated nutmeg; bake in cups.

CHARLOTTE RUSSE.

Extract the flavour of a vanilla bean by boiling it in milk, of which take half a pint; the milk must then be strained, and when cold mix with it a quarter of a pound of loaf sugar; beat the yolks of four eggs very light and stir them into the mixture; heat it over the fire for five minutes until it becomes a custard, but take great care that it does not boil; boil an ounce of isinglass with a pint of water, the isinglass must be thoroughly dissolved before fit for use, and one half of the water boiled away; the custard being cold drain the isinglass into it and stir them hard together; leave them to cool while you prepare the rest of the mixture; whip a quart of cream to a froth (the cream should be rich) and mix it with the custard; in whipping the cream great care should be taken to make it quite light; the safest way is to remove the froth with a strainer as fast as it gathers until the whole is whipped; take two round slices of almond sponge cake, glaze them with the beaten white of eggs mixed with sugar; lay one on the bottom of a circular mould and reserve the other for the top; cut some more sponge cake into long pieces, glaze them carefully with the egg and line the sides of the mould with them; each piece should lap a little over the other, or the form will not be perfect; the custard will by this time be just beginning to congeal; pour it gently into the mould and cover the top with the piece of cake which had already been prepared; the cake around the sides must be trimmed evenly, so that the upper pieces will fit without leaving any vacancies; pound some ice and throw it into a tub, covering it well with coarse salt; the mould should then be set in the midst of this ice and remain there an hour; prepare an iceing with powdered sugar and the beaten white of egg, flavouring it with lemon juice, or essence of lemon, or orange rose water, according to your taste; the charlotte russe is then turned out into a handsome dish and iced over; it should be moved about as little as possible; to insure success in preparing it, the utmost care should be taken to follow the above directions.

CHARLOTTE POLONAISE.

Beat together the yolks of six eggs which must be perfectly fresh, mix with them two table-spoonsful of flour, boil a pint and a half of cream and stir the eggs with it, great care being taken that the flour is not in lumps; the cream must be still kept over the fire, and it may boil slowly for ten minutes or more, stir it continually, and be sure the fire is not too hot; divide the mixture into two separate pans; scrape six ounces of chocolate quite fine, break up a pound of maccaroons and add them to two ounces of powdered sugar; mix this with the ingredients of one pan, boil it a few moments, stir as before, take it from the fire, stir a little longer and leave it to cool; blanch a dozen bitter almonds and four ounces of shelled sweet almonds; pound them in a mortar with a little rose water until they are quite fine, add an ounce of chopped citron and pound them again; pour the contents of the mortar into a dish and add to them four ounces of powdered sugar; stir this mixture into the other half of the cream, and let it boil gently; take it off and put it in a cool place; cut a sponge cake (it should be a large one) into slices about half an inch thick, spread alternately one with the chocolate cream and another with the almond cream; pile them evenly on a china dish until the slices have all been used; whip together the whites of six eggs until they become a stiff froth, mix with it six ounces of powdered sugar, twelve drops of oil of lemon, some persons prefer rose water, but it is not generally considered as good; pour this mixture lightly over the pile of cake, using a spoon to distribute it evenly, and then sift some sugar (not too finely powdered) over it. It should be left in a slow oven until the outside is browned; if the oven is too hot it will become deeply browned, and will not look well. It may be ornamented with slices of peaches or quinces cut in fanciful shapes, or drops of jelly, or raspberries preserved whole; should the chocolate cream be too thin, thicken it with crumbled maccaroons; should the cream be too thin add in more pounded citron; should either of the mixtures be too thick, dilute it with cream. Some persons prefer a charlotte polonaise to a "charlotte russe," as it has a more delicate and more decided flavour.

GOOSEBERRY CUSTARD.

Stew ripe gooseberries in as little water as possible, stir and mash them through the colander; stir in while the pulp is hot a spoonful of butter, and sugar to sweeten it; beat six eggs very light, then simmer the pulp very slowly, and stir in the eggs gradually; when it comes to a boil, take it off, stir very hard and set it to cool; serve in glasses cold, grate a little nutmeg over each glass.

FROSTED FRUIT.

Take large ripe cherries, plums, or grapes, cut off half the stalk; have ready in one dish some beaten white of an egg, and in another some fine loaf sugar, sifted. Dip the fruit in the egg, then roll into the powdered sugar; lay a sheet of white paper on the bottom of a reverted sieve, and set it on a stove.

ANGEL'S FOOD.

Stew tart apples, strain them, sweeten with white sugar, mix four whites of eggs, (saved from the custard,) add the stewed apples, and the eggs beaten to a stiff froth; make a boiled custard, pour it into a glass dish, and drop on the custard the beaten apples and eggs.

CHOCOLATE MANGE.

Three ounces of French isinglass, dissolved in a very little cold water; put on a quart of new milk to boil, grate half a cake of vanilla chocolate, and stir in the milk; then let it simmer, and add the dissolved isinglass; let this all simmer five minutes; then pour into a mould, and when cold and jellish, turn out and serve with cream.

COCOANUTS STEWED.

Grate two cocoanuts very carefully; dissolve one pound and a half of white sugar in very little water; when dissolved, let it simmer slowly five minutes, when the watery particles are all evaporated, stir in the grated cocoanut; add one wine-glass of white wine, one wine-glass of rose water, stir these well; have ready some paste puffs baked, and when wanted for table, fill them with the stewed cocoanut.

RUM JELLY.

To one quart of white wine add one pound of crushed sugar; dissolve one ounce of isinglass thoroughly in cold water; strain through a sieve; mix this with the syrup of sugar when the syrup is milk warm, and when nearly cold pour in the white wine, stir these well together, then add one wine-glassful of the best Jamaica rum, pour it into moulds to get cold; this is very nice for evening parties, and is used on the continent.

MADEIRA WINE JELLY.

Soak for half an hour three ounces of the best French isinglass, stir it into one pint of hot water; cut the rind of one fresh lemon thinly and put in, let it simmer fifteen minutes; stir in one quarter of a pound of crushed sugar, and one quart of Madeira wine, let this warm only, then strain through a jelly bag or strainer into moulds; it is very fine.

LEMON JELLY.

Cut the rind of three fresh lemons and their juice; soak for half an hour two ounces and a half of French isinglass, pour on the lemon rind and juice one quart of boiling water, put it into a clean saucepan; let it simmer five minutes, then stir in the isinglass; when dissolved add three-quarters of a pound of crushed sugar, let this simmer fifteen minutes; beat up the whites and shells of three eggs, and stir in one pint of good sherry wine; it only requires one simmer after the wine is added; remove it from the fire and let it stand five minutes only to settle, then pour it slowly through the "jelly strainer" or bag into the moulds; when jellied it is ready for use.

ARROW-ROOT BLANC-MANGE.

Put in a very clean saucepan one quart of milk and a piece of vanilla bean; cover tightly or else the flavour will evaporate; stir into half a pint of cream a tea-cupful of arrow-root, and a very little salt; mix this smoothly; pour into this through a hair sieve the quart of boiling milk, stir it well; return it to the saucepan and let it simmer for ten minutes, sweeten to the taste; put into moulds to cool; serve with cream.

CALVES' FEET BLANC-MANGE.

Put a set of calves' feet nicely cleaned and washed into four quarts of water, and reduce it by boiling down to one quart; strain and set it to cool, when cold take off all the fat and remove all the settlings at the bottom, then put to it one quart of new milk, sweeten to the taste, let it simmer a few minutes, and add a few drops of essence of almonds, or one large spoonful of orange flower water, but this flavoring is to be added after it is removed from the fire; strain it through a sieve into the mould, and set it to harden.

NEW YORK CUSTARD.

Boil one quart of new milk and a piece of vanilla bean, while it is simmering cover tightly as the flavour will evaporate if it is not; mix five large table-spoonsful of rice flour with a little cold milk, stir it quite smooth, pour it into the boiling milk, stir it well and boil for fifteen minutes, then take it from the fire and break in two eggs, stirring very rapidly; take out the bean; sweeten to the taste, pour it into moulds; serve with cream.

PEACH MANGE.

Take three tablespoonsful of nicely preserved peaches; rub them carefully through a sieve; then stir in well one quart of rich cream; dissolve three-quarters of an ounce of best French isinglass in half a pint of water, and simmer it; when entirely dissolved and cool stir it into the mixed peaches and cream; then put all into a mould, and when quite firm turn it out. In summer it must be made the day before, and kept on ice to harden and be cold.

ALMOND TRIFLE.

Put on to boil one quart of new milk, blanch and bruise a quarter of a pound of sweet almonds; put them into the milk; beat the yolks of six eggs and two large spoonsful of sugar well together; and when the milk boils stir in the yolks as for a custard; remove it from the fire—pour it into a dish, and cover the top with rather thin slices of almond sponge cake; beat the six whites to a very stiff froth with six large spoonsful of sifted loaf sugar, and add three or four drops of essence of bitter almonds; when quite stiff spread it over the cake smoothly with a large knife; then put it in a moderately heated oven for twenty minutes to brown nicely; set it aside to cool. This is a nice dessert.

ALMOND GUST.

Two ounces of almonds, blanched and pounded to a paste, with a large spoonful of orange-flower water, or rose-water—to prevent oiling; put on a pint of new milk to boil, beat the yolks of six eggs, with a quarter of a pound of crushed sugar; and when the milk boils stir in the eggs and sugar, and then add the almonds; mix all well together, and set it aside to cool; then whip one quart of cream to a stiff froth, with a quarter of a pound of pulverized sugar; lay the froth on a sieve to drain; lay some slices of sponge cake in a dish, and on them spread either quince or apple jelly; on this pour the cold boiled custard; and on the custard place the froth of the whipped cream This is a nice and handsome dessert.

MARIA'S DESSERT.

Beat very lightly six eggs, together with a tea-cup of pulverized sugar; sift into a pan four tea-cups of best flour, and one teaspoonful of cream of tartar; then stir it with a knife—the eggs and sugar; mix them well together; dissolve half a teaspoonful of soda in a very little warm water; grate the oily part of the rind of two fresh lemons, the third of a grated nutmeg; mix these well together and beat them until quite light; have ready six pie plates, and put into each two large spoonsful; bake them a nice brown; when quite cold spread over three of these cakes quite thickly either grape, raspberry, or any nice jam, and then lay the other three on those with the jam, having the brown side up. Make a nice boiled custard, and serve with the jam and cake.

CHERRY PUDDING.

Sift into a pan one pint and a half of corn meal; on this pour sufficient boiling water to wet the meal; stir this well, adding half a teaspoonful of salt; cut and shred very finely a quarter of a pound of nice beef suet, and stir into the meal; beat very light three eggs, and add to the meal and suet; dissolve one teaspoonful of soda in a cup of new milk; beat these all well together until quite light; then add a pint of fresh morello or pie cherries, stoned, and with the juice and one teaspoonful of ground ginger stir well through, and pour in lastly a teacupful of the best molasses and one pint of new milk; pour this mixture into a well greased pan, and bake slowly one hour. Serve with wine sauce.

NEST PUDDING.

Make the foundation of the nest of jelly or blanc mange, rasp the skin of three lemons and preserve it; then lay it around and on the jelly like the straw; take out the contents of four eggs through a small hole, and fill the shell with blanc mange; when cold break off the shells and lay the mange eggs in the nest. A pretty ornamental dish.

APPLE SNOW.

Select eight or nine good sized tart apples; core them, and put them into a pan and just cover them with cold water; whilst they are cooking slowly, make a nice boiled custard of the yolks of four eggs and one quart of milk; set it aside to cool; when the apples are quite soft lay them carefully on a sieve and remove the skins; then put the pulp into a bowl, and whip to a stiff froth four whites of eggs and three large spoonsful of pulverized sugar, then beat the apple-pulp to a stiff froth, and add it to the whipped whites; beat them then until they resemble snow; when done pour the cold boiled custard into a glass bowl and heap on the whipped snow; finish by sprinkling on colored nonpareils; this is a beautiful and palatable dessert. Flavor the boiled custard when cold with a few drops of essence of lemon.

RICE BLANC MANGE.

Put a teacupful of the best rice into a half pint of cold water; let it stand until the rice cracks and looks perfectly white; then add one pint of new milk, and one tablespoonful of white sugar; stir it and let it gently simmer until all the milk is absorbed, stirring frequently; then pour it into a mould to cool; eaten with preserves it is very nice. The rice may be flavored with essence of lemon, and eaten with cream.

STRAWBERRY AND OTHER SYRUPS.

Juice one pint, water one pint, refined sugar three pounds.—After squeezing the juice from berries, take the pulp and pour the water on and let it come to a boil; strain this and make up the pint with water, if wanting; pour this on the sugar, put it over the fire till the sugar is dissolved, and comes to a boil; take it off the fire and add strawberry juice; stir well again, and place on the fire and let come to a boil (or nearly); when cool, strain and bottle. Three quarts of ripe berries make the above quantity. Pine apple, raspberries, &c., as above.

DRINKS AND FOOD FOR THE SICK.

Beef Tea.

Take a piece of lean juicy beef, wash it and cut it into small pieces an inch square; salt a very little; put them into a wide mouthed bottle; set the bottle into a kettle of cold water and let it gradually heat to boiling, keep the kettle boiling three hours, then take out the bottle and strain off the juice; this concentrates more nourishment than any other method.

Chicken Tea.

Take a leg and thigh of a chicken, lay it in cold water, say one pint, set it on the fire to simmer for twenty minutes, cover tightly, skim it well, add a little salt, and strain it; toast a piece of bread, cut it into small squares; put these into a bowl and pour on the boiling tea.

Chicken Broth.

Clean half a chicken, on it pour one quart of cold water, and a little salt; put in a spoonful of rice; boil this two hours very slowly and tightly covered; skim it well; just before using it throw in a little chopped parsley.

Chicken Jelly.

Cut up a cleaned and washed chicken; put it into a stone jar, break all the bones; cover it very closely; set the jar into a kettle of boiling water; keep it boiling three hours and a half; strain off the liquor; season with salt, and a very little mace, or lemon and sugar; return the chicken to the jar and boil again, it will produce just as much jelly again; an old fowl answers as well as a young one; this is very nutritious.

IRISH MOSS.

Steep one-quarter of an ounce of moss in cold water for a few moments only; then take out the sprig from the water, shake them, and then put them into one quart of new milk; simmer it until of the consistency of warm jelly; strain, and sweeten to the taste with either honey or white sugar; set it away to cool; it is very palatable for an invalid.

BREAD JELLY.

Toast five slices of stale bread a light brown, take off the crust before toasting; lay them in two quarts of boiling water; slice a lemon thinly and lay in also; let it boil to a jelly; strain and sweeten to the taste; this is nice for young children as well as invalids.

RICE JELLY.

Boil a quarter of a pound of the best rice flour with half a pound of loaf sugar in a quart of water, until the whole becomes one glutinous mass; strain off the jelly, and let it stand to cool; this is nutritious and light.

RICE CAUDLE.

Wash with care a tea-cup of rice, on it pour one quart of boiling water, and a very little salt; let this cook slowly for an hour; then pour off the water and let it boil, while scalding add a wine-glass of wine and the yolk of an egg beaten to a cream with a large spoonful of white sugar; stir this in slowly so as not to curdle; remove it from the fire; pour into a bowl and grate nutmeg over it; this is light and nutritious.

SLIPPERY ELM BARK JELLY.

Four large spoonsful of ground bark; pour on it one quart of cold water; let it stand all night, stir it and let it settle; the next morning pour off the water; pare the rind of a lemon very thinly, and with the juice put it into the water strained, let it simmer very gently fifteen minutes, then sweeten, and pour in a mould to cool and harden; take out the rind before putting into the mould.

ALMOND MILK.

Blanch about a dozen almonds, put them into a stone mortar with a couple of lumps of sugar to prevent them from oiling; when tolerably well crushed add to the almonds about a wine-glass of scalding water, pour it into a piece of muslin and squeeze into a bowl, pound the almonds again, and add more hot water and squeeze again in this way; pour over the almonds by degrees about a pint of hot water; set it away to cool; when ready for drinking it is nutritious and palatable.

BARLEY WATER.

Two ounces of the best pearl barley; wash it clean in cold water; put it into a half pint of boiling water; let it stand for five minutes only, then pour it off and add one quart and a pint of boiling water, a little salt, six or eight nice figs sliced, a handful of cut raisins, a little stick of liquorice, let this all simmer fifty minutes, strain it, and when prepared add a little sweetening, although it is better for the stomach without this; this is a delightful nutritious drink.

WINE WHEY.

Boil a pint of new milk; add to it a glass or two of white wine; put it on the fire until it just boils again, then set it aside till the curdle settles; pour off the clear whey; sweeten to the taste; cider is as good as wine to curdle if it is good country cider.

CORN MEAL GRUEL, OR OATMEAL.

Put in a clean saucepan one pint of water to boil, when boiling mix of oatmeal two large spoonsful in a half pint of milk and a little salt, stir this into the boiling water, stir it well, let it simmer thirty minutes, then strain it through a hair sieve; if the patient can bear it a large spoonful of the best brandy stirred in after it is strained and sweetened, and a little grated nutmeg; if cornmeal is used, stir the dry cornmeal into the boiling water, two large spoonsful to a pint of boiling water and a half of new milk; season as the other; cornmeal requires more cooking.

JELLY FOR INVALIDS.

Cut the crumb of a penny roll into thin slices, toast them a light brown, then boil gently in a quart of water until it jellies, strain it upon a few shavings of lemon peel; sweeten and add if liked a little wine and nutmeg.

EGG BROTH.

Beat the yolk of one egg with a spoonful of white sugar to a cream, put this into a bowl, and pour on it, stirring all the time, half a pint of either boiling new milk or water, add a spoonful of good brandy and grated nutmeg over it; this is very nourishing for an invalid.

EGG NOGG.

Take the yolks of eight eggs, beat them with six large spoonsful of pulverised loaf sugar; when this is a cream, add the third part of a nutmeg grated; into this stir one tumbler full of good brandy and one wine-glass of good Madeira wine; mix them well together, have ready the whites beaten to a stiff froth, and beat them into the mixture; when all are well mixed add three pints of rich milk.

ANOTHER FOR SUMMER.

Beat the yolk of one egg and a spoonful of white sugar in a bowl to a cream; add a tumbler full of crushed ice; put the ice in a clean cloth and pound it with a mallet as fine as hail, stir this into the egg, add one spoonful of wine or good brandy and grate a little nutmeg over it; stir this all well; this is refreshing and nutritious as a drink.

PANADA.

Cut two slices of stale bread half an inch in thickness; cut off the crust; toast them a nice brown; butter both sides with good fresh butter while they are hot; cut them into squares of two inches in size; lay them in a bowl, sprinkle a little salt over them, and pour on a pint of boiling water; grate a little nutmeg.

CRACKER PANADA.

Grate four water crackers into a saucepan; to a spoonful of white sugar add a little salt, stone and cut in half two large spoonsful of bunch raisins; over this pour one pint of boiling water; let it slowly simmer five minutes; pour it into a bowl, and it is ready for the invalid.

TAPIOCA.

Soak two table-spoonsful of very clean tapioca in two tea-cups of cold water over night; in the morning add a little salt; one pint of milk, or water if milk cannot be taken; simmer it until quite soft; stir well while cooling; when done pour into a bowl, and if allowed add sugar, a spoonful of wine, and a little nutmeg.

ARROW ROOT.

Bermuda arrow root is the best, but it is, unless purchased from a reliable person, much adulterated; put in your saucepan to boil one pint of milk; stir very smoothly into a cup of cold milk two spoonsful of arrow root, and a little salt; when the milk boils stir in the arrow root; continue to stir until it is cooked, which will be in five minutes; then remove it from the fire, and sweeten to the taste; if allowed, a little grated nutmeg; it is very nice cold and eaten with cream.

SAGO JELLY.

Select clean nice sago, wash it in cold water; put it to soak over night; a small cupful of sago, in half a pint of cold water; in the morning put the sago in one pint of hot water; pare the rind of a fresh lemon very thin, and squeeze the juice into the sago; let it simmer twenty minutes slowly; then sweeten, and if wine is allowed add one wine-glass of sherry; pour it into a mould.

FOR A COUGH.

Put a quarter of a pound of pearl barley into two quarts of water, boil until reduced to one quart; then add half a pound of the best figs, a quarter of a pound of sugar candy, and simmer all, and strain; take a wine-glassful cold frequently, whenever the cough is troublesome.

ENGLISH CAUDLE.

Make a fine smooth gruel of oatmeal, when done strain it, stir it at times till cold; when wanted for use add sugar, wine, and lemon peel, with some nutmeg, according to taste; you may add if you please, besides the wine, a spoonful of brandy or lemon juice if allowed to the patient

CAUDLE, BROWN.

Boil the gruel the same as for white caudle, with six spoonsful of oatmeal, and strain it; then add a quart of good ale, not bitter, boil it, then sweeten according to your taste, and add half a pint of white wine; when you do not put in the white wine let it be half ale.

CAUDLE, WHITE.

Mix two spoonsful of oatmeal in a quart of water, with a blade or two of mace, and a piece of lemon peel, stir it often, and let it boil full twenty minutes, strain and sweeten it, add a little white wine, nutmeg and a little lemon juice.

PANADA.

Put into a clean saucepan one pint of hot water; set it on the fire; add one wine-glassful of white wine; a spoonful of white sugar, the rind of a lemon very thinly pared, and a very little grated nutmeg; as soon as it comes to a boil stir in two large spoonsful of stale bread crumbs; stir this until well mixed, then take out the lemon peel, and pour the panada into a bowl.

SYRUP FOR A COUGH.

Take one pound of brown sugar; one pint of vinegar; boil together until it becomes a thick syrup; a short time before it is done, add half a pound of raisins seeded; one tea-spoonful is sufficient for a dose unless the cough is very troublesome, then take two every two hours; this is most excellent.

TOAST WATER.

Cut a slice of stale bread half an inch thick a finger length long; cut off the crust, and toast it quite brown, but not scorched; while hot put it into a half pint pitcher; pour over half a pint of boiling water; cover it tightly, and when cool remove the bread.

SCOTCH TOAST.

Lay in a pan three or four hard water crackers; the "Trenton cracker" is the best for soaking; pour on them boiling water to cover them; sprinkle a little salt over when well softened; then put on each a piece of good sweet butter, and set it in the oven for ten minutes, and if allowed a little cream poured on.

LEMON WATER.

Cut the rind of a fresh lemon very thinly, and squeeze the juice of half the lemon; put it into a pitcher and pour on one pint of boiling water; cover it tightly until cold; then sweeten to the taste.

PEACH WATER.

A small cupful of dried peaches washed carefully; put them into a pint pitcher, and pour on one pint of boiling water; cover tightly, and when quite cold strain; it is an acceptable drink in fever.

QUINCE WATER.

When preserving quinces save the cores if not wanted for jelly; cut the core as whole as possible, string it and dry it; as there is nothing which makes so delightful and healthy a mucillaginous drink as the cores steeped in hot water, for a cough it is most soothing. Take four or five slices of dried quinces, and pour on them half a pint of boiling water; cover it tightly; when cold strain, and it is a most acceptable invalid's drink

COOL SUMMER DRINK FOR AN INVALID.

Gather green tansy fresh; put eight or nine leaves in a pint pitcher of water; let it stand for a couple of hours in a cold place, and in a fever it is most refreshing, so is green sage.

A HOT DRINK FOR A COLD.

Make a strong sage tea; beat up the yolk of an egg, and stir in a large spoonful of good honey; mix it well with the egg, and pour the boiling hot tea on the egg and honey; stir it well and take hot.

APPLE WATER.

Roast three good tart apples with care and preserve all the juice, put them into a quart pitcher when done, pour on it nearly a quart of boiling water, cover and when cold it is a pleasant drink.

RICE MILK JELLIED.

Wash very clean a large cup of rice, put it into a clean saucepan, pour on it three pints of new milk and add half a teaspoonful of salt; cover it closely and let it slowly simmer three hours; then take it from the fire; mash it well with a spoon, and put it into small moulds to cool; it will keep in a cool place for two or three days; eat with cream.

MULLED WINE.

Put cinnamon or alspice (to the taste) into a cup of hot water to steep, add three eggs well beaten with sugar; heat to a boil a pint of wine, then put in the spice and eggs while boiling, and stir them until done, which will be in three minutes.

A HINT TO OYSTER EATERS.

When too many oysters have been incautiously eaten, and are felt lying cold and heavy on the stomach, we have an infallible remedy in hot milk, of which half a pint may be drank, and it will quickly dissolve the oysters into a bland, cream jelly. Weak and consumptive persons should always take this after their meals of oysters.

SYRUP OF VINEGAR.

Take eleven ounces of French vinegar, obtained at the druggists, and fourteen ounces best loaf sugar; cover the vessel tightly and let them simmer slowly fifteen minutes, stirring occasionally; when the sugar is entirely dissolved, pour it into a bottle for use, and cork tightly; this is very refreshing in ice water in fevers, and can be added to barley water.

A VEGETABLE SOUP.

Take an onion, a turnip, two pared potatoes, a carrot, a head of celery; boil them in three pints of water till the vegetables are cooked; add a little salt; have a slice of bread toasted and buttered, put it into a bowl, and pour the soup over it. Tomatoes when in season form an agreeable addition.

CARRAGEEN MOSS.

To one quart of milk add half an ounce of moss; boil it till thick; strain it, and pour it into moulds; flavor it with anything you prefer.

SCOTCH BROSE.

Stir into a pint of nice chicken broth half a pint of best oatmeal, and a little salt; let this cook until the meal is entirely done, stirring continually. When done, if the invalid can take it, a little sweet butter is nice stirred in; this is nutritious and palatable.

GUM WATER.

Put a quarter of a pound of best white gum arabic, a quarter of a pound of rock candy, and one large sized fresh lemon thinly sliced, into a pitcher; on these pour one quart of boiling water, stir well, and let it stand in a warm place until the gum is dissolved; this is delightful for colds or a fever.

MUTTON BROTH.

Select two nice tender mutton chops, not too fat; put them into a saucepan, and pour one quart of cold water and a little salt; cover them, let them cook slowly for two hours; then skim off all fat, and add one tablespoonful of rice, one pared white potato, one turnip, and a little very finely chopped parsley; let this simmer for three quarters of an hour, remove all the fat, take out the chops and pour into a bowl; this is very nutritious and palatable for an invalid.

BRAN FLOUR JELLY.

Moisten with cold water half a pint of best bran flour; then stir it into a quart of boiling water; let it boil slowly, stirring frequently, to prevent scorching, for half an hour; then pour it through a very coarse sieve into a mould; when cold turn it out, and eat with cream.

MISCELLANEOUS RECEIPTS.

POP CORN.

Put some nice fresh lard into a pan; when boiling, drop in the corn and cover tightly, to prevent it popping out of the pan; when done popping, remove the corn from the pan and put them into a colander to drain; have ready some nice steam syrup, heat it and flavour with either seville orange juice or lemon juice; when simmering drop in the corn; let it simmer for ten minutes; take it out in large lumps and lay on buttered dishes to cool.

FOR CHILLBLAINS.

Cut up two white turnips without paring into thin slices; put the slices into a tin cup with three large spoonsful of best lard; let it simmer very slowly for two hours, then mash this through a sieve, when cold spread it on a soft linen cloth, and apply to the chillblain at night; one or two applications will cure the most inveterate chillblain, or frost feet.

TO DESTROY CATERPILLARS.

Hang pieces of woollen cloth amongst the bushes and shrubs; the caterpillar will during the night take shelter on the cloth, and in that way thousands may be destroyed every morning.

PATENT LINEN POLISH.

One pint of flour starch, two ounces of gum-arabic, one ounce and a half of white bees-wax, a small piece of alum, stirred in while boiling; boil one hour slowly

COLOGNE.

Oil of lemon, bergamot, cloves, cinnamon, rosemary, musk, ten drops each, put all in one pint of alcohol; this is a very nice receipt.

WALNUTS A FAMILY MEDICINE.

Every one eats walnuts, everybody knows how to make pickle of walnuts; few, however, know the medical virtue of walnuts. Now, the fact is, walnuts, when properly prepared, are an excellent medicine and alterative, and this is the way to prepare them: Get the green walnuts fit for pickling; put them in a stone jar filled up with sugar, in the proportion of half a pound to a score of walnuts; place the jar in a saucepan of boiling water, for about three hours, taking care that the water does not get in, and keep it simmering during the operation. The sugar, when dissolved, should cover the walnuts; and if it does not, add more, cover it close, and, in six months, it will be fit for use; the older it gets the better it is. One walnut is a dose for a child six years of age, as a purgative; and it has this great advantage over drugs, that while it is an excellent medicine, it is, at the same time, very pleasant to the palate, and will be esteemed by the young folks as a treat.

TO TAKE OUT MILDEW OR WINE STAINS.

Wet your article and rub it well with soap, then rub powdered chalk thickly on, and lay it in the sun; wet it when it dries, and repeat it next day.

TO PREVENT INSECTS IN CORN.

Soak your corn for planting a few hours in one ounce of salt petre, dissolved in one gallon of water, and cover a small part of your corn-hill, as it is coming up, with plaster of paris.

DISINFECTANT FOR A SICK ROOM.

One of the best disinfectants is dried raw coffee beans pounded in a mortar and sprinkled on a shovel, heated quite hot and passed through a room; it removes all unpleasant odours.

TO REMOVE MARKING INK, OR STAINS.

Take the piece of marked linen and immerse it in a solution of chloride of lime, when in a few minutes the characters will pass from black to white, owing to a new preparation of silver being formed, namely, white chloride of silver, which still remains in the fabric, but owing to its solubility in solution of ammonia it may be entirely extracted by immersion in that liquid immediately it is removed out of the first, and allowing it to remain in it for a few minutes; after this it only requires to be well rinsed in clean water, which completes the process.

TO RENDER HARD WATER SOFT.

For every hundred gallons take half a pound of the best quick lime, make it into a cream by the addition of water, then diffuse it through the hard water in a tank or reservoir, and allow the whole to stand; it will quickly be bright, the lime having united with the carbonate of lime, which makes the hard water, will be all deposited. This is a most beautiful application of the art of chemistry.

HERBS FOR DRYING.

The best state in which balm, thyme, sage, and other kitchen or medicinal herbs can be gathered for drying to preserve for winter use, is just as their flowers are opening, at that period of growth they are found to contain more of the essential oil, on which their flavours depend, than at any other. Put them in paper bags and keep in a cool dry place.

WASHING DELICATE CHINTZ AND LAWNS WITHOUT FADING, AND ALL WOOLLENS AND BOMBAZINES, &C.

Put one large spoonful of fresh beef's gall into one gallon of warm water, mix it well, then wash the article well in this, use no soap; rinse in clear tepid water, and hang in the shade to dry. If the woollen article is greasy, wash it first in warm soap suds, and then in the gall water, finally rinse in warm water. Sugar of lead in the rinsing water will keep the colour of black calico.

CURE FOR CORNS.

Infallible.

Take equal parts of pulverized Indigo of the best quality, common brown soap, and tallow; of these make a soft ointment by rubbing well together; spread it on a piece of soft leather, and apply it to the corn; keep it on until relieved.

SOFT SOAP, VERY SUPERIOR.

Twenty pounds of potash, twenty pounds of fat, and thirty-two gallons of water, reduced to twenty gallons by slow simmering.

ANOTHER WAY.

Sixteen pounds of potash, and twenty-five pounds of good fat, to a barrel of water; a part only of the water to be put to the potash and fat at first; when the fat is destroyed add the remainder of the water; this makes a very strong and white soap.

AN ADMIRABLE WHITE-WASH.

Six quarts of lime slacked with hot water, and covered to keep in the steam, then strain it through a sieve, add one-quarter of a pound of whiteing or burnt alum, pulverised; one pound of nice brown sugar; three pints of rice flour, mix all into a thin paste, and add one pound of glue which has been well dissolved first in cold water, and then boiled over a slow fire; to the whole add five gallons of hot water; if for an inside wall it must be pu on cold; if for an outside wall with a large paint brush.

TO PREVENT IRON FROM RUSTING.

Warm your iron until hot, and then rub it with clean new white wax, put it again to the fire, till it has soaked in the wax; when done rub it well with a piece of serge or coarse woollen cloth.

ANOTHER GOOD SOAP.

Nine pounds of fat; nine pounds of potash, boiled with four gallons of water until all the potash is dissolved, then fill the barrel with hot water.

BANE FOR INSECTS.

Whale oil soap is a great bane to insects; dissolve two pounds in fifteen gallons of water; mix the soap at first in a little water and then dilute; try this on trees, vines, &c.

TO REMOVE GREASE.

A weak solution of potash and lime water applied with a sponge to cloth will remove grease, then rubbed with clean cold water.

TO BRIGHTEN FIRE ARMS.

Fire arms can be kept bright by rubbing them with alum dissolved in the strongest vinegar; Montpelier is the best.

TO PREVENT MILDEW ON GOOSEBERRIES.

Train your gooseberry bushes so as to admit the air, and have through them a free circulation; manure about the roots, and sprinkle the bushes, before they blossom for three or four weeks, well with soapsuds.

HINTS TO LOVERS OF FLOWERS.

A most beautiful and easily attained show of evergreens in winter may be had by a very simple plan, which has been found to answer remarkably well on a small scale. If geranium branches are taken from healthy and luxurious trees just before the winter sets in, cut as for slips, and immersed in soap and water, they will, after drooping for a few days, shed their leaves, put forth fresh ones, and continue in the finest vigour all the winter. By placing a number of bottles filled in flower baskets, with moss to conceal the bottles, a show of evergreens is easily insured for a whole season; they require no fresh water.

TO REMOVE RUST FROM STEEL.

Rub the article with olive oil well, then sprinkle a little hot slacked lime over, lay the steel article then in a dry place for forty-eight hours; take some finely powdered fresh unslacked lime, and rub on it quick and hard until the rust all disappears, then polish with dry whiting and a soft leather.

COLD CREAM.

Two ounces of the oil of sweet almonds; half an ounce of spermaceti; half an ounce of white wax, melt these together, then stir in two large spoonsful of rose water, and while hot put into little pots; this is very nice for chapped lips.

SUPERIOR METHOD OF KEEPING BUTTER.

Take two quarts of the best dairy salt; one ounce of good sugar; one ounce of saltpetre, mix these well together; then one ounce of this mixture to one pound of the best made butter, work this well into the butter, and when all the butter is worked with this proportion put it into stone vessels tightly covered, and keep in a cool, dry place; it is not impregnated with the salt before a month. Butter thus prepared, if of a good quality, retains all its original flavor and no saltness, and will keep for a year sweet and fresh.

A SUPERIOR POMATUM.

Half a pound of nice beef marrow; three large spoonsful of best quality leaf-lard, free from salt; put them into a half pint of cold water in a very clean saucepan, let it simmer for ten minutes, then strain it through a hair sieve into a basin of cold water; when cold remove it carefully from the surface of the water, and put it into a clean bowl, and add fifteen drops of cantharides and a few drops of any kind of agreeable essence, bergamot, or attar of rose, merely for perfume, then beat all together with a silver spoon until it is a cream; put into jars and keep in a cool place.

BRILLIANT WHITE WASH.

Take half a bushel of nice unslacked lime, slack it with boiling water, covering it during the process to keep in the steam; strain the liquid through a fine sieve or strainer, and add to it a peck of fine salt previously well dissolved in warm water; three pounds of ground rice, boiled to a thin paste, and stirred in boiling hot; half a pound of powdered Spanish whiting, and a pound of clean glue, which has been previously dissolved by first soaking it well, and then hanging it over a slow fire in a small kettle, within a large one filled with water; add five gallons of water to the whole mixture, and white vitriol two pounds dissolved in warm water; stir it well, and let it stand a few days kept free from dirt; it should be quite hot; for this purpose it can be kept in a kettle on a portable furnace; it is said that one pint of this mixture will cover a square yard upon the outside of a house, if properly applied. Brushes more or less large may be used, according to the neatness of the job required. It answers as well as oil paint for wood, brick, or stone, and is cheaper; it retains its brilliancy for many years; there is nothing of the kind that will compare with it, either for inside or outside walls.

Coloring matter may be put in, and made of any shade you like; spanish brown stirred in will make it red or pink, more or less deep according to the quantity; a delicate tinge of this is very pretty for inside walls; finely pulverized common clay, well mixed with the spanish brown before it is stirred into the mixture, makes a lilac color; lamp black in moderate quantities makes a slate colour, very suitable for the outside of buildings; lamp black and spanish brown mixed together, produce a reddish stone colour; yellow ochre stirred in makes a yellow wash; but chrome goes further, and makes a color generally esteemed prettier. In all these cases, the darkness of the shade will of course be determined by the quantity of coloring matter used. It is difficult to make a rule, because tastes are very different; it would be best to try experiments on a shingle, and let it dry. I have been told that green must not be mixed with lime. The lime destroys the colour, and the colour has an effect upon the whitewash, which makes it crack and peel.

When walls have been badly smoked, and you wish to have them a clean white, it is as well to squeeze indigo plentifully through a bag into the water you use, before it is stirred into the whole mixture.

If a larger quantity than five gallons is wanted, the same proportions should be observed.

TO KEEP A STOVE BRIGHT FOR SIX MONTHS.

Make a weak alum water; mix with it the british lustre, about two tea-spoonsful of the lustre to a gill of alum-water; when the stove is quite cold brush it well with this mixture, then polish it with a dry brush; should any part become dry before it is polished moisten it with the mixture and then polish; this, if properly done, requires being done only once in five or six months, and retains the polish.

SIMPLE AND SUPERIOR POLISH FOR PLATE.

Wash the articles in hot soapsuds, then make a paste with camphene or burning fluid and finely powdered rotten stone, mixing in equal proportions; put this on the articles of silver or plate, then with a soft cloth or chamois skin polish them; this produces a very beautiful polish; door-knobs can thus be kept in fine order with very little trouble.

FOR FROZEN FEET AND CORNS.

Dissolve half a pound of alum in a gallon of warm water; immerse the hands or feet in this alum water and let them remain ten or fifteen minutes; repeat it until relief is obtained, and it will prove an effectual cure, and then apply the turnip salve for chilblains; for corns the salve is not required.

TO CLEAN CANE CHAIR BOTTOMS.

Turn up the chair bottom, and with hot water and a sponge wash the cane-work well so that it may become completely soaked; should it be very dirty, you may add soap. Let it dry in the open air if possible, or in a place where there is a thorough draught, and it will become as tight and firm as when new, providing that it has not been broken.

TO CLEAN DECANTERS.

Roll up in small pieces some coarse brown paper, then wet and soap the same, put them into the vessel with a little lukewarm water, and some common soda, shake them well, then rinse with clean water, and it will be as bright and clear as when new.

CLEANING FLOOR CLOTHS.

After sweeping and cleaning the floor cloth with a broom and damp flannel in the usual manner, wet them over with milk, and rub them till beautifully bright with a dry cloth; they will thus look as if they were rubbed first with a waxed flannel and afterwards with a dry one, without being so slippery, or so soon clogging with dust or dirt.

TO CLEAN MATTING.

Put a double-handful of salt into a bucket of cold water, with this wash over the matting, a small piece at a time, and rub it well with a coarse cloth, then the remainder in the same manner until all is done; avoid treading on the matting until it is dry.

TO CLEAN AND BRIGHTEN THE COLORS OF BRUSSELS OR ANY WOOLLEN CARPETINGS.

Obtain from the beef-butcher a fresh beef-gall, break it into a clean pan, pour one-half into a very clean bucket and nearly fill it with lukewarm water; take a clean coarse cloth, and having brushed the carpet well, rub it hard with the cloth thoroughly wet with the gall-water; do a small piece at a time, have ready a dry coarse cloth, and rub the carpet dry, so proceed until the whole carpet is cleaned.

A CEMENT USED BY THE ALGERINES.

Two parts of ashes, three parts of clay, and one part of sand; it is called by the Moors *fabbi*, is mixed with oil, and resists the influence of weather better than marble.

GOOD GREASE BALL.

Moisten fuller's earth with lemon juice, add powdered pearl-ash, and mix well, make it into little balls, dry well in the sun, use it by moistening the spots with water, rub on the ball, then dry, and brush off well.

DISINFECTOR.

A handful of copperas thrown in a basin, and on this pour a pint of hot water, which creates a vapour, which will correct disagreeable odours in rooms, vaults, and cellars; and for cess pools the very best is to dissolve twenty-five pounds of soda ash in boiling water, and one peck of common lime, slacked separately; then mix the two and pour it down the privy.

SNAILS.

These can be destroyed in cellars by sprinkling coarse salt freely on the places where they are.

TO CLEAN PAINT.

Make a paste of whiting and hot water, dip a flannel cloth into it, and rub it well on the paint, have ready a piece of clean flannel and wash the paint off with clean tepid water, this removes spots and cleans better than soap.

TO KEEP POULTRY FREE FROM INSECTS.

Keep their houses well cleaned with care; whitewash the box inside in which their nests are placed; make their nests fresh, and have plenty of ashes, sand or loose dirt, in which they can at all times dust themselves.

TO KILL INSECTS IN POULTRY.

Boil as many onions several hours as may be required for the number of fowls; when they are reduced to a perfect pulp, thicken with corn-meal, and give it to the fowls.

REMEDY FOR CANCER.

Take an egg and break it, put it in salt, and mix with the yolk as long as it will receive it; stir them together until the salve is formed; put a portion of this on a piece of sticking plaster, and apply it to the cancer about twice a day.

A HINT.

A very pretty and economical finish for sheets, pillow-cases, &c., may be made from the cuttings of bleached muslin, by cutting one and a half inch squares, and folding them bias, from corner to corner, then fold again, so as to form a point, seam on to the straight side on raw edge, and face on a strip to cover the seam.

HOW TO TREAT YOUR BOOTS AND SHOES WHEN PARTIALLY BURNED.

On one of the coldest days of the present month, I pulled off my boots and set them close to a stove which was very hot. The room was filled with a smell as of something burning. Turning round, I saw my boots smoking at a great rate. I seized them and immediately besmeared them with soft soap, much of which, owing to their highly heated condition, quickly disappeared in the leather. When they became cold, the leather was soft and pliable; and now, after several days of subsequent wear, they exhibit no marks of having been burned.

A HINT FOR HOUSEKEEPERS.

A few drops of carbonate of ammonia, in a small quantity of warm rain-water, will prove a safe and easy anti-acid, &c., and will change, if carefully applied, discolored spots upon carpets, and indeed all spots, whether produced by acids or alkalies. If one has the misfortune to have a carpet injured by whitewash, this will immediately restore it.

TO GREASE EGGS FOR WINTER.

In the spring when eggs are plenty and cheap, it is very well to put up several hundred, to use in the winter, when it is very difficult to get them, even in the country.

Grease each egg with melted lard, and as you do so, lay them in a keg or jar, or old tin vessels that are out of use; put them in a dry closet, and keep them covered over; if they are put in the cellar, they are liable to mould, which spoils them entirely. Do not put in any cracked ones, or they will injure the rest.

In this way they have been known to keep a year, and were nearly as good for puddings, or batter cakes, as fresh eggs. They do not do to boil, or make pound or sponge cake, as they lose part of their lightening property.

TO KEEP EGGS IN LIME WATER.

Pour two gallons of hot water on a pint of lime and half a pint of salt; put the eggs in a jar or keg, and when it is cold, pour it over them, and put them in a cellar to keep; be sure that there are no cracked ones.

TO CLEAN WHITE KID GLOVES.

Take one teaspoonful of chloride of soda, and two tablespoonsful of water; use a sponge.

DURABLE INK.

One hundred grains of lunar caustic, one dram gum arabic, into one ounce of soft water.

Preparation for wetting the linen; one ounce of salsoda, two ounces soft water; a small quantity of gum arabic will stiffen the linen.

LAVENDER COMPOUND.

Take three pints spirits of lavender, one pint rosemary spirits, half an ounce nutmeg, half an ounce cinnamon, and three drams of cochineal; digest them in a good hot sun, or good sand heat for twenty-four hours, at least, and then strain it for use.

ECONOMICAL WHITE PAINT.

Skim two quarts of milk, eight ounces of fresh slacked lime, six ounces of linseed oil, two ounces of white Burgundy pitch, three pounds of Spanish white; the lime to be slacked in water, exposed to the air, and mixed in about one fourth of the milk; the oil in which the pitch is dissolved, to be added a little at a time; then the rest of the milk, and afterwards the Spanish white; this quantity is sufficient for twenty-seven square yards, and the expense a mere trifle.

VOLATILE SOAP,

And Directions for Washing Clothes.

Cut up five pounds of country hard soap into one quart of strong ley; simmer it over the fire until the soap is dissolved, and add to it three ounces of pearlash; pour it into a stone jar, and stir in half a pint of spirits of turpentine, and a gill of spirits of hartshorn; cover the jar tight, and tie a cloth over it.

To use the soap, have a tub half full of water as hot as you can bear your hands in; assort the clothes, and, beginning with the cleanest of them, rub a small quantity of the soap on the soiled parts of each article, and immerse them in the water one by one, until it will cover no more; let them soak for fifteen or twenty minutes, then stir them well for a few minutes, and boil them for half an hour in eight or ten gallons of water, to which a tablespoonful of the soap has been added; rinse them, using blue water where it is required as usual, and they are ready for drying. After the white clothes are finished, the same waters will answer for the colored ones, adding hot water and more soap. By the use of this soap, most of the rubbing can be dispensed with, and it is not injurious to the texture of the clothes. It has been proved that the clothes washed in this way are more durable than with the common soaps, and the rubbing required in connection with them.

It is particularly recommended for washing flannels and calicoes. The above quantity is sufficient for a family of four or five persons for a month, varying slightly as the clothes are more or less soiled. Its cheapness recommends it to all housekeepers.

SOAP.

A Blessing to Women.

Take two ounces of pulverized ammonia, put it into a bottle with one pint of turpentine; shake them well together, and in half an hour it is fit for use. For an ordinary wash, use one quart of soft soap in warm water sufficient to make strong suds and four tablespoonsful of the mixture; put in the clothes, and let them remain twenty minutes, stirring them occasionally; then rinse them out in the usual manner, *without the use of a wash-board.*

A FAMILY SOAP.

Soft Soap from Kitchen Grease or Scraps.

Dissolve and strain into a pork barrel any refuse grease of twenty-five pounds, into this put eighteen pounds of best potash; on these pour two pailsful of boiling water; stir this with a long stick well; let this stand three days, and then add another pail of water; when all has set well, fill up the barrel with water; stir well, and frequently. This supplies the family with cleaning soap at a small expense.

TO MAKE PRIME BUTTER.

In each pan of milk put sufficient sour milk to make it very sour and thick in thirty-six hours; in moderate weather two or three tablespoonsful will answer; in cold weather it should be kept in a room at summer heat: skim it every morning and night; skim the cream in a pot, and before putting it in the churn scrape off the top with a knife, as it will make the butter strong; work most of the buttermilk out, then salt it; then work it well with a cloth till there is no more milk in it—print it, throw it in water awhile, then set it away in a cool place.

When the churn is new, cleanse it well with a churning of sour milk; also scald, then cool the paddles.

This is the receipt given to us by Mr. E. G. Passmore, who is so celebrated in the Philadelphia market for his very superior butter, and who always commands a price from twenty-five to thirty-three per cent. higher than his neighbors for it.

FAMILY VINEGAR.

Mix five quarts of warm rain water with two quarts of New Orleans molasses and one quart of good yeast. In four weeks a capital vinegar is the result, for all purposes, pickling, &c.

FOR STAINING FLOORS OF PIAZZAS, &c.

Make a strong ley of boiled wood ashes; let it settle and pour off the ley; then add as much common copperas as will stain the floor a light shade of oak; the quantity of copperas must be decided by experimenting on the floor; the wash is to be put on with a mop dipped in the ley, and the boards well wet; if too light add more copperas, and when dry, well varnished. This will last a season, and is easily renewed.

A SUPERIOR STARCH FOR DRESSES, MUSLINS AND SHIRTS.

Pour on two ounces of white gum arabic, one pint of boiling water; let it stand all night; in the morning when all is dissolved, pour it off from the dregs into a clean bottle, cork it and keep it in a cool place; when wanted for use, one tablespoonful of this gum water stirred into a pint of the best starch made in the usual way, will give lawns either black or printed a fresh new appearance, and is the best kind of stiffening for bobinet or muslins, of course much diluted for them.

A DISINFECTING LAMP.

Take an ordinary fluid or camphene lamp, with the usual wick, only a fresh one; fill the lamp with "chloric ether;" light the wick in the place where the odour exists, and in a very few minutes the disagreeable and unwholesome odour will be entirely over come. It is one of the best methods for correcting unpleasant smells

SUGGESTIVE HINTS TO YOUNG HOUSE KEEPERS.

It is often a subject which causes great dilemma, the deciding on the meats and desserts in a private family, so as to have a necessary change on an economical system. An attempt is here made to aid an inexperienced housekeeper, in providing for her household the required varieties. Our markets afford such a field for selection to the experienced caterer, that to them these may appear unnecessary; but as cook books are intended to instruct those who do not know, it is necessary to inform on all domestic points, which can contribute to the comfort and health of the household, over which it is woman's peculiar privilege and right to exercise authority; and to be enabled to fulfil the duties of that most important position, she must have power to obtain knowledge, and every little avenue sought by which she can procure this, to her, necessary information.

"One who looketh well to the ways of her household," is always provident in caring for the morrow; inspects her larder daily without reference to its size, large or small, both demanding equal attention, both requiring to be kept supplied; if that is done, the unlooked-for addition of one or two creates no inconvenience or irritation; a guest is sometimes made to feel "de trop" from the apologies of the hostess, and all the pleasure of an unexpected visit is destroyed by having caught the family on a "short day;" in well regulated households there should be no such days, but should they occur, have something in reserve to be quickly gotten up, and thereby save guests and hosts.

We shall divide the seasons into four, commencing with the Autumn, and as one week will answer for the remaining twelve of that season, we give the seven days' fare for a family consisting of ten persons, one or two, more or less, makes but little difference. A roast should always be for a Sunday's dinner; beef, mutton, lamb, or veal in season; it answers for a nice cold

Monday's dish, and the gravy and trimmings left will make nice soup for Monday; no soups on Sundays, as every considerate mistress regards her domestics, and as an evidence of that should render their Sabbath labour light, consistent with the comfort and health of the household.

This "bill of fare" can of course be added to, or retrenched; it is only a nucleus for the catering ideas of a young mistress of a household so as to vary each day's provision; soup should be a daily dish at the board; it can be made in small or large quantities, and if prepared with care is acceptable and nutritious, particularly to the aged, who have no longer the full powers of mastication; it is economical as it is better made from gravies and broths, than in any other way. The family health is very much promoted by changing the food, and on the mistress this of course depends, to the inexperienced it is often very perplexing to effect this.

Made dishes of course cannot be included in this limited "bill of fare," and as the receipts afford a great variety, the housekeeper cannot be at a loss to make an addition to the table when one is required, and a nicely prepared stew or mince is often preferred to a joint.

With regard to desserts they must be varied according to taste, the book provides a great number of excellent puddings, pies, and light fancy desserts; in the summer fruits relieve from all difficulty on that score. Stewed fruits can be prepared at all seasons, and are generally not in sufficient use in families, they are much preferable to preserves, more healthy, and retain if rightly prepared more of the flavour of the fruit, particularly the apple and peach.

Corn bread is not enough honoured at Northern tables; the difficulty of having it well prepared has been one of the causes, as all who go South enjoy it; it is stated that a difference exists between the Northern and Southern meal, there is something in that; but it can be very deliciously prepared here if the mistress will superintend the compounding, her success will reward her for the labour.

AUTUMN.

MONDAY.

Breakfast. Corn bread, wheat bread, broiled ham, poached eggs, and fried potatoes.
Dinner. Soup, cold joint, cutlets, vegetables.
Dessert. Custard, pie, or fritters.
Tea. Cold bread, toast, salt or smoked fish, sago cheese grated—always on table in a covered glass.

TUESDAY.

Breakfast. Warm bread, cold bread, nice hash, boiled eggs, fried hominy.
Dinner. Soup, roast mutton and jelly, a made dish, stew or hash, vegetables.
Dessert. Pudding, &c.
Tea. Cold bread, milk-toast, stewed fruit, soused pigs' or calves' feet.

WEDNESDAY.

Breakfast. Corn and wheat bread, pork steaks, fried potatoes.
Dinner. Soup, boiled fowls, with oyster sauce, boiled corned pork, vegetables.
Dessert. Pie, &c.
Tea. Cold bread and Scotch toast, frizzled beef, light cake.

THURSDAY.

Breakfast. Warm and cold bread, chops, fried hominy, omelet.
Dinner. Soup, fish, beef steaks, vegetables.
Dessert. Pudding, and fruits stewed.
Tea. Corn bread, cold bread, sliced meats, stewed fruit.

FRIDAY.

Breakfast. Warm and cold bread, fried liver, boiled eggs, fried potatoes.
Dinner. Soup, roast poultry, boiled tongue, vegetables.
Dessert. Pudding, &c.
Tea. Cold bread, toast, sandwiches, fish.

SATURDAY.

Breakfast. Corn bread, cold bread, meat cakes, omelet.
Dinner. Soup, boiled mutton, caper sauce, cold tongue, vegetables.
Dessert. Custard, &c.
Tea. Cold bread, toast, sliced tongue, stewed fruit.

SUNDAY.

Breakfast. Cold bread; chops, boiled eggs.
Dinner Roast pork, cold meat, vegetables, apple-sauce.
Dessert. Pie, blanc-mange, and preserves.
Tea. Cold bread, toast, sliced meat, stewed fruit, light cake.

WINTER.

MONDAY.

Breakfast. Corn bread, cold bread, stew, boiled eggs.
Dinner. Soup, cold joint, calves' head, vegetables.
Dessert. Puddings, &c.
Tea. Cold bread, milk toast, stewed fruit.

TUESDAY.

Breakfast. Hot cakes, cold bread, sausages, fried potatoes.
Dinner. Soup, roast turkey, cranberry sauce, boiled ham, vegetables.
Dessert. Pie, &c.
Tea. Corn bread, cold bread, stewed oysters.

WEDNESDAY.

Breakfast. Hot bread, cold bread, chops, omelet.
Dinner. Boiled mutton, stewed liver, vegetables.
Dessert. Pudding, &c.
Tea. Hot light bread, cold bread, fish, stewed fruit.

THURSDAY.

Breakfast. Hot cakes, cold bread, sausages, fried potatoes.
Dinner. Soup, poultry, cutlets, vegetables.
Dessert. Custards and stewed fruit.
Tea. Corn bread, cold bread, frizzled beef, stewed fruits, or soused calves' feet.

FRIDAY.

Breakfast. Hot bread, cold bread, chops, omelet.
Dinner. Soup, fish, roast mutton and currant jelly, vegetables.
Dessert. Pudding, &c.
Tea. Hot light bread, cold bread, stewed fruit.

SATURDAY.

Breakfast. Hot bread, a nice hash, fried potatoes.
Dinner. Soup, roast veal, steaks, oyster pie, vegetables.
Dessert. Custards.
Tea. Corn bread, cold bread, stewed oysters.

SUNDAY.

Breakfast. Cold bread, croquets, omelet.
Dinner. Roast pig, apple sauce, steaks, vegetables.
Dessert. Pie, jelly.
Tea. Cold bread, stewed fruit, light cake.

SPRING.

MONDAY.

Breakfast. Warm bread, cold bread, broiled ham and eggs, fried mush, or hominy.
Dinner. Roast mutton, currant jelly, cutlets, vegetables.
Dessert. Pudding, &c.
Tea. Corn bread, cold bread, radishes, ham sandwiches.

TUESDAY.

Breakfast. Warm bread, cold bread, fish, boiled eggs.
Dinner. Clam soup, roast pork and beans, beef steak, vegetables.
Dessert. Pie, &c.
Tea. Cold bread, toast, cream cheese, cold tongue.

WEDNESDAY.

Breakfast. Warm bread, cold bread, fried liver, boiled eggs.
Dinner. Boiled fowls, egg sauce, boiled corn, pork, cutlets, vegetables.
Dessert. Puddings or floating island.
Tea. Corn bread, cold bread, radishes, fish.

THURSDAY.

Breakfast. Warm bread, cold bread, broiled ham and poached eggs.
Dinner. Chicken pie, boiled tongue, calves' head, vegetables.
Dessert. Pie, custard.
Tea. Bread, toast, cream cheese, cold tongue.

FRIDAY.

Breakfast. Warm and cold bread, clam fritters, boiled eggs.
Dinner. Fish, roast lamb, mint sauce, vegetables.
Dessert. Pudding, &c.
Tea. Corn bread, cold bread, cold ham, preserves.

SATURDAY.

Breakfast. Warm and cold bread, fish, and fried hominy.
Dinner. Fricasseed chicken, boiled ham, veal cutlets, vegetables.
Dessert. Pie, &c.
Tea. Milk toast, cold bread, fish, preserves.

SUNDAY.

Breakfast Cold bread, broiled ham and poached eggs.
Dinner. Roast beef, boiled calves' feet, parsley-sauce, vegetables.
Dessert. Pie, blanc-mange or jelly.
Tea. Cold bread, cottage cheese, preserves, light cake.

SUMMER.

MONDAY.

Breakfast. Cold bread, fish, boiled eggs.
Dinner. Lamb and peas, calves' head, vegetables,
Dessert. Fruits.
Tea. Cold bread, light cake, fruit, curds and cream.

TUESDAY.

Breakfast. Cold bread, broiled ham, poached eggs.
Dinner. Ochra soup, fried chickens, calves' feet boiled, parsley sauce, vegetables.
Dessert. Fruit, floating island.
Tea. Cold bread, corn bread, fruits.

WEDNESDAY.

Breakfast. Cold bread, chops, boiled small hominy.
Dinner. Roast lamb, mint-sauce, green peas, boiled pigs' feet, parsley sauce, boiled tongue, vegetables.
Dessert. Pie, trifles.
Tea. Cold bread, toast, cream cheese, fruits.

THURSDAY.

Breakfast. Cold bread, fish, fried mush.
Dinner. Lobster, boiled mutton, stewed liver, vegetables
Dessert. Pudding and fruit.
Tea. Corn bread, light cake, stewed fruit.

FRIDAY.

Breakfast. Cold bread, clam fritters, boiled rice, and boiled eggs.
Dinner. Fish, beef steaks, vegetables.
Dessert. Pudding, fruit.
Tea. Corn bread, cold bread, fruit, cream cheese.

SATURDAY.

Breakfast. Corn bread, cold bread, fish and boiled eggs.
Dinner. Boiled fowls, egg or celery sauce, tongue, cutlets, vegetables.
Dessert. Pie, floating island, &c.
Tea. Cold bread, sliced tongue, fruit.

SUNDAY.

Breakfast. Cold bread, boiled ham and eggs, and small hominy.
Dinner. Roast beef, fricasseed chicken, vegetables.
Dessert. Fruit, jelly, or blanc-mange.
Tea. Cold bread, fish, fruits, light cake.

WEIGHTS AND MEASURES.

Avoirdupois Weight.

16 drams . . .	1 ounce,
16 ounces . . .	1 pound,
28 pounds . . .	1 quarter of hundred,
4 quarters, or 112 pounds, .	1 hundred,
20 hundred, . . .	1 ton.

A quart of flour weighs just one pound; a quart of corn meal, one pound two ounces; a quart of butter, one pound one ounce; a quart of loaf sugar, one pound; a quart of white sugar powdered, one pound one ounce; a quart of best brown sugar, one pound two ounces; ten eggs weigh one pound; sixteen tablespoonsful make a half pint; eight make a gill; four, a half gill, &c.

Liquid Measure.

4 gills . . .	1 pint,
2 pints . . .	1 quart,
4 quarts . . .	1 gallon,
63 gallons . . .	1 hogshead,
2 hogsheads . .	1 pipe or butt,
2 pipes . . .	1 tun.

Dry Measure, for Grain, Fruit, and Potatoes.

2 pints . . .	1 quart,
8 quarts . . .	1 peck,
4 pecks . . .	1 bushel,
8 bushels . . .	1 quarter

INDEX.

Date

THE END.